The Mature Student's Guide to Writing

3rd edition

Jean Rose

palgrave
macmillan

First published 2012 by
PALGRAVE MACMILLAN

Palgrave Macmillan in the UK is an imprint of Macmillan Publishers Limited, registered in England, company number 785998, of Houndmills, Basingstoke, Hampshire RG21 6XS.

Palgrave Macmillan in the US is a division of St Martin's Press LLC, 175 Fifth Avenue, New York, NY 10010.

Palgrave Macmillan is the global academic imprint of the above companies and has companies and representatives throughout the world.

Palgrave® and Macmillan® are registered trademarks in the United States, the United Kingdom, Europe and other countries

ISBN: 978–0–230–29787–6

This book is printed on paper suitable for recycling and made from fully managed and sustained forest sources. Logging, pulping and manufacturing processes are expected to conform to the environmental regulations of the country of origin.

A catalogue record for this book is available from the British Library.

A catalog record for this book is available from the Library of Congress.

10   9   8   7   6   5   4   3   2   1
21   20   19   18   17   16   15   14   13   12

Printed and bound in the UK by
Charlesworth Press, Wakefield, West Yorkshire

Contents

Part Four: Moving On

Acknowledgements

The author would like to thank the following:

The *Daily Telegraph* for permission to quote from 'Tory tipple more compassionate and hangover-free' by Andrew Gimson, 1 March 2006.

Devon Life for permission to quote from the following features: 'Class Glass', 'The Trading House', 'The Rich Earth' and 'A Plant Phenomenon'.

A. C. Grayling for permission to reprint 'Why a high society is a free society', *Observer*, 19 May 2002.

Pan Macmillan Ltd (London, UK) for permission to quote the poem 'Tea' from *Rapture* by Carol Ann Duffy.

Penguin Group (UK) for permission to quote from *The Psychology of Perception* by M. D. Vernon.

All the adult students I have taught (without whom this book would not have been written), and especially students who were kind enough to let me use some of their work here. All names have been changed.

Every effort has been made to trace all the copyright holders, but if any have been inadvertently overlooked the author and publishers will be pleased to make the necessary arrangements at the earliest opportunity.

Who Is this Book For?

This book is for adults. You're likely to be a mature student, but you might be studying anything from IT to drama or from business studies to building construction. Perhaps you're about to begin a full-time course in higher education – or you might be studying part-time or be enrolled on an Open University course or be taking another distance-learning course. Maybe you're starting an Access to Higher Education programme.

You might be a science student who has always found English baffling. Perhaps your early studies were undertaken in a different country and you now need to check up on British procedures. Perhaps you're not a student at all, but you just want to brush up your writing skills. Whatever you're doing, you'll find lots of tips here to help you with writing well and improving your style.

This book will give you a sound basis from which to move forward. If you're having difficulties with your written English, but can't work out what's wrong, you'll find lots of simple explanations to help you. If you missed out at school or you've forgotten some of the basic rules of good writing, you'll probably find the answers here.

You might have tried looking at books that give grammatical rules but then found that you couldn't understand them or relate them to your own situation. This book explains the kinds of writing you'll be required to do at college and university and it does this in a simple, conversational style. All the explanations and examples have been kept simple too so that the process will be as stress-free as possible for you.

How to Use This Book

There are a number of different ways you can use this book. What you do will depend very much on your individual circumstances – on how much you remember from your previous education, for instance, or on what particular assignments you have to cope with. You'll probably find that there are some things you just need to brush up on and others that you need to look at more carefully. You might find that you'll need to cover one or two issues immediately and others as they arise in relation to your course or other work.

Each chapter in this book begins with a brief introduction. This is followed by explanations and, sometimes, activities for practice. At the end of the chapter, you'll find a summary of the main points you need to remember. Let's suppose you've been asked to write a letter for an assignment. You're likely to want to look at Chapter 6, in Part Two, so that you can get the main structure right straight away. When your tutor has seen and commented on the letter, you might find that you need some help with understanding how verbs work. That will be the time to turn to Chapter 12 on verbs. This chapter will show you how to use verbs accurately in your sentences.

If you just need to brush up on your knowledge of verbs, you might like to scan the first few pages in Chapter 12 and then turn to the summary at the end of the chapter to see if it makes sense to you. If it rings bells and you feel fairly confident, you could turn back to the activities and try one or two to test yourself. This might be all you need. If, however, things are not coming back easily, or if an item is quite new to you, you'll probably want to work through the whole chapter. It would be a good idea to take one section at a time when you have a spare half hour, rather than trying to do too much at once. This way, you won't overload yourself with new information.

You can also use the book as a quick reference tool. Perhaps you want to know what an adjective is, or how to use a semicolon. Just turn to the index and this will refer you to the page you need.

Always give new information time to sink in. Learning to improve your writing is not like learning a set of dates. You'll need to practise each skill that's new to you. So don't be alarmed if you continue to make mistakes for a little while. Expect to improve gradually. When your tutor marks an error in your writing, go back to the rules so that you understand *exactly* what went wrong. It's through fully understanding our errors that we are able to make most progress.

PART ONE

When you return to study, the thing that's likely to be uppermost in your mind is submitting your first essay. It might be years since you wrote one, and you're probably aware that more will be expected of you now. Chapter 2 will take you slowly through the essay-writing process, explaining everything you need to do and how to do it. In order to write the essay, however, you're going to need to have written some useful notes. So Chapter 1 helps with this and shows different methods for note-taking. Essay-writing also involves giving references, so Chapter 3 will talk you through the referencing process.

PART TWO

Part Two covers particular writing tasks you're likely to be doing such as summaries and reports. Chapter 4 on style forms a basis for each of the other chapters in this part of the book. Besides explaining some techniques on improving your writing in general, Chapter 4 contains important material on how to adjust your writing for different types of assignment.

If, for example, you need to write a letter about a faulty freezer, you'll need to include specific details of the fault and of where you bought the item. If, however, someone writes an article comparing several freezers, it will be likely to include details of performance, and may also give background information on the process of refrigeration and on market trends. But if a freezer features in a detective novel because it contains a corpse, the emphasis will be on the horror of the situation. Whatever we write, we need to be clear on the purpose of the piece so that we can write in a suitable mode. Chapters 5 to 10 explain what's necessary for a variety of purposes.

PART THREE

You might need to refer to items in Part Three at any time. It's full of basic rules on grammar and punctuation. So dip into it whenever you're unsure of something or whenever your tutor comments on something you need to revise. Correct punctuation, for example, is essential for helping to get your meaning across. Part Three shows you how to be sure that your writing is easily understood. An essay that is full of good ideas can fail to get a good mark if it's difficult to follow.

PART FOUR

Part Four of the book looks beyond your life as a student to give you help with applying for jobs. You're likely to be making applications from the spring of your final academic year. You might, however, need to look for part-time work while you're studying, or you might want to gain some valuable experience (whether paid or unpaid) in your chosen field. So this part of the book might be useful at any time in your studies. Chapters 15 and 16 will show you how to construct a useful CV and how to approach the writing of application letters. Preparing a CV can be a time-consuming process, but the good news is that once you've put one together, it can be changed and updated as you go along. It will be with you for life.

If You Think You Might Be Dyslexic ...

There are many forms of dyslexia. As well as causing problems with reading and writing, these can affect various other activities, particularly your ability to organise your work. Sometimes, well-meaning friends can suggest that a person is dyslexic just because his or her spelling isn't good. If you're at all concerned, contact the study-support section at your college or university and arrange to see an expert who'll be able to discuss things with you.

If you already know that you are dyslexic, you might need to ask a dyslexia specialist how you might make use of this book. You might not be able to work with it in the same way as a student who is not dyslexic. So make sure that you take advice. This book does *not* contain any specific help with dyslexia.

Nowadays, colleges and universities understand the problems that dyslexia can cause and they're keen to do all they can to help. Even students in some evening classes can get help if they're studying for an exam. Sometimes, notes and handouts can be provided in a special format for those who are dyslexic, and sometimes a laptop computer can be obtained for a student's personal use. Extra time can be allowed in examinations, and sometimes a student can be allocated someone to help take notes in class sessions.

All this takes time to organise, however, so it's important to get checked out as early as possible in the academic year – or as soon as you are accepted on a course. If you leave it too late, you might have fallen so far behind that it's difficult to catch up.

Part One
The Big Picture

1 Taking Notes

This chapter explains how to:

- ▶ manage your note-taking in lectures
- ▶ make useful notes from written sources
- ▶ read and analyse academic material

INTRODUCTION

In lectures, some of us hope to rely on our memories and some of us try to write down absolutely everything. But unless you have a brilliant memory, the first method won't work, and if you try the second, you'll exhaust yourself and your notes might not make much sense. You need a method that picks up key points without having to write too much.

Note-taking from written materials involves a different procedure. You'll be taking notes for an assignment and aiming to find just those things that will serve your purpose. So you need to analyse what you're reading as you go along. The better you become at understanding a text, the better your notes will be and, consequently, the better your essays.

NOTE-TAKING IN LECTURES AND CLASS SESSIONS

In any class or lecture session, you need to spend some time considering what's being said. Lecture sessions sometimes include brief periods of discussion too, so your mind needs to be free to follow these. What you need is a set of notes that give you outline information in a very readable format. So notes written in sentences aren't going to make things easy for you. You'll need to get into the habit of writing down individual words and phrases. Listen out for names, dates, technical terms and other key words. This might take a bit of practice.

* note down names, dates, technical terms and key words and phrases

Watch, first of all, for the way a lecture is structured. Some tutors start by telling you what will be covered. So if you're told there will be three sections, mark them out as you go along. Your syllabus may also give you some clues as to the important areas to concentrate on, so check it out before the lecture and then listen out for key topics.

You might be given a hand-out showing the main areas of the day's lecture. This is an invaluable guide. There may even be spaces for you to fill things in as you go along.

* think about the structure of a lecture and put headings in your notes

Quite often, the way a lecturer speaks can give a clue to important points: a tutor's voice might rise, he or she might stress certain words very strongly, he or she might pause before an important point or even repeat a phrase or two. Note these down and either underline or ring them as you go along. You'll probably want to leave out extras such as full descriptions and details of examples, because there just isn't time to record everything.

It's possible to use your page rather like a drawing-board, ignoring the printed lines if you find that easier. Spreading out your notes and leaving space on each page is especially important. After the lecture, or even months later or when you're revising, you might come across something else you need to add. It's infuriating if there's no space. Not only that, a cramped page can be hard to read later. It can look very daunting, too, and there'll be no clear sense of an overall structure.

* watch for clues from the way a lecturer stresses points

Here's how Helen might have begun to make notes from a lecture on the Founding Fathers from her course on American Studies before she'd learnt some new and easier methods of note-taking:

Founding Fathers – America

Country gents / upper class / those in commerce – had influence & power –
  e.g. Thomas Jefferson (7,500 acres) & wife (11,000 acres).
The colony was governed separately from Britain – the Governor
  appointed by the Crown.
Governor app. a Council. Council app. local assemblies.
There was more representation of the people than in Britain because
  more land available.
N. States – 75% males voted
S. States – 50%   "   "
Most colonists were loyal to the British Crown. When there were
  difficulties, they blamed Parliament (not the King).
There were some tensions over taxes. Britain passed acts to
  recoup expenses – e.g. for British troops in N. America – to
  protect against Indians & French.
Colonists resisted the Stamp Act and the Townsend Act (which
  led to problems in Boston).

Below, you can see what Helen actually did, because, by the time she took these notes, she'd had a bit of practice in using a clearer layout that gives space to add things later:

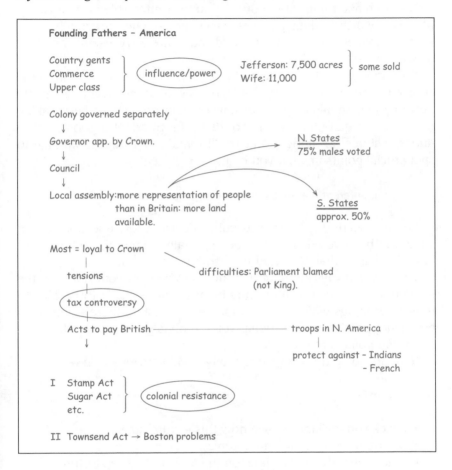

The main things to notice here are:

- only a few key words are written down
- lines are drawn to link points
- there's space to add more later
- these notes are very easy to read

It's also possible to use mind maps (see Chapter 2), where you start in the middle of the page and work outwards. There can be a problem with using mind maps for lecture notes, however: it can be hard to link to a second page when you've filled one up. For this reason, I tend to favour Helen's method of working down the page. Diagrams are good, too. Whatever method you use, you can add colour after the lecture to make things stand out. If you're comfortable with drawing, it's even worth adding pictures, since visual cues are really good memory-joggers. By the way, mind maps are very useful for other tasks.

It's important to find a method that works for you in relation to the course you're on and the type of lectures you attend. Trying out some new methods should help you discover what's going to be best. Taking notes can be quite hard work, so it's useful to adopt a good posture during lectures. Sit upright and you'll remain alert and more able to spot crucial points in what you hear.

* try out different methods of note-taking in lectures

Before a lecture, it can be useful to devise a few questions about what will be covered. This can be especially helpful for getting your brain in gear so that it's easier to absorb the material.

There will always be things you miss. So go over your notes on the same day if you can to fill in any blanks. You're likely to be able to remember things while your memory is still fresh. If there's time for a brief study session with a friend, you'll probably come up with all the important points between you.

Here are some tips for getting the best value from a lecture:

beforehand:

- check your syllabus to see how this lecture fits in
- do some pre-reading on the topic
- write down three questions on the topic before the lecture
- talk to other students about likely topics

during:

- note key headlines on any handouts provided
- pay special attention to the introduction
- listen for words or phrases that are stressed
- write down dates, technical terms, key phrases, etc.
- leave plenty of space on each page

afterwards:

- debrief with another student
- discuss any contentious points
- add items you missed

All the following can help you to remember things more easily:

- patterns
- colour
- pictures
- diagrams
- lists

- highlighting
- underlining
- boxing
- ringing
- arrows for linking

Make use of as many basic abbreviations as you can, because these are great time-savers. For example: *hist.* for history, *psych.* for psychology and *trad.* for tradition. There are symbols too, of course:

therefore	∴
because	∵
is	=
isn't	≠
nineteenth century	⑲
twentieth century	⑳
more than	>
less than	<

If you need to get in some practice at note-taking before starting a course, you might try listening to a radio programme on a subject linked to your studies. Go for radio rather than TV programmes so that you won't be distracted by pictures.

READING AND ANALYSING ACADEMIC MATERIAL

Obviously, you'll have more thinking time when you take notes from books than when you're in a lecture theatre and there are various strategies you can use to make the process easier. Read only what you need, look for journal articles and for relevant chapters in books – even a specific section of a chapter, and use contents lists and indexes to direct you relevant pages. Scanning and skimming (see below) can also help you to locate the parts of a text that deal with the topic you're studying.

Just as with a lecture, it's a good idea to ask yourself some questions about what's likely to be in the text before you start. Try to think up three or four, such as:

- Will I find out about x?
- What details will there be on y?
- What's the writer's view on z?

Then scan the material very quickly. Look at headings, sub-headings, diagrams, graphs and any illustrations. This will help you feel more comfortable because your brain will be starting to become familiar with the territory. You might also be able to pick out some of the sections that you'll want to read in detail.

* scan headings, sub-headings, diagrams and graphs

Then you can skim. Read the first and last paragraphs of a chapter – the introduction and conclusion. This should give you a better idea of the areas covered. Then go a little deeper by reading the first and last sentences of each paragraph. This will show you more clearly which bits you need to focus on.

* to skim, read the first and last paragraphs of a chapter and the first and last sentences of all paragraphs

In order to work through the following section, please now read the article 'Why a high society is a free society' by the philosopher A.C. Grayling (originally published in the *Observer*). I've numbered the paragraphs so that you can refer to things easily.

Why a high society is a free society
A.C. Grayling

1 One measure of a good society is whether its individual members have the autonomy to do as they choose in respects that principally concern only them. The debate about heroin, cocaine and marijuana touches precisely on this. In my submission, a society in

which such substances are legal and available is a good society not because drugs are in themselves good, but because the autonomy of those who wish to use them is respected. For other and broader reasons, many of them practical, such a society will be a better one.

2   I have never taken drugs other than alcohol, nicotine, caffeine and medicinal drugs. Of these, I have for many years not taken the two former. I think it is inimical to a good life to be dependent for pleasure and personal fulfilment on substances which gloss or distort reality and interfere with rationality; and yet I believe that heroin, cocaine, marijuana, ecstasy and cognates of these should be legal and available in exactly the same way as nicotine and alcohol.

3   In logic [there] is no difference between legal and currently illegal drugs. Both are used for pleasure, relief from stress or anxiety, and 'holidaying' from normal life, and both are, in different degrees, dangerous to health. Given this, consistent policy must do one of two things: criminalise the use of nicotine and alcohol, in order to bring them in line with currently illegal substances; or legalise currently illegal substances under the same kinds of regime that govern nicotine and alcohol.

4   On civil liberties grounds the latter policy is preferable because there is no justification in a good society for policing behaviour unless, in the form of rape, murder, theft, riot or fraud, it is intrinsically damaging to the social fabric, and involves harm to unwilling third parties. Good law protects in these respects; bad law tries to coerce people into behaving according to norms chosen by people who claim to know and to do better than those for whom they legislate. But the imposition of such norms is an injustice. By all means let the disapprovers argue and exhort; giving them the power to coerce and punish as well is unacceptable.

5   Arguments to the effect that drugs should be kept illegal to protect children fall by the same token. On these grounds, nicotine and alcohol should be banned too. In fact there is greater danger to children from the illegality of drugs.

6   Almost everyone who wishes to try drugs, does so; almost everyone who wishes to make use of drugs does it irrespective of their legal status. Opponents say legalisation will lead to unrestrained use and abuse. Yet the evidence is that where laws have been relaxed there is little variation in frequency or kind of use.

7   The classic example is Prohibition in the USA during the 1920s. (The hysteria over alcohol extended to other drugs; heroin was made illegal in the USA in 1924, on the basis of poor research on its health risks and its alleged propensity to cause insanity and criminal behaviour.) Prohibition created a huge criminal industry. The end of Prohibition did not result in a frenzy of drinking, but did leave a much-enhanced crime problem, because the criminals turned to substances which remained illegal, and supplied them instead.

8   Crime destabilises society. Gangland rivalry, the use of criminal organisations to launder money, to fund terrorism and gun-running, to finance the trafficking of women and to buy political and judicial influence all destabilise the conditions for a good society far beyond such problems as could be created by private individuals' use of drugs. If drugs were legally and safely available through chemist shops, and if their use was governed by the same provisions as govern alcohol purchase and consumption, the main platform for organised crime would be removed, and thereby one large obstacle to the welfare of society.

9   It would also remove much petty crime, through which many users fund their habit. If addiction to drugs were treated as a medical rather than criminal matter, so that addicts could get safe, regular supplies on prescription, the crime rate would drop dramatically, as argued recently by certain police chiefs.

10   The safety issue is a simple one. Paracetamol is more dangerous than heroin. Taking double the standard dose of paracetamol, a non-prescription analgesic, can be dangerous. Taking double the standard medical dose of heroin (diamorphine) causes sleepiness and no lasting effects.

11   A good society should be able to accommodate practices which are not destructive of social bonds (in the way that theft, rape, murder and other serious crimes are), but mainly have to do with private behaviour. In fact, a good society should only interfere in private behaviour in extremis.

12   Until a century ago, now-criminal substances were legal and freely available. Some (opium in the form of laudanum) were widely used. Just as some people are damaged by misuse of alcohol, so a few were adversely affected by misuses of other drugs. Society as

a whole was not adversely affected by the use of drugs; but it was benefited by the fact that it did not burden itself with a misjudged, unworkable and paternalistic endeavour to interfere with those who chose to use drugs.

13   The place of drugs in the good society is not about the drugs as such, but rather the freedom and the value to individuals and their society of openness to experimentation and alternative behaviours and lifestyles. The good society is permissive, seeking to protect third parties from harm but not presuming to order people to take this or that view about what is in their own good.

---

autonomy	freedom to determine one's own actions
inimical	unfavourable, hostile
cognates	related things
analgesic	pain killer

▶ Key sentences

In any paragraph, everything is likely to revolve around one topic, and the paragraph will contain a key sentence concerning that topic. This sentence will be the most important statement in that paragraph and everything else will follow from it. It's often the first sentence. Once you've found this key sentence, understanding meaning becomes a lot easier. We'll look now at finding the key sentences throughout Grayling's article.

* every paragraph has a main topic and a key sentence

The introduction is the point where a writer explains what the text is going to cover. Grayling's first sentence in **paragraph 1** prepares the reader with the words 'good society' and 'autonomy'. We begin to get the message that he has a particular ethical stance and that he's in favour of the freedom of the individual. Sentence two gets straight to the main topic: drugs. Then, in sentence three, he gives an immediate clue that this is the core of the paragraph by saying, 'In my submission'. He's clearly going to set out his stall here. This is what the article is going to be about so it's the key sentence in this paragraph. Sentence 4 adds a little elaboration.

In **paragraph 2**, the key sentence is the long one beginning 'I think …'. The first two sentences are merely personal information. (Note that in an essay you won't generally mention yourself – see Chapter 2.)

In **paragraph 3**, the key sentence is the third. The first two sentences give explanation necessary to understand the argument that's put forcefully in the third sentence – that society must either criminalise nicotine and alcohol or legalise illegal substances.

In **paragraph 4**, the key sentence is the first. It picks up and underlines the final point from the previous paragraph on 'legalis[ing] currently illegal substances'. The remaining part of this paragraph gives further elaboration on and explanation of this statement. In **paragraph 5**, the key sentence is the first and in **paragraph 6**, it's the last.

In **paragraph 7**, the key sentence is the third: 'Prohibition created a huge criminal industry.' This is followed by details of unintended negative consequences of Prohibition.

In **paragraph 8**, the key sentence is the first. The remainder of the paragraph goes on to explain this statement and suggest a cure. In **paragraph 9**, the key sentence is also the first which neatly follows from the comments on organised crime in paragraph 8 with a clear statement on petty crime.

In **paragraph 10**, it's the first sentence again: 'The safety issue is a simple one.' Grayling follows this with explanation and examples. The same goes for **paragraph 11** where Grayling comes back to his argument about the 'good society'.

Sometimes it can be really tricky to decide on a key sentence. **Paragraph 12**, where Grayling notes the legal situation in previous times, hangs on the first sentence which states the area he's discussing. But the last sentence contains a very strong plank of his overall argument, so you might choose that one.

In the conclusion – **paragraph 13** – it's really tricky to decide which is the key sentence since the second sentence restates the first in different words. I think the first is a slightly clearer statement so I'd go for that one.

The key sentence in any paragraph will be the logical base on which the paragraph rests. The remainder of the paragraph will explain and exemplify it. But here's a word of warning: the key sentence might not necessarily be the one that interests you most in relation to the particular assignment you're working on (see 'Selecting information' below).

► Punctuation as a useful guide to meaning

Whenever you're faced with reading a complex text, following the punctuation can be a help towards understanding it. Sentences are a paragraph's building blocks and a writer will be expecting you to absorb the meaning one sentence at a time. So if you find a paragraph hard to understand, go back to the beginning and take it one sentence at a time. Watching for commas can also help you with picking out meaning as they mark off different parts of a sentence, showing which bits fit together logically (see the section on commas in chapter 14). Reading a sentence aloud, pausing at each punctuation mark can often help you over a difficult patch.

* punctuation helps with meaning & shows you which parts of a sentence fit together

► Implication, suggestion and bias

It's important to be alert for bias in things you read – for statements that result from a writer's personal views. Seemingly simple things like repetition or the use of a term as though it had academic significance can be used to sway readers.

Grayling repeats the phrase 'good society' a number of times, and uses it as though it has a specific meaning that we can all agree on. But your definition of a good society may not be the same as his – or mine – even though we'd probably agree that such a society would be founded on sound ethical principles.

Grayling is an experienced writer, so this repetition cannot have occurred by chance. When he comes to his conclusion, Grayling subtly strengthens the effect by changing from the non-specific '*a* good society' to the specific '*the* good society' (my italics). He's not only given the term prominence by repetition but has finally enforced its validity with the word 'the'.

Explicit language says exactly what it means:

The train for Brighton leaves at 15.00 hours.

Implicit language contains some kind of suggestion:

We're told that the train for Brighton leaves at 15.00 hours.

That sentence is not so straightforward. By beginning it with the words, 'We're told that', the speaker suggests that the information might not be accurate – that in this case, there might be some delay. There's a further possible implication – that trains to Brighton are often late. So there's an implied criticism of the service on this line – or possibly of the whole rail network.

Look at this sentence:

> Easton's MP has been seen lunching with high-ranking members of the Opposition on three occasions in the last fortnight.

The implication here is that the MP in question is about to leave his party. But this wasn't stated outright, so if a sentence like this appeared in a newspaper, there could be no accusations of libel. The writer has stuck to observable facts, but has put them forward in such a way that readers will draw the conclusion that defection is imminent. It's important to be aware of this kind of trick in what you're reading.

▶ Things that writers omit

When a writer wants to put forward a particular view, he or she will frequently omit to mention facts and arguments that might detract from it. Grayling's piece on heroin was written for a newspaper (the *Observer*) and is an 'opinion' piece. This means that he didn't need to include detailed evidence or give references for his assertions. The article is useful as a means of discovering Grayling's views and as a way, perhaps, of broadening our perspective on the drug issue. What it doesn't do is provide much material on the current state of heroin use that could be used to support an academic argument on legalising drugs in an essay.

* writers sometimes omit things that would detract from their argument

NOTE-TAKING FROM WRITTEN SOURCES

There are various ways you can make notes, and what you do will depend partly on the subject you are studying and partly on what the notes are to be used for. Find the method that suits you best.

You'll be guided, in part, by the task or assignment you've been set.

You're likely to be either writing an essay or preparing to give a short talk or a seminar paper. Never spend time on books that are only vaguely related to your topic, and never make notes on a whole chapter unless it's brim-full of ideas and data relevant to your work. Choose just those things that will be useful for you.

If you own the book you're working from, do underline things and make notes in the margin. Books you've bought for your studies are your tools. So make them work for you. If you use pencil, you can always rub things out later. It's best not to use a highlighting pen since highlighting can't be changed if you find you've made an error.

Always copy the bibliographical details of books and journals that you work from. You can't use ideas or quotations in your assignments without saying where they came from. So without publication details (see Chapter 3), your work would be wasted.

* Copy bibliographic details of every book you use at the top of your first page of notes

Keep a running tally of page numbers in your left-hand margin. These are essential for referencing (see Chapter 3) and for finding your way back to a point you might want to check or expand on later.

If you have ideas of your own or want to note down a comment on what the writer says, use a consistent method of showing this in your notes, otherwise it can be hard to differentiate your own observations from what the writer actually wrote. I put my own comments in square brackets and add my initial.

Wherever possible, make notes in your own words. This helps you to fully understand the material and will be useful for essays where you'll need to demonstrate that you understand a topic. It's fine, however, to copy occasionally where the writer has put something especially well or when it would be difficult to reduce something to simple terms – as long as you use quote marks and give a reference.

* keep a running tally of page numbers in your margin as you make your notes

▶ **Full notes**

When you make full notes, it's generally best to omit explanations, examples, humorous asides and personal stories. Go for the core of the writer's ideas. If you were to make full notes on Grayling's article, they would probably look something like those below. (Numbers here refer to Grayling's paragraphs.)

1 Soc. where all drugs legal = gd: freedom of individual.
2 'good life' shd. not depend on 'substances which … distort reality'. But: hard drugs shd. be treated like nicotine & alcohol.
3 Legal/illegal drugs = used for: pleasure, stress relief, escapism. Both = 'dangerous to health' but shd. be treated same.
4 Only practices that harm soc. or 'unwilling third parties' shd. be illegal. Legal coercion of private behaviour is wrong.
5 Children more at risk when drugs illegal.
6 Drug-taking not prevented by laws.
7 Prohibition in USA caused increase in crime.
8 Organised crime = threat to society: money-laundering, terrorism, vice rings, buying political influence. Ans. = controlled sale of hard drugs in chemists.
9 If addicts got supplies on prescription, petty crime & overall crime rate = down.
10 Overuse of standard painkillers – more dangerous than hard drugs.
11 If a practice isn't dangerous to soc. – shd. not be illegal. Only restrict private behaviour 'in extremis'.
12 Hist. shows no more damage to soc. from drug use than alcohol + no 'paternalistic … interfere[nce]' with private behaviour.
13 Freedom to choose lifestyles (while protecting third parties) = essential in 'good society'

You'd probably only do such comprehensive work on an article, however, if you had to summarise it (see Chapter 5) or write a critique of it. When you're making notes for an essay, you'll look for just those things that relate to the particular essay question.

▶ Selecting information

In most situations, you won't want to take notes on a whole article or chapter. You'll be selecting information for a particular task. Let's suppose you've been given the following essay question:

Heroin should be legalised. Discuss.

Your essay would probably look at facts and statistics on drug use: health, NHS costs, crime, particular examples and the views of various professionals and commentators. So if you wanted to mention Grayling, you'd need just his main ideas. You might make the following notes from his article:

1 A 'good society' protects freedom of the individual.
5 Children more at risk when drugs illegal.
7 Prohibition (US) caused increase in crime.
8 Legal availability through chemists wd. reduce organised/ petty crime.
11 Gd. soc. restricts 'interfere[nce] in private behaviour'.
12 Hist. shows little damage to society as a whole from drug use.

These notes that go straight down the page are called linear notes. You could, of course, organise your notes in a mind map (see above and Chapter 2). Or you might like to put them in the form of a table – something like this:

Grayling on Heroin

'Good Society'	Children	Historical evidence
individual autonomy (1)	more at risk when drugs illegal (5)	Prohibition (US) resulted in worse crime problem
protects third parties (4)		little damage to society from drugs (12)
doesn't interfere in private behaviour (11)		

If you argued in favour of legalising heroin in your essay, you might note the reasonableness of Grayling's position and stress his points on less damage to children and the lack of historical evidence showing any harm to society. If, on the other hand, you became convinced by your reading that heroin should not be legalised, you might still want to refer to Grayling's article because, in order to discuss the proposition on legalisation, you'd need to show a range of views. You could then use various other items of evidence to argue against him.

SUMMARY

This chapter has covered:

Note-taking in lectures
- what to do before, during and after a lecture
- looking for structure and using headings
- listening for key terms
- leaving space on your page
- using abbreviations

Reading and analysis
- scanning and skimming the material
- finding key sentences
- using the punctuation as a guide to meaning
- watching for implication, suggestion and bias
- noticing what writers omit

Note-taking from written sources
- recording the bibliographic details
- taking full notes
- taking notes for a specific essay
- linear notes, mind maps and tables

2 Writing an Essay

This chapter will show you how to:

▶ structure an essay with a clear plan
▶ form an argument
▶ use evidence
▶ plan a paragraph
▶ draft your work
▶ proof-read

INTRODUCTION

Writing your essays is likely to be a time-consuming process at first, and many people become extremely worried about them. Sandra, one of my students, was afraid that I would think her work was childish. Another student, Bill, felt he had to prove himself first time round.

Neither student should have worried. Sandra needed to realise that everyone has something useful to say, even if at first they have difficulty expressing their ideas on paper, and Bill soon found out that we learn to write essays through practice.

At college or university, you're likely to find that things are rather different from what many of us did at school five, ten, twenty or more years ago. When we were given the title for an essay, we usually went away and wrote as much as we knew on the subject. Now, you'll be given a very specific question. Instead of writing all you know on a topic, you'll need to select information that's relevant to that particular question and argue the case for your carefully considered opinion on it. There are two examples of essays at the end of this chapter.

Writing an essay is a process that contains different stages. You'll spend time gathering information, working out what you think about various aspects of what you've studied, and finding out how best to get the crucial issues on paper. Essays grow. You'll almost certainly find that some parts go well, while with others you feel you're wading through treacle. The answer is to take things in stages. Aim to give yourself plenty of time to work on an essay (sometimes for quite short periods at a go) over a week at least – more if possible.

* writing an essay is a process with specific stages

Different subjects have different ground rules. If you're studying history, for example, there'll be great emphasis on events, on texts written in the period you're studying and on various accounts by later commentators. In sociology, the emphasis is likely to be on theories about society and on surveys of different societies or parts of a society. If your subject is English literature, you'll have found that you need to analyse language very closely. If you're studying a science subject, you'll need to focus on data, to show clear results, and to demonstrate how these are arrived at.

PREPARATION

► Analysing the question

Essay questions can often seem very complicated, and sometimes, people are put off by this. Most questions turn out to be a lot less complex than they at first appear, however, but if you're already feeling nervous, a difficult-looking question can seem like a cast-iron reason for giving up a course.

Questions often look difficult because they are written in rather formal language. There are two reasons for this. The first is that the tutor has probably tried to be as precise as possible and to write something that can't be misunderstood. She or he has actually tried to be as helpful as possible. The other reason is that the question will have been set out in such a way as to put boundaries on what you do. If the topic is not restricted, you wouldn't know where to stop. Oddly enough, it sometimes turns out that questions which look easy prove to be harder to answer than those which appear more complex. A tightly structured question will help you organise your work and keep on track.

> * a question that looks difficult can often help you structure your essay clearly

Many people have learned the hard way that it is absolutely essential to *underline the key words* in an essay question before you do anything else. If you get things wrong at this stage, all your work could be wasted. There are two reasons for underlining: you need to understand *exactly* what is wanted and you need to eliminate the possibility of making errors that would send you off in the wrong direction. It's so easy to misread a word or even to answer the question that you hoped you would be asked. Underlining also helps to get your brain in gear so that you start work painlessly.

Let's suppose that you've been asked to write an essay with the following title:

Discuss the case for having increased censorship in the media.

Here are my underlinings:

<u>Discuss</u> <u>the case</u> for having <u>increased censorship</u> in the <u>media</u>.

You'll notice that I've underlined nearly everything. This often makes people feel that it would be quicker to underline the whole thing and be done with it. But that would defeat the object, which is to break up the question into its separate parts.

It's important to be clear on what is *not* asked. The question does not, for example, ask for a full survey of current censorship. Nor does it ask for a historical survey or a detailed analysis of practice in one area. Taking any of those approaches could lead to a low grade, although brief mention of them could be useful. For example, a couple of sentences summing up what's happened in the past could help to give background information in your introduction. Detailed analysis, too, will be essential in your essay – though it needs to be on something that's particularly relevant to the question.

If an essay question relates to a wide area, it's perfectly reasonable to put boundaries on what you write. You can't cover everything. Of course, you will need to make sure that you don't omit anything vital, but, generally speaking, as long as you address the topics from the question and make clear in your introduction what your essay will cover, there should be no problem. It's sometimes a good idea, however, to check with your tutor before you start that what you plan to do is acceptable.

The process of writing essays is a process of training our minds to think clearly. A good essay is one which sticks like a limpet to the key issues and so does exactly what it says on the tin (the essay question). If, by any chance, you're not sure what the question is asking for, go back to your tutor for clarification. S/he would far rather spend five minutes with you before you begin than have to mark an essay that gets things all wrong. In fact, most tutors find that answering questions makes them feel wanted.

* an essay needs to focus closely on the issues mentioned in the question

You may sometimes need to use a dictionary for accurate definitions of certain key words in the question. Be careful, however, over words that can have specific meanings for your subject area. Use a subject-specific dictionary for these. It's possible, however, that the words you need explained are in a handout you've been given or that they've been defined in a seminar. Check your notes.

It was important to underline the word 'Discuss' in the essay question because this gives the instruction on how to angle the essay. You will often be asked to *discuss*. This means that your essay needs to consider the question from different angles, using evidence, ideas and/or quotes from key writers. Then you need to include your own judgement on which is/are the more reasonable. Here's a list of different instructions you might be given:

analyse	pull a topic apart to show its constituent parts and look at these in detail
argue	make a case for something, using evidence and examples, and draw a clear conclusion
assess	weigh something up and consider how valuable it may be
comment	explain something, giving a brief judgement on it, with reasons
compare	show the similarities between two items or ideas
contrast	show the differences between two items or ideas
criticise	show the good and bad points of something, looking at any implications
define	give the precise meaning of
describe	give a detailed account of
discuss	explain and analyse various angles on a topic, showing which is most reasonable
evaluate	explain the worth of something, giving reasons
explain	make clear with reasons, showing any implications
explore	examine thoroughly from different viewpoints
illustrate	give fully explained examples of something in order to make it clear
interpret	explain, showing key features and implications
justify	give good reasons why something has been said or done, answering possible objections
outline	give a broad description of the main issues of something
review	give a general survey, noting key features and commenting on their value
trace	set out the history or development of something, explaining the stages
verify	check out and report on the accuracy of something

► Generating ideas

The next stage is to spend some time *thinking* about the topic. It's a stage that often gets missed out. We tend to jump in and start an essay too quickly, kidding ourselves that if we've got started, we're making headway.

Well at this stage you might be in a state of confusion, and that's fine. In fact, it's a good thing. The whole point of essay-writing is to go through a process of learning more about a topic and organising our thoughts about it. Writing an essay develops our understanding.

    * thinking-time is vital

So it can be a good idea to start with a mind map. In this book, *mind maps* are used to help with two different processes – getting ideas and making notes. Here, we're looking at the process of getting ideas. A mind map is said to mimic the way our brains work, making connections that look more like a web or net than items on a list. Constructing a mind map is a way of trawling for ideas in order to see what we know and where we need to find out more.

It's important to think in broad terms at this stage and to throw down absolutely everything that comes to mind – good, bad and indifferent. What you want is the big picture. Here's my map of ideas for the censorship essay (mentioned above):

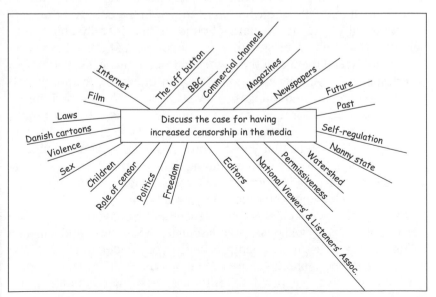

The important thing is to keep your thoughts moving and not to stop yourself from writing anything that seems wrong. Assessing yourself at this point can result in putting your brain on a 'go-slow' or sapping your confidence. What you're after at this point is a completely free flow of ideas. Seemingly daft thoughts can sometimes lead on to really good ones that have been lurking in your subconscious. So keep writing.

A word here for tidy people: there are times when tidiness is highly valuable, but this is not one of them. Creativity won't occur when you are busy dotting i's, crossing t's and using a rubber.

At this stage, it's a good idea to gather together any class notes, lecture notes, photocopies and handouts that will be relevant to the essay and to glance through them to remind yourself of the territory. Now, bearing in mind the question, look at the ideas that have turned up on your mind map together with your understanding of what the course has covered so far on this topic. At this point, you'll begin to see where you need to do more reading.

* use your mind map to direct your reading

▶ Gathering further information

If you've not been given a reading list, ask your tutor to recommend something. If that fails, see what you can find in the college or university library. If you're stuck, there's bound to be a friendly librarian to help you. Don't, however, go out with a great pile of books. You won't have time to read them and the mere sight of the pile is likely to make you despair. You're not even going to read one book from cover to cover. Use contents and indexes to get straight to relevant sections.

You'll be looking for relevant ideas and theories as well as for facts, figures, explanations of areas that have confused you and useful points from reputable sources that you can quote to back up your argument. Don't be fooled, however, into assuming that writers and critics in any field are always right. When you're sure of your ground, it's quite acceptable to challenge their ideas in your essays.

It's important to get plenty of notes together before you start to write (see Chapter 1). This will give you material to choose from and will also ensure that your essay has depth because your understanding of the topic area will be more developed. You may use only a small proportion of your notes, but you'll have a good overview of the topic and you'll be able to choose just the most fitting items. Notes that you don't use for your essay may well come in handy at exam time, so don't feel that your work has been wasted.

> * you might need only a small proportion of the notes you make

You'll undoubtedly want to make use of the Internet as this is so useful for finding relevant articles – many of which will have been printed in reputable newspapers and journals. These can be extremely useful for evidence (and for saving you time), but confining yourself to using the Net is no substitute for learning to work from books that are key texts in your subject. Many items on the Internet, while interesting, can have purely temporary interest and a limited viewpoint as well as lacking a firm basis in research. (See Chapter 3 for more information on using the Internet.)

> * use material from the internet with care

▶ Planning

When you've read up on the main areas you'll be covering, it's time to make a plan. This is the hardest part of writing an essay, and the most important. It will give you a structure to work from. Careful planning is the key to writing a good essay (and I wish I'd known this when I was an undergraduate). Once you've written a good plan, you'll not only find that writing the essay is easier; you'll almost certainly get good grades. And the better your plan, the fewer drafts you're likely to need.

> * a strong plan results in a strong essay

Whatever the topic, your plan is going to fall into three broad sections.

Introduction
- statement of the main issues involved
- brief background information
- statement of the ground the essay will cover and the conclusion it will come to

Main body of the essay
- three to five numbered headings for the main topics/areas your essay will cover
- a list of sub-points (which can show as bullet points) under each heading

Conclusion
- a summing-up of the main points made in the essay
- a link to the central point(s) of the essay question to demonstrate you've covered them

The meat of your plan lies in the middle section – between the introduction and conclusion. You'll need to think carefully about the order in which you set out the topics you'll cover. Each topic needs to follow helpfully from the previous one so that essay will hang together well. Having a useful order will also make it easy for you to put a clear link at the beginning of each paragraph.

* the meat of your plan will be in the middle section

You can leave your introduction blank to start with. You probably won't have a clear idea of what will go in it until you've completed the middle section. You can even write up the first draft of the middle section of your essay before planning your introduction. The same goes for your conclusion. But do plan those paragraphs before you write them up.

Your plan will be a working document; you might need to adjust it as you go along. If it turns out to be restrictive or unhelpful in any way, change it. Sometimes, students feel that there's no point making a plan in the first place if it's likely to be changed. But it's only when you have created a structure that you can begin to find out what does and doesn't work. The tighter your plan, the better your essay will be – and the easier it will be to write.

* a good, tight plan will help you write your essay

There are many ways to produce a good assignment. What you do will depend partly on your own interests as well as on the topic and your individual way of working. There are three simple rules, however, for writing a plan:

A plan needs to:

- be set out in single-line spacing (the essay itself will be in double)
- be written in note form without sentences
- fit on one side of A4 paper

Aim to use as few words as possible. This will force you to think really hard about what will be in your essay and the result will be a stronger piece of writing. And if you're tearing your hair out by this stage, you're clearly normal. Planning is hard work. Here's the basis of Pete's plan for the essay on press censorship which you'll see later on (I've omitted his items of evidence and argument for now):

Discuss the case for having increased censorship in the media

PLAN

Introduction
democracy & the media
censorship is alien to democracy
the problem of events

1 Privacy rights of the individual
- anonymity of offenders
- place of the legal system
- human rights

2 Self-regulation
- media can self-regulate where necessary
- TV warnings of disturbing material
- watershed
- difficult areas
- press rights

3 Public opinion as regulator
- a free press is not without restrictions
- reaction to Danish cartoons of Muhammad
- *Jyllands-Posten*'s apology

Conclusion
media must be free to make mistakes
legal frameworks & self-regulation are sufficient
public opinion is the ultimate regulator

As you work on your plan, aim to fill in some very brief notes on the evidence you'll use and on the argument you'll put forward. This will keep you firmly on track.

It's often helpful, when you've decided on the structure of your plan, to colour-code the relevant sections in your notes, handouts, etc. This can save a lot of time because it means that you can easily find items you need when your mind is otherwise engaged on the writing process.

▶ Argument and evidence

There are two crucial elements that make a good essay: the plan and the argument. Writing an argument doesn't mean that you need to get heated, however. It means that you need to look at the evidence objectively, set out what you feel is the most valid interpretation of the issues involved, and comment clearly on the topics you raise as the essay progresses.

One thing you want to avoid at all costs is telling a story. If, for example, you are writing a history essay, you won't need to recount everything that happened. Aim to pick out just those items that you can use for a discussion of the essay question. You'll be graded on the way you interpret, analyse and discuss, not on your ability to reproduce a narrative of events. Do be guided by your tutor, however, over the amount of factual information you'll need to include in your particular subject area.

In a nutshell, writing an argument entails explaining to the person reading your essay what you want him or her to *think* about the material you cover as you go along. In a court of law, counsels for the prosecution and defence will question the same witnesses, but they might draw very different conclusions from witness testimonies. Your tutor needs to understand your particular angle on the material. So spell it out.

* your argument will explain what you want your reader to *think* about issues you cover

Back up your argument with evidence, demonstrating how each point you make helps to answer the essay question. Your evidence might be facts, figures, information from reports and/or quotes from a specific text or from respected sources. When you look for evidence, you'll want to use trusted sources that can be relied on. When you write your own essays, you're practising being a trustworthy source yourself. So act like the professionals: be sure that your argument holds water and your sources are sound.

* always back up your argument with evidence

Putting argument into your essay means writing persuasively (see also Chapter 4). Everyday life is full of persuasion, but we generally engage in it orally. If, for example, you have a 13-year-old son or daughter who wants to become a regular whisky drinker, you're going to want to show that this wouldn't be a good idea. Teenagers can be very persuasive themselves, of course, so you'll need a good argument, and you'll probably trot out some facts: selling alcohol to under-18s is illegal, an early drink habit can lead to alcoholism, too much in the way of spirits can damage the liver. We could plan out your line of attack like this:

1 the law
2 alcoholism
3 other health issues

As you mention each topic, you'll argue your case:

1 the law: the law is for everyone's protection and law-breakers often go to prison
2 alcoholism: this could ruin your life – your job, relationship and home could be at risk
3 other health issues: it's important to look after your body

Let's suppose it's a good day and you're feeling calm. You might introduce your argument by saying something like this:

> "There are lots of reasons why I can't let you drink whisky. Let me explain ..."

You might conclude by saying something like this:

> "So I'm sorry, but I really can't let you do this because it's my duty to help you abide by the law and protect your health."

That, in a nutshell, is the shape of an argument: there's an introduction, key topics are covered, comment is given on each and there's a conclusion that sums up your position. Persuading a teenager not to drink whisky is, of course, rather one-sided. In this instance, you probably wouldn't want to put forward any evidence for an alternative viewpoint. In your essays, however, you're generally going to need to look at things from more than one angle. Including other viewpoints can even be a way of strengthening your own stance. You can come across as level-headed by demonstrating what's reasonable about a writer's stance and then picking holes in the remainder of their argument.

People sometimes try to reduce an essay to two sections – points for and points against – but this method generally has problems. It forces you to put everything in one section or the other without allowing for grey areas and a full discussion. It can also result in two huge, unwieldy sections – or worse, one tiny and one enormous one. Splitting the essay up by topic areas and commenting on each as you go along will result in a much more balanced and effective piece of work.

People also sometimes feel strongly about a topic and want to put their personal opinions into essays. Others actually worry about using their own opinions. Well, what's wanted is your considered opinion after you've looked at the facts and at what specialists in the field have said about the topic. Once you've looked at the evidence and considered the topic from different angles, you'll be giving an academic opinion. So be sure to include facts and quotes from reliable sources to back up what you say.

> * a good argument entails consideration of the facts and whatever specialists have written

▶ **Grey areas**

There's no need to be categorical, however, if you're writing about something that's a bit of a grey area or if, even after doing your reading, you feel that there's no straight answer. This is where some of the following phrases can come in handy:

- it seems as though …
- some evidence suggests that …
- it's possibly the case that …

And it's quite reasonable to say that on the one hand, writer X says *this* while on the other, writer Y says *that*. Then show which view you are more inclined to agree with – and why.

STARTING TO WRITE

Many people find that one of the hardest parts of writing an essay is starting to write the first draft. Well, the good news is that since this is a first draft, it doesn't matter what it looks like – and you don't even have to start at the beginning. As long as you've got a clear plan, you can, if you wish, start by working on the section that interests you most or that you find easiest. Your enthusiasm will then have a spin-off effect and you'll find it easier to do things you'd felt were more difficult.

You might like to think of your essay as a jigsaw puzzle. You gradually need to get all the pieces in the right places, but you can add a piece whenever you spot where it will fit. The main thing at first is to cover the ground – to get the whole thing on paper *somehow* without worrying about making it look perfect.

* you can start by writing the easiest bits

It doesn't even matter if you're not quite sure what you think before you begin writing. One of the functions of essay-writing is to force us to think harder as we go along and to clarify things in our own minds. We often don't know what we really think until we've tried to express it on paper. As you work on your assignment, you'll almost certainly find that your ideas become clearer.

If you're really stuck, start by writing down something that your tutor – or another student – has said on the topic. You can always cross this out later. What you'll be doing is tricking your mind into getting started. If you're handwriting the essay, use one side of the paper only. Then when you come to redrafting, you can, if necessary, cut the thing up and put it together in a different order just as if you were working on a computer.

By the way, don't fall into the trap of thinking that, because your tutor knows the subject inside out, you don't need to spell things out. The only way for a tutor to find out whether *you* understand the topic fully is for you to write it down. The fact that you were able to discuss the issue competently in a class session will not count. Marks can be given only for what you actually put on paper.

* spell out your ideas clearly

▶ Paragraphing

A paragraph will always contain a key sentence – that is, a statement (possibly a statement of argument) on what the paragraph is about. The key sentence is very often the first, and in order to make things easy on yourself, you might like to use that format. The rest of the paragraph will elaborate on the key sentence and bear out what it states through adding explanation and argument and providing proof in the form of facts, data and/or a quote. Your final sentence in a paragraph can then pull together the points discussed in it. So a paragraph can sometimes be thought of as a mini essay – with an introduction (the key sentence), main body (the argument and evidence) and conclusion.

You might like to look back at the analysis of Grayling's paragraphs in Chapter 1, but bear in mind that Grayling was writing an article for a newspaper where it would be fine to have some paragraphs that are quite short. Also be aware that Grayling has written an opinion article – not an assessed essay. This means that he has had more leeway to advance his personal views than is possible in an essay.

* a paragraph always has a key sentence, and it can be the first one

Some people find it helpful to plan out paragraphs at the essay-planning stage, deciding exactly what is going to go into each one. I prefer to stick to planning sections so that any section will contain as many paragraphs as are necessary to explain and develop it. But either method will work, so choose what feels right for you.

▶ Paragraphs that are too long

If there's too much going on in one paragraph, a reader may start to get bogged down. So aim to cover just one topic or, perhaps, one aspect of a longer topic. If you have a handwritten paragraph that is a page or more long, check to see whether it contains more than one issue and could helpfully be broken into two. The same goes for a word-processed paragraph of much more than about twelve lines.

▶ Paragraphs that are too short

If a paragraph covers only three or four lines or is composed of only one or two sentences, it's almost certainly too short. There are two possibilities here: it might fit better as part of the preceding or the following paragraph, or it might need expansion. It very possibly needs expansion. You're likely to have raised a new idea that now needs explanation, examples and comment. The fact that you've written very little on it may indicate that you know less about this than other issues covered in your essay. It's no good, however, raising an issue and then leaving it hanging in mid-air. Perhaps you need to do some extra reading. If you've got no clue on how to expand a short paragraph and it won't fit into the preceding or following one, you're probably going to have to be ruthless and cut it out.

▶ Linking

Clear linking of one paragraph to the next is essential. Linking helps whoever is reading your essay to understand how one point leads to another and where the essay is going. A well-structured piece of writing will be put together in such a way that each section follows smoothly from the one before in a logical manner. You can do this by the use of specific linking words and phrases:

Despite the evidence above	In addition
In contrast to this	As a result
The above X shows that	Similarly
This X also relates to	Therefore
It follows from this that	Conversely
Smith, however, disagrees with this analysis	

The word *this* can be very handy, especially when you use it with a re-statement of the topic you've been discussing in the previous paragraph. For example, *this view of x ...*, *this result ...*, *this type of behaviour*, *this survey ...*, and so on.

Good paragraphing with strong links will carry an essay's argument clearly and so can make the difference between a forceful essay that gains a high grade and one that never really gets off the ground. A. C. Grayling's article is a particularly good example of linking. He spells out his links clearly throughout the entire piece. This is very good practice, and the process is so important for your own work that its worth looking at all the links in his article:

Paragraph	Method of linking
2 linked to 1	By the simplest means. Grayling re-uses a word from his previous paragraph early in the first sentence: 'drugs'.
3 linked to 2	By the reuse of the word 'legal'. He has just been talking about making substances legal.
4 linked to 3	Through the phrase 'the latter policy'. At the end of 3, he has given a choice of policies. Now he refers to one of them.
5 linked to 4	With the phrase 'by the same token'. This refers specifically to what he's just mentioned – the argument that good laws protect the vulnerable and bad ones merely adhere to dogma.
6 linked to 5	Less obvious. He moves in this paragraph to consideration of the opposing position to his own. The word 'legalisation' links to the whole of his argument up to this point, and the introductory sentence brings the argument from theory into practice.
7 linked to 6	Very neatly by giving an example of what he means by what he's just said about issues around drug use. The words 'The classic example' make that link clearly.
8 linked to 7	With the word 'Crime' – the topic that was mentioned at the end of 7.
9 linked to 8	By using the word 'also'. In 8, he shows how 'organised' crime figures might be improved. In 9, he moves on to petty crime. The word 'also' forces the reader to make the link.
10 linked to 9	Implicit. Paragraph 9 mentions 'medical' matters. The 'safety issue' is obviously relevant here.
11 linked to 10	Implicit. Paragraph 10 plays down the effects of heroin. Paragraph 11 goes on to state that the effects of drug use do not damage society as a whole.
12 linked to 11	By giving an example – in this case, from history.
13 linked to 12	The opening reference to society – the topic that has been central to paragraphs 11 and 12.

▶ Introductions

Your introduction will consist of just one paragraph. As I explained earlier, it's often easiest to write this after you've written the main body of the essay. You will need to:

- identify the issues your essay covers
- outline how the essay will deal with these issues
- give *brief* background information to set the scene for the essay
- state your overall conclusion very briefly

There are also two things you mustn't do in your introduction:

- don't include any quotations
- don't include any argument

As well as a little background information, your introduction needs to state what areas the essay will cover and what its conclusion will be. Many people find it helpful to include a sentence that begins: *This essay will ...* In that sentence you can state exactly what's in the essay. You can see how this is done in the two student essays at the end of this chapter.

   * an introduction needs to state what's in the essay

▶ Conclusions

Like your introduction, your conclusion will consist of just one paragraph, and you can check this out in the student examples just mentioned. The conclusion is where you sign off, so to speak, by underlining your main points and tying up your argument. You will need to:

- summarise the main points you've made
- state your general conclusion
- relate your conclusion to the essay question

By relating your conclusion to the essay question, you're indicating to your tutor that you've done what you were asked to do, and this will get you more Brownie points.

There are a couple of things here that you must *not* do:

- don't introduce any new ideas/material
- don't use quotations

► Language and clarity

When you write the final draft of your essay, you'll need to be sure your sentences are grammatical. Good essays are those which make the writer's ideas really clear to the reader – in this case, your tutor. It makes no difference that he or she may have been teaching for twenty or thirty years and knows the subject inside out. S/he needs to be helped to understand exactly what *you* are getting at.

> * good essays make their ideas clear to the reader

You don't need to try to sound like a textbook; just aim to write in a simple and straightforward manner. It's a good idea to keep in mind that your work should be understandable to an intelligent reader from a *different* subject specialism. This means that you'll use technical terms only when necessary, that you'll explain your ideas fully, and that you'll be as precise as possible (see Chapter 4, Style).

Academic writing is logical and unemotional, formal, factual and precise. Because of the need for precision, we have to be especially careful not to state that something is the case if there is the least chance that it might not be so. A good way of getting around this particular problem is to say things such as:

>   It is *likely* that x is the case

Or

>   x *seems* to be the case

Saying things in this way allows you to show both that you know the possibilities and that you're aware of the pitfalls. Don't overdo this trick, however. You don't want your tutor to complain that you always sit on the fence.

▶ Writing impersonally

Nowadays, some tutors are happy to accept essays containing the word *I*, but your work will be more sophisticated if you learn to write impersonally. We call this writing in the third person. Some people feel that they *must* write in the first person. "I must admit that the views in the essay are mine", they say. The simple answer to this is that if an essay has your name on it, it's very clear that the views in it are yours. Don't worry about sounding authoritative. Your tutors are looking for essays that show strength of purpose. An essay that doesn't contain the word 'I' actually comes across much more forcefully. Notice how the statement:

Education for adults is essential.

seems somehow to have more validity than the statement: *I think education for adults is essential.*

The words *I think* introduce an element of doubt. They seem to imply that you feel that maybe you've got things wrong and that perhaps anyone who holds opposing views to yours has a more reasonable case. The first statement is adamant, although it contains no unnecessary emotion.

It's also best to omit the word 'you' from essays because doing that tends to personalise things and can sound a bit pushy. It can often be helpfully replaced by the word 'people'. So, instead of writing: *You want a good education for your children*, put:

People want a good education for their children.

▶ Writing objectively

It's very important, in academic writing, to omit personal views and to give evidence for your argument. Look at the following emotive piece of writing:

Fox-hunting is a cruel and barbaric sport. It is undertaken by upper-class types who don't care about hurting an animal. People who lose their jobs get what they deserve.

The views contained in those three sentences could be put across much more persuasively by omitting emotion and including some factual material:

> Fox-hunting is considered by many people to involve cruelty. The fact that the sport is traditional should not be used as a reason to ignore any pain suffered by foxes. Links to a network of rural employment, however, make the issue of banning fox-hunting more complicated. The answer is diversification. Farmers, for example, have frequently boosted their incomes by developing nature trails and other leisure pursuits that bring tourism to an area. There are numerous ways in which declining rural economies can rejuvenate themselves; those who have relied on occupations directly allied to fox-hunting need to reinvent their working lives.

▶ Clichés and slang

Clichés are over-used, worn-out phrases that have lost their bite – such as *in this day and age, tried and tested, the bottom line,* and so on. They can be a problem for new writers because we all start by expressing what we want to say in the words we've picked up from TV, newspapers, and whatever else we've heard and read.

Whenever you can, say things clearly in your own way. I've almost certainly used a few clichés in this book, but I'm not writing a strictly academic work. Since I want to chat to you, a few clichés are bound to have crept in. It's also important to avoid slang in essays. This is language that is often felt to be inappropriate or not polite and whose meaning is not sufficiently specific, such as *dead cert, dodgy, loaded.* Slang can spoil the texture of your work and even make it look as though you're not thinking clearly.

▶ Tense

Changing tense (see Chapter 13 on verbs) by mistake is another common problem. If you're discussing a topic in the past tense, don't change to the present, and *vice versa.* You'll find out whether you've done this if you look for it specifically when you proofread (see below). It's a particular issue for those who are studying literature. When talking about a character in a book, it's fatally easy, for example, to swap backwards and forwards between *she did* and *she does* without realising what we're doing.

▶ Abbreviations

Generally speaking, abbreviations should not be used in essays. Things like *i.e.* and *e.g.* are not admissible. You might, however, be given some assignments in which particular abbreviations are acceptable, especially in science or technology. Check with your tutor. It's also the case that you can use just the relevant initials for an institution or corporation if you give those initials in brackets immediately after your *first* use of the institution's full name. For example, it's OK to write the following in an essay:

> The Royal National Institute for the Blind (RNIB) grew from the British and Foreign Society for Improving the Embossed Literature for the Blind.

Then you can subsequently use the initials RNIB throughout the essay. You won't need to give the full name again.

▶ Raising questions

Some people feel that formulating questions can be a useful means of drawing attention to particular arguments. When giving a talk, this is fine, but in written work, it can end up being more trouble than it's worth. And you're likely to find that your tutor is not too keen on you putting questions in your essays. Assuming you've remembered to use the question mark itself (and this frequently gets forgotten), there are further problems to negotiate. Asking questions rather than making statements can give the impression that you don't really know what you're talking about. But that's not all.

When you're writing an essay, you're already grappling with a question you've been given. That's usually a hard task in itself. Raising more questions can just make the whole thing more complicated because once you've asked a question yourself, you really need to try to answer it – or you can appear to be less than clued-up.

Technically speaking, raising questions can get you into a real minefield – especially because of difficulties with the grammar of individual sentences and with construction of the essay itself. Students sometimes tie themselves in knots trying to answer extra questions that they've raised themselves while still struggling to answer the main essay question.

* make statements instead of asking questions

Sometimes, however, you'll need to talk about questions that other people have raised on various issues, and it's important that you set these out really clearly. For this, you need to understand the difference between the question itself and a statement of this question.

Let's assume that you've been asked to write up a report on a seminar discussion on the subject of poverty in the Third World, and that during the discussion, one student, Tom Rush, said, "How can governments co-ordinate a global approach?"

When you write your piece, you *could* merely repeat Tom's question:

> One student said, "How can governments co-ordinate a global approach?"

But a more sophisticated way of doing it would be to *report* what Tom said (see the section on reported speech in Chapter 16). This means that you'll rephrase the question so that it becomes a statement – like this:

> One student raised the question of how governments might be able to co-ordinate a global approach.

Notice that when I've used the student's *actual words,* I've used a question mark, but that when I've *reported* his question, I've used only a full stop. This is very important. A question mark should be used *only* after a question, never after a statement of the question or a 'translation' of it into reported speech.

One thing you want to avoid at all costs is *combining* a question with a statement like this: *One student said how governments would be able to co-ordinate a global approach to the problem of Third World poverty?*

That is very bad practice. *Either* use the exact question (with speech marks and a question mark) *or* report it (*without* speech marks, the word *said*, or a question mark).

Now you may be feeling that it's essential to mention questions that frequently come up in relation to certain topics. You might want to show that you're aware of these. Or you might want to show that a particular view is not foolproof and that questions *should* be asked about it.

You can cope with this in a similar way to the reporting of Tom Rush's question. Suppose you're writing an essay on the current state of secondary education in Britain. You've mentioned the relevant Acts of Parliament and various other government initiatives, and you've looked at classroom practice. Now you want to tie up your argument by asking the following questions:

1 Why isn't more money spent on education?
2 Why are parents not expected to be more involved in schools?
3 Why doesn't Britain try to learn more from European education systems?

You can turn those questions into statements – like this:

> The most useful measure that government could take to improve education in our secondary schools would be to spend more money. If parents were then routinely involved much more closely in their children's education, the public would become far more aware of the cost of good systems and would accept the inevitable increase in taxes. Finally, it is clear that Britain could learn a good deal on structuring an education system from its near neighbours, France and Germany.

That simple process has transformed the questions into a forceful argument.

THE FINISHED PRODUCT

▶ Redrafting

Redrafting enables you to have a finished product which is clear and neatly organised. This is a process through which any serious writer will go. No published book or article arrives on the author's desk fully formed. Everybody adds things, deletes, makes changes, and puts whole sections in the bin. So be prepared to write two or more drafts.

Don't worry too much about grammar and punctuation in your first draft, just keep going. When it's done, leave it on one side for a day or two. Then you'll look at it with a fresh eye and you'll be able to spot problems more easily. First of all, look at structure. Check that each section follows clearly from the one before and that each paragraph follows easily from the preceding one. Then check that your argument is logical and that you have sufficient information and evidence – facts, theories, examples and quotes – to back it up. Check that your introduction sets the scene and states what the essay sets out to do and that your conclusion sums up your main points. Then check that you have full referencing in place (see chapter 3).

* make checks on structure, argument, evidence, introduction, conclusion, and referencing

Keep an eye out for anything you've written that doesn't specifically answer the question – such as details of another topic that you happen to be interested in but which doesn't actually fit the essay. Unrelated information can lose you marks because it suggests that you are not thinking clearly. So delete it.

In your final draft, use 10-point print in Ariel font or Times New Roman. Put your essays in double line-spacing, leave an extra line between paragraphs, and indent the first line of each paragraph by three spaces. Doing that makes your work look really neat, enables anyone reading it to see clearly where new paragraphs start and, crucially, gives tutors space to add comments. Whether you write by hand or use a computer, keep all your drafts and printouts until you've submitted your assignment. You might need to retrieve something you'd binned.

▶ Proofreading

Your final draft needs to be checked for grammatical problems, spellings and other minor errors. It's sometimes easiest to do a separate read-through for each type of error so that you can concentrate on one at a time. You'll focus much more easily if you're looking for just one thing. Some people find that it helps at this stage to read their work aloud, stopping briefly after each sentence. Check, particularly, for errors that have been picked out in your work on previous assignments.

You'll want your work to read smoothly. So if you find that you have some long, unwieldy sentences that don't seem to say quite what you mean, you'll need to sort this out. It can often be done by splitting the sentences up into shorter ones. Remember, everything must be crystal clear for whoever is marking your work.

* split long, awkward sentences into shorter ones for clarity

▶ Learning from feedback

Comments on your work are your own personal tuition. They're designed to help you to make progress and they're like gold dust. You'll sometimes find that your tutor has also added factual items and useful analysis on your scripts. These might come in handy for your exams. So aim to treat comments as valuable information rather than as harsh criticism. If you can't follow what's been said on your work, do ask for explanation. Understanding what's been written may be crucial for your next assignment, and tutors are always happy to explain things. Most of them love doing it.

As your course progresses, keep a note of tutors' comments on your work and of the errors that you've made. You're very likely to find that you keep making similar mistakes. This is quite usual, but it will go on happening until you address the particular issues consciously. So make yourself a list of problems that keep cropping up. Stick it on a piece of card and have this by you when you work. That way, you'll progress really fast.

* tutors' comments are your personal guide to making good progress

If there are an awful lot of corrections on your work or if you've got a very bad grade, even though you've worked hard, try not to despair. It really is all part of the learning process. I once nearly gave up all my studies quite early on over a bad grade. I'm very glad I didn't.

There are gurus in the business world who state categorically that if you're not making mistakes you're not likely to make progress and that an expert is someone who has made more mistakes than anyone else. They're far happier to see employees working creatively and getting some things wrong than playing safe and never opening up new horizons. Getting things wrong is the first step to getting them right.

EXAMPLES OF STUDENT ESSAYS

Here are two very good essays written by students on the case for censorship of the media. They take rather different positions on the question. Both constructed a detailed plan that acted as a route map for them and kept them on track while they were working. I've omitted their bibliographies as all aspects of referencing are dealt with in Chapter 3.

The essays followed the furore that ensued when some Danish newspapers printed cartoons of Mohammed in 2005. So the two students focused on freedom of the press. The more recent issue of phone-hacking by journalists has brought newspapers into the news yet again. If you were writing a similar essay in the aftermath of the most recent furore, you would doubtless include in your argument some discussion of the means of gathering information as well as of material that is printed.

I've given a running commentary (in blue) on the two essays in order to point up how each is put together to achieve flow, good structure and, above all, an argument that builds well. Notice how both students frequently make a statement of argument at the start of a paragraph and end the paragraph with a re-statement of their position on that particular issue.

Here is Sadie's essay:

Discuss the case for having increased censorship in the media

PLAN

Introduction
newspapers:
    power of owners
    tabloids stretch truth
    self-regulation

this essay will argue:
* increased censorship necessary for religious beliefs/privacy
* freedom of reporting necessary otherwise

	Evidence	Argument
1 Danish cartoons of Mohammed		
Muslim response	deaths	respect for
European reprints	£millions lost	others: essential
results: Muslim	*Hamshari's* threat	
demonstrations &	*Guardian*: Tabish Khair	
boycott of goods		
2 Journalists' concerns		
defence of freedom	*Reporters Without*	regulation cd. have
causing offence	*Borders*	prevented extreme
	Guardian 2006	responses
	British govt. response	
intruding on privacy	Kate Adie 2002	
	Seierstad 2004	
3 Privacy of the individual		
Human Rights Act 2000	Jonathan Aitken	benefits of
possible problems with	*Mass Media: Press*	increased
censorship	*Complaints*	censorship
	Commission 2006	
4 Demand for sensational reporting		
increase in newspaper		appropriate
sales		censorship would
journalists under		end pressures on
pressure		journalists

Conclusion
increased censorship would:
    prevent problems re. religion & privacy
    alleviate pressure on journalists

Discuss the case for having increased censorship in the media

Newspapers in Britain are owned by a small group of formidable corporations that have power over a large market. We all obtain information and entertainment via these newspapers which convey to us the values, opinions and codes of behaviour considered necessary for us to fit into our society. While we have a free press that can operate without government interference, we also have some of the most notorious tabloid papers in the world, known for publishing controversial material and for their stretching of the truth, especially concerning people in the public eye. Newspaper owners have power without responsibility, a view often expressed today. The British press has more freedom than its broadcasting equivalents, being self-regulatory, with voluntary codes of practice which are often reinterpreted or ignored. This essay will argue that increased press censorship is necessary in order to deal with the sensitive, contentious issues of religious beliefs and privacy, while on the other hand accepting that the press also need freedom to work openly to report the truth.

- This is a pretty good introduction. It sets the scene very clearly, noting the current situation of the press in Britain. Sadie's main argument is set out in the final sentence: she'll cover two main areas – religious beliefs and privacy.
- Since the essay title used the word 'media', Sadie needed to state clearly here that she would be limiting her essay to a discussion of print journalism (because that is what she goes on to do). She hints that she won't cover broadcasting, but doesn't spell this out.
- It would have been useful to mention that the essay will show how the effects of journalism in Europe can spread beyond its borders.

Respect for religious beliefs has rarely troubled the mainstream press. Recent caricatures printed in a Danish newspaper, mocking the Prophet Muhammad, caused a furore among Muslims who repeatedly asked the newspaper editor to stop printing the cartoons. The requests were ignored. Muslims called the cartoons blasphemous because Islam bans all ridicule of Muhammad. Newspapers in Europe felt justified in reprinting the cartoons, even though their doing so was deeply offensive to millions of Muslims.

These cartoons have now been republished in almost every major European country, setting off angry demonstrations amongst Muslims from Denmark to the Far East. Several people have been killed and moderate Muslims have suffered the backlash of intolerance. Boycotts of Danish goods in Muslim countries are costing Danish companies millions of pounds. One Iranian paper, *Hamshahri*, is threatening to retaliate by running Holocaust cartoons. 'The western papers printed these sacrilegious cartoons on the basis of freedom of expression,' says *Hamshahri's* graphics editor, 'so let's see if they mean what they say, and also print these Holocaust cartoons.' [Farid Mortazavi, 06.02.2006] Freedom of speech must go hand in hand with respect and consideration for the feelings of others. This applies equally to the press and everyday life. Reporting for the *Guardian*, Tabish Khair states that:

> Freedom of expression is necessary not because it is a God-given virtue, but because if you let authorities start hacking away at it you are liable to be left with nothing. But along with the right to express comes the duty to consider the rights of others. This applies as much to *Jyllands-Posten* [the Danish paper that published the cartoons] as to the mobs in Beirut.

- This paragraph opens with a strong statement – that (up until the time of writing) the press were unconcerned with offending people in regard to religious beliefs. What follows is an explanation of the situation following the Danish paper's printing of cartoons satirising Mohammed and two quotes showing some journalistic responses to the affair.
- Sadie ties up her argument neatly at this point with the sentence beginning 'Freedom of speech must go ...' (and its following one).
- Quotes: one split apart and neatly embedded into the writer's sentence and following easily from the previous sentence. The other, longer quote, is carefully introduced and then indented.

Reporters Without Borders has defended the media's right to make fun, but many European newspapers argue that free speech is not an excuse for unwarranted insults. The *Guardian* argues that 'newspapers are not obliged to republish offensive material merely because it's controversial' (03.02.2006). Indeed, the British government has praised its country's media for acting in a prudent manner by not publishing the cartoons in their own newspapers.

Appropriate press regulation and censorship of European newspapers could have stopped the publication of these cartoons, a simple thing that would have prevented the volatile demonstrations, boycotts of Danish goods, loss of innocent lives and the racial conflict that followed.

- This paragraph develops Sadie's argument further using information on certain journalists' concerns. The point on 'unwarranted insults' in the first sentence follows smoothly from the *Guardian* quote at the end of the preceding paragraph that mentions 'the rights of others' and leads easily to another quote from the *Guardian* on 'offensive material'.
- The final sentence on the value of 'Appropriate press regulation' makes a strong statement of argument at this point. Note that Sadie uses a key term from the essay question – 'censorship' – so demonstrating clearly that she is addressing that question.
- Quote: neatly embedded into the writers' sentence.

Of course, free speech is important, but the fact that some journalists are so keen to write intrusively about people's private lives is also an area of concern. Writing about her time in Iraq, Kate Adie reveals that:

I was bothered by the tabloid press ... at least one paper had sent a reporter to track my moves and get a few embarrassing snaps ... some journalists wrote ridiculous fiction ... it comes with the turf. (Adie, 2002: 386)

The press argue that it is in the public interest, but there are a number of journalists who will not support associates whose writing is too concerned with gossip and scandal:

We are now far too sensationalistic. You can read any amount of lies in the papers every day ... I direct my reporters to tell people what is actually happening, not what they think should be happening. (Seierstad, 2004: 65)

- The opening reference to free speech links the discussion to the topic of the preceding paragraph. The reader is being shown that there's more to say here – in terms of misuse of that freedom.
- Sadie uses quotes from two useful sources to back up her points.

Such writing is said to challenge the tradition of wide-ranging journalistic public discussion, which is important in any democratic society. In October 2000, the Human Rights Act was introduced. The act contains a right to respect for a private family life. However, some journalists believe censorship and prior restraint could prove disastrous for investigative journalism. This is aptly demonstrated by the following comment:

> Was the lying politician, Jonathan Aitken, on a private holiday when he was in Paris? If he was and the Human Rights Act on privacy had been law at the time, how could the *Guardian* legally have discovered who paid his hotel bill? (Mass Media: Press Complaints Commission, 2006)

Despite the Human Rights Act, there is still public and journalistic disquiet over the reporting of personal details regarding people's private lives. Increased press censorship could protect privacy, promote meaningful journalism and allay concern over intrusive newspaper reporting.

- By opening the paragraph with the words 'Such writing', Sadie makes a neat link to her previous paragraph.
- Sadie uses this paragraph to put an alternative argument to her own (giving a pertinent quote from *Mass Media*). That's good practice because the essay question asks for discussion of the topic. But since her own argument is for an increase in censorship, it would have more strength if she had made some attempt to demolish the alternative suggestion – or at least to pick holes in it. The problem here is that the quote she's given on Aitken would make a really useful point in an argument *against* further censorship – and she's not contested it.

In the aftermath of disaster or tragedy, newspaper sales increase dramatically. People often want to know the personal angle, therefore journalists could be said to be meeting readers' demands. Conversely, there are journalists who state that such writing is used as justification for selfish, unethical behaviour, and that it is more important to think about what is appropriate in the circumstances. It should, however, be borne in mind that journalists working for the tabloids are under a huge amount of pressure from editors who want powerful pieces of journalism in order to increase their newspaper sales. Many journalists are not happy with such invasive journalism which makes them feel guilty about their ruthless behaviour. However, they know that their survival depends on producing the kind of material that editors demand. Appropriate regulation and censorship should prevent such invasion into private grief. Editors would no longer be able to put journalists under such tremendous pressure to produce this emotive and intrusive writing.

- Mention of 'the personal angle' in the second sentence makes a good link to the previous paragraph.
- Sadie again can be seen to be looking at the issue from various angles. But this time, she counters the opposition very well in her final two sentences that underline the essay's argument on the need for increased censorship.

   To summarise, increased press censorship could prevent potential problems when dealing with concerns such as religious beliefs and privacy. Appropriate censorship would have checked the publication and repeated printing of the satirical cartoons depicting the prophet Mohammed, thus averting the anger and demonstrations amongst millions of Muslims. In turn, lives would not have been lost, people would not have suffered the backlash of intolerance and millions of pounds' worth of Danish goods would not have been boycotted in Muslim countries. Press censorship should preclude journalists from writing intrusively about people's private lives. Many journalists are not happy with writing that includes too much gossip and scandal, or that intrudes into private grief, but they are under huge pressure from their editors to produce the pieces of journalism that the public seem to demand. Increased press censorship to stop this sort of writing would alleviate pressure on journalists to deliver such work, thus lessening public concern over invasive journalism.

- Sadie could omit the phrase 'To summarise' because the final paragraph in an essay will always be expected to be the conclusion that summarises the essay.
- This is a very good conclusion. The essay's argument is re-stated clearly, forcefully and comprehensively, covering both religious sensibilities and invasion of privacy.

Here is Pete's essay (with my comments in blue throughout):

Discuss the case for having increased censorship in the media

PLAN

Introduction
democracy & the media
censorship is alien to democracy
the problem of events

	Evidence	Argument
1 Privacy rights of the individual anonymity of offenders place of the legal system human rights	Higham 2001	• freedom to print names might discourage reform • individuals might be at risk • the law is a safeguard • further censorship is unnecessary
2 Self-regulation media can self-regulate where necessary	Press Complaints Commission 2005 Ofcom 2006	
TV warnings of disturbing material watershed difficult areas – Ken Bigley – avoid aiding kidnappers press rights	Preston 2004 PCC 2005	• no need for censorship
3 Public opinion as regulator a free press is not without restrictions	Hillsborough tragedy as reported in the *Sun*	• public opinion is powerful regulator • many Muslims are natives of West
reaction to Danish cartoons of Muhammad	results on BBC News	• cartoons showed religious stereotyping
Jyllands-Posten's apology	Herber – 2006 *Reporters Without Borders* – 2005 *Daily Telegraph* 03.02.2006 *Guardian* 03.02.2006	• public opinion reacts quickly to ill-advised editors

Conclusion
media must be free to make mistakes
legal frameworks & self-regulation are sufficient
public opinion is the ultimate regulator

Discuss the case for having increased censorship in the media

Freedom of expression is one of the pillars of democratic societies. By definition, democracy is government of the people, by the people and, for the most part, it is through the media of broadcasting, newspapers and, more recently, the Internet, that people's views are represented and debated. For this reason, increased media censorship would be unwelcome, as clearly, this would undermine the principle of free speech. No democracy would surrender these values in favour of those prevalent in many Middle Eastern or Asian countries where media sources are tightly controlled by governments (*Reporters Without Borders*, 2005). However, such a polarised world view is often tested by events, which cause even those living in democratic societies to question whether sections of the media are able to equalise the tension triangle that exists between their right to free speech, its accompanying responsibilities and their commercial objectives. This essay will focus on the broadcast and printed news media in the United Kingdom and seek to show that, in such a democracy, the inherent safeguards of the legal system, self-regulation and public opinion, obviate the need for increased censorship.

- This introduction sets out very clearly the ground the essay will cover – broadcast and print media in the UK – and what it will argue – that there should be no increase in censorship.
- Its final sentence states the essay's argument clearly.
- Items that need referencing should not normally appear in an introduction. Pete gets away with it here because he's using the item as an important part of his scene-setting.

   When child murderers Robert Thompson and Jon Venables were released from secure accommodation in 2001, many newspapers disputed the court's decision to grant them anonymity. They argued that 'in the interests of open justice and freedom of expression, all criminals should be identified' (Higham, 2001). The danger with this argument is that it burdens offenders with the 'once a criminal always a criminal' tag and may discourage those who wish to reform. Without doubt the press were frustrated by the court's decision, which prevented the media circus they needed in order to sell more newspapers. However, after such an emotive and high-profile case, the men's safety was at risk, should their identities be revealed. Although their crime was horrific, the responsibility for sentencing rests with the legal system. Whatever one's view on the adequacy of that sentence, once it has been served, the men are entitled to protection from the threat of harm as a basic human right (Higham, 2001). The legal system, therefore, acts as a safeguard, preventing the media from exhibiting disproportionate emphases in favour of its commercial interest and right to free speech over its responsibilities to individuals and the wider community. Ultimately, further censorship is unnecessary.

- Pete has opened his essay with a high-profile case and a very strong argument which looks at the issue from both sides. Each sentence adds to his explanation of the situation, and the final two sentences state his argument with great clarity.
- The term 'media circus' insufficiently factual for an academic essay.
- One quote is embedded neatly.

   In addition, the media can avoid censorship through self-regulation. The Press Complaints Commission (PCC) is charged with 'enforcing ... [a] Code of Practice ... framed by the newspaper ... industry ...' (PCC, 2005). Similarly, while the office for Communications (Ofcom) has statutory powers to regulate the UK communications industry, it operates 'with a bias against intervention, but with a willingness to intervene promptly and effectively where required' (Ofcom, 2006). This allows broadcasters to regulate themselves on many issues. Typically, therefore, a warning that 'viewers may find some of the images upsetting' precedes potentially disturbing news items. Similarly, programmes containing colourful language or nudity are also preceded by warnings and are shown after 9 p.m. so as not to be viewed by young children. Generally this works well. However, there are difficult areas: for example, the broadcasting of the kidnappers' videos of hostage Ken Bigley. Such episodes are a relatively new development and broadcasters must weigh their responsibility to inform against the danger of handing the kidnappers their desired publicity, while having regard to the distress suffered by those close to the hostage (Preston, 2004). That said, there is no need for censorship. The press 'have a right to report on events in a robust ... fashion ... balanced by responsibility. In doing this [the press] can demonstrate the strength of effective self-regulation' (PCC, 2005).

- Pete manages the necessary link at the beginning of this paragraph with the words 'In addition'. That's not a very sophisticated link, but it's adequate now and again.
- The opening sentence on self-regulation of the press forms a point of argument on which the rest of the paragraph elaborates, using sound evidence from reputable sources. Pete does, however, show his awareness of an area where problems could arise.
- Pete closes the paragraph with a quote from the Press Complaints Commission that makes a reasonable response to the problems and so bolsters his own argument – that further media censorship is unnecessary.

   In the absence of self-regulation and legal restrictions, the media would seem to have carte blanche to target any section of society, shielded by the principle of freedom of speech. However, such an attitude can have serious consequences should their target decide to fight back. In 1989, the *Sun* newspaper misreported incidents concerning the Hillsborough stadium disaster when 96 Liverpool football fans were killed. The front-page article implied that the fans' own drunken behaviour had contributed to the disaster. The story led to a boycott of the paper in Liverpool that has lasted for 16 years, costing the *Sun* tens of millions of pounds in lost sales (BBC News, 2005). Latterly, a full-page apology was published, and although this came long after the event, it demonstrates that public opinion can be a powerful force in the regulation of the media.

- Pete's link here is the repetition of the term 'self-regulation' – from the last line in the previous paragraph. He now strengthens his argument that further censorship is unnecessary by giving evidence of a high-profile case where public opinion acted as judge and jury. His final statement on the force of public opinion bolsters his main argument.

   The violent reaction to the publication, in Denmark, of cartoons depicting the prophet Muhammad is a further illustration of the sensitivity of public opinion and the potentially destructive nature of its response. Supporters of increased media censorship would point to this as evidence for their case. However, as Lord Justice Sedley declared in a High Court judgement in 1999, 'the freedom only to speak inoffensively is not worth having' (Herbert, 2006). Denmark tops the World Press Freedom Index 2005 (Reporters Without Borders, 2005). However, by exercising this freedom without the required responsibility, *Jyllands-Posten*, along with its European counterparts who reprinted the cartoons, failed to have regard for the changing cultural constituencies of their societies. Furthermore, it is misleading to argue, as the *Daily Telegraph* does, that 'Muslims who cannot tolerate the openness and robustness of intellectual debate in the West have perhaps chosen to live in the wrong culture' (leader, 03.02.2006.). A great many Muslims are natives of the West; the depiction of the prophet of Islam as a bomb owes little to intellectualism and more to religious stereotyping, misrepresenting most Muslims' attitude to violence and increasing their sense of persecution. As the *Guardian* editorial points out, 'the right to publish does not imply any obligation to do so' (03.02.2006.). Nor does this impact only on Muslims in the West. Geographical borders are no longer a barrier to the flow of information. A weakness of the public opinion safeguard is that, almost inevitably, offence has already been caused before it can have an effect. However, if such incidents illustrate an editor's lack of understanding of the issues prior to publication, that understanding is rapidly enhanced by the subsequent public reaction, hence *Jyllands-Posten*'s hurried apology.

- The link here is information on another case where public reaction acted as a regulator. Pete starts by countering the opposing argument with a quote from Lord Justice Sedley, and goes on to give a detailed discussion of various relevant issues on both sides of the Danish cartoons debate with an array of pertinent quotes and references.
- The paragraph is rather long and might have been usefully split before the word 'Furthermore', which would have made a useful link.

In summary, in a democracy, the media must be allowed to make their own mistakes as society strives for tolerance and understanding. Increased censorship is both unwelcome and unnecessary where the safeguards of legal frameworks and self-regulation stand sentry.

Furthermore, those editors and journalists who insist on living by the mantra 'publish and be damned' learn quickly that public opinion will not allow them to flaunt their precious freedoms irresponsibly, nor to use them as a conceit in the quest for commercial gain.

- Pete needed to omit the words 'In summary' (see my comments on Sadie's conclusion).
- Pete pulls his argument together neatly and forcefully, revisiting his main points. It's a good conclusion.

SUMMARY

This chapter has covered the steps for essay-writing

- analyse the question
- make a mind map
- gather information
- write a plan
- write your first draft
- take a break
- rewrite as necessary
- proofread and edit
- write final draft

Issues to keep in mind:
- the essay question
- facts, figures, etc.
- theories
- your argument
- evidence and quotes
- paragraphing
- linking and clarity
- benefiting from your tutor's feedback

3 Quoting and Referencing

This chapter will show you how to:

▶ set out quotations
▶ put citations in the body of your essay
▶ avoid committing plagiarism
▶ write references in the Harvard, MHRA and MLA systems

INTRODUCTION

When you produce an academic piece of work, it's very important to show where your ideas and data have come from, to reference your quotations clearly and to set everything out according to particular rules. There's a reason for this: anyone who does academic work needs to be able to understand references in someone else's work with ease. They need to be able to decide whether they trust the source and, if they wish, find the original book or journal to do further reading. Getting everything right will give your assignments a professional appearance, demonstrate that you're applying academic rigour to your work and even enhance your grades. This chapter will give you the basics to get you going.

There are several different methods of referencing and it's essential to know which one you need. Here, you'll find **Harvard** (the most commonly used), **MLA**, and **MHRA** (a numeric system that uses footnotes). It's best to check out only the one you'll be using so that you don't confuse yourself by looking at other methods. If, by any chance, the system you'll need isn't here, you can still use this chapter's general notes on referencing because these apply to all systems.

You'll also find a section below on plagiarism (using other people's work without acknowledgement). Colleges and universities are very much alive to the problem of plagiarism now – especially in relation to work found on the Internet. Many of them now have electronic systems of checking students' work, so getting clued up on how to avoid problems could save you a lot of heartache.

* correct referencing is essential and can enhance your grades

HOW TO QUOTE

Obviously, quotes aren't any good by themselves. Each one needs to be carefully introduced and you need to show why you feel it's useful. You might use only a small proportion of the quotes you've noted from your reading, but that's fine. If you have plenty of material to choose from, you'll be able to take the most appropriate items.

There's no hard and fast rule on how many quotes are needed. If you're analysing a novel or a poem, you'll be quoting from it constantly. The same goes for full analysis of other texts. Some subject areas need only two or three quotes or references to trusted sources per page; others want considerably more.

Your tutors will want to be sure you've understood what you've read, and to do this they need to see your own explanations of topics. Sometimes, it's useful to summarise longer sections and then to use the occasional quote as illustration. But this can vary considerably, so do check on what's expected in your particular subject area.

* check out the average number of quotes per page expected in your subject area

Let's assume I have to write an essay on A. C. Grayling's article, 'Why a high society is a free society' (see Chapter 1). I might want to quote his comment on the similarities between legal and illegal substances. So I might have a sentence that runs something like this:

Grayling feels that both legal and illegal drugs '… are used for plea-

sure, relief from stress or anxiety, and 'holidaying' from normal life,

and both are, in different degrees, dangerous to health.'

Notice that I've used single quotation marks and that I've started with three dots to show that I've missed out the beginning of Grayling's sentence. I've introduced the quote with my own words in such a way that it flows smoothly from them. I've also carefully copied all Grayling's punctuation. You'll also notice that he has put a word in quote marks himself – 'holidaying' – to show that he's giving it a slightly different meaning from the usual one. It was crucial that I copied this accurately too.

It's quite acceptable to start and stop a quote wherever you like in order to suit the purpose of your own writing. It's essential to show any punctuation that appears within the quote, but you may terminate your quote before a punctuation mark if it makes sense to do that. So it would be perfectly OK to write this:

Grayling states that both legal and illegal drugs 'are, in different degrees, dangerous to health' and should therefore have equal status under the law.

I've terminated my quote *before* Grayling's full stop after 'health' because I wanted to continue my own sentence. If it suits your meaning, you can miss out a few words from the middle of a sentence. The missing words are shown by three dots, like this (see Grayling, paragraph 11):

Grayling states that 'A good society should be able to accommodate practices which are not destructive of social bonds ... but mainly have to do with private behaviour.'

It's also acceptable to add or change a word to make things make sense within your own sentence, provided that you put any additions in square brackets to show that they are your own (see Grayling, paragraph 1):

Grayling believes that heroin should be freely available because 'a good society' is one in which 'the autonomy of those who wish to use [drugs] is respected.'

By the way, although the lines or single words that you copy from a book are called a quote, they only turn into a quote when you've copied them – or when you repeat them aloud to someone else. In their printed form in the text, they are not quotes. People sometimes get confused over this.

▶ Indenting

When quoting two lines or more, it's best to indent. This means having a wider margin than usual on the left (sometimes on both sides) of the page and leaving a line both before and after a quote. For this method, you use single-line spacing for the quote and you won't need to use quote marks as each quote will show up clearly on your page, like this:

> Grayling argues that there is no logical difference between legal
>
> and illegal drugs:
>
> > Both are used for pleasure, relief from stress or anxiety, and 'holidaying' from normal life, and both are, in different degrees, dangerous to health.
>
> His stance on this is, perhaps, unusual, but his meaning is clear:
>
> there is no valid reason for splitting drugs into different categories.

▶ The problem of the half-way house

It's very important to make a clear difference between putting something in your own words and quoting directly from what you've read. Sometimes, students get muddled and seem to try to do both at once. The following sentence suffers from this problem (see Grayling, paragraph 6):

> Grayling says, 'people who want to try drugs do so irrespective of their legal status'.

The final five words in the quote above are an accurate quote from Grayling, but the first eight are not an accurate copy and so must not be put in quote marks. I didn't copy accurately and I didn't show a clear difference between Grayling's words and my own representation of them. Sorted out, that sentence above might become:

> Grayling explains that people intent on trying or using drugs do
>
> so 'irrespective of their legal status'.

Now I've quoted just a few words from Grayling, so it makes sense to terminate my quote before Grayling's full stop and to use my own – after the quote. If at first you find it difficult to fit quotes neatly into your own sentences, don't worry. The simplest way to do it is to precede your quote with a simple introductory statement followed by a colon – like this:

Brown states that:

Then you can give the quote, indented, without any alterations. This is not a very sophisticated practice, but it usually avoids serious mistakes. Be sure to put a colon after your introductory words.

▶ Using the Internet

You'll need to be particularly careful over using material from the Internet. The World Wide Web has revolutionised our ability to research topics at speed, and it's now highly unlikely that anyone would attempt to produce a serious piece of work without making use of it. But there are certain dangers in working from the Net. To begin with, it's essential to reference work from the Net as fully as if it came from a book or journal (see the information below).

There are two other important issues which frequently get over-looked. First of all, there's the possibility that ideas published one week will be disproved the next. People tend to publish work in progress so that the ideas they put forward may have a very limited shelf life. The likelihood that information will be superseded also applies to current events. Even experienced broadsheet journalists can make mistakes in the fast-moving media world.

The other problem is that theories and experiments you find on the Net might not have been reviewed by the writer's peers. That is to say, the information given might not have been scrutinised by other experts who are in a position to show whether or not it's valid. Even material found on *Wikipedia* can fall into this category. So you'll need to be on your guard against using material that doesn't have a sound academic basis.

* material found on the Internet can be inaccurate or out of date

▶ Quoting from literature

If you're an English literature student, you're going to have to quote very frequently from the texts you're studying. There are specific rules on how this is done and it varies according to the kind of text you quote from.

NOVELS

Quoting from novels or from commentary on these by critics presents no difficulties because they are written in prose (that is, paragraphs are used and the sentences follow straight on from each other along each line). Use the procedure outlined above, with quotation marks for short quotes within your paragraphs and indentation for longer ones.

POEMS

When you quote from a poem, a rough guide is that quotations of up to a line and a half can be incorporated into your own paragraphs, while those of two or more lines look better indented (see *Indenting*, above).

Aim to limit your quotes to about three lines at most – never quote great chunks of a poem in one go. You need to analyse small sections at a time, showing exactly what it is in the lines that causes you to say what you do. When indenting, keep to the same lines as the original. The titles of poems should be put in single quote marks when you refer to them in the body of your essay.

Take special care when quoting more than one line but not indent-ing. You will need to use a slash (/) to show where a line ends. Here's an example taken from Pattie's essay on William Blake's poem 'The Chimney Sweeper' from his book *Songs of Innocence*:

> Tom dreams that an angel sets the child sweeps free so that 'leaping
>
> laughing they run/And wash in a river and shine in the Sun'.

The original lines in the poem look like this:

> Then down a green plain leaping laughing they run
> And wash in a river and shine in the sun.

DRAMA

It can be easier to quote from drama than from poetry, as you don't need to stick to the same line layout as shown in the text unless, as with much of Shakespeare's work, the play is written in verse form (for which you follow the rules for quoting from poetry). You need to make clear to your reader who it is that is speaking, but you don't need to put the character's name at the side of the page in addition. Here's an extract from David's essay on Ibsen's play *A Doll's House*:

> Ibsen shocked Scandinavia with his character Nora. At first shown as a small-time housewife, she finally throws off her repressive marriage with the bald statement:

> Well, that's the end of that.

> He undercuts the tradition of melodrama at the same time as analysing the role of women.

PLAGIARISM

Plagiarism is the act of using someone else's words or ideas as if they were your own. Every time you quote, or mention ideas you've gleaned from a writer or speaker (whether from a book, magazine, tape, disk, radio, TV, film or the Internet) you must make acknowledgement and use quotation marks where relevant. This is crucial. An essay containing plagiarised material might result in a grade of 0 being given. Clearly, that's not something worth risking. There are three possible offences:

- copying from a text without acknowledging your source
- putting an extract from a text in your own words without acknowledgement
- using someone's ideas without acknowledgement

Copying without acknowledgement is often blatantly obvious to a tutor who will frequently either know the book that has been used or will be able to spot the difference in writing style between your essay itself and unmarked quotes from another writer. There's even a computer programme that can now be used by tutors to assess the likelihood of a piece of work being plagiarised. So make sure that you have all your references in place. Forgetting to do that could get you in as much trouble as doing it on purpose.

Here's a checklist of items that need to be referenced:

- someone's particular ideas or theories

- their special way of writing or explaining them

- statistics, tables and diagrams

- facts that are relatively unknown

- particular examples

There are one or two exceptions, however. You don't need to reference definitions of well-known items from dictionaries unless you're copying the exact words, nor do you need to give proof for things like the fact that, for example, the earth goes round the sun or other facts which are common knowledge.

▶ Changing parts of a quote

Let's suppose I'm writing an essay on drugs and I say the following:

> There is no justification in a good society for using the police to monitor people's behaviour unless they are suspected of things such as rape and murder.

This is plagiarism because I've rephrased what Grayling wrote and I've failed to acknowledge him (see paragraph 4 in the article in Chapter 1). So I'll change my wording to include Grayling's actual words and I'll indent my quote so that I won't need quote marks. I'll also show that I've changed a phrase in order to make the words make sense here by putting square brackets around it:

Grayling states that:

> On civil liberties grounds [legalising currently illegal drugs] is preferable because there is no justification in a good society for policing behaviour unless, in the form of rape, murder, theft, riot or fraud, it is intrinsically damaging to the social fabric, and involves harm to unwilling third parties.

My work is acceptable now, but it's essential that I also give a reference (see the *References* section below). Once a reference is in place, it will be totally clear that I'm not trying to pass off another person's writing as my own.

▶ Acknowledging a writer's ideas

Using someone's ideas without acknowledgement is seen as an underhand practice. Let's suppose I include the following in an essay on drugs:

> Freedom of the individual is essential in a fair society. It has been shown that use of the law to ban mind-altering substances does not protect children, or reduce crime or the number of users. Monitoring supplies to addicts, however, would result in a measurable reduction in both serious and petty crime.

Here, my offence is to sum up Grayling's ideas without admitting that they are his, not mine. I *must* say where I got them. When you refer to someone's idea or to the results of an experiment or survey that someone has conducted, you need to show clearly that the material is not your own. You need to give the author credit for it just as you do when quoting someone's exact words (see below).

REFERENCING

Below you'll find tables showing how to use the following systems: Harvard (the most commonly used), MHRA (Modern Humanities Research Association) and MLA (Modern Language Association of America). They are quite similar in some ways, so read only the one you'll be using in order to avoid getting confused. Check on which you'll need with your college or university (I hope yours is one of these three).

Different departments within a college or university – and sometimes even individual tutors – sometimes have their own preferences.

The bad news is that, whichever method you use, you'll need to get it exactly right. Every name must be correct, the order of items must be correct, and commas and full stops need to be in the right places. You'll need to spend a little time getting to grips with the system you use, but once you've got into the referencing habit, things will be much more straightforward.

> * every comma and full stop needs to be in the right place

There are two places in your work where you need to acknowledge that you are quoting from someone else or using their ideas:

- in the **body of your essay** at the point where you quote or refer to their work
- at the end of your essay in a **References** list

Occasionally, you'll also be asked to provide a **bibliography** showing all the texts you've looked at but have not actually used in your work.

When using the tables below, look up the item you need in the relevant left-hand column. Then copy exactly the *pattern* of the reference as set out in the right-hand column. This means that you must get all the names, dates and article, book or journal titles in the right order.

▶ Referencing in the body of your essay (in-text citations)

Whenever you quote from or refer to someone's work in the body of your essay, you need to include a very brief reference there and then. (See the tables below for how to do this.)

QUOTING FROM LITERATURE

If you quote from a novel, you'll need the page number after each quote.

If you include quotes from various short poems in one essay, give the relevant titles in single quote marks; if your essay involves a close analysis of one poem, give the line number after each quote.

If you quote from a play, you'll need to show the act in Roman numerals, the scene in lower case and the line in Arabic figures, like this quote from *Hamlet*:

> To be, or not to be, that is the question (III.i.56)

▶ Reference lists (all systems)

- Put **titles of books, magazines, journals, newspapers, films, plays and full-scale musical works** in italics (underline them if you are writing by hand).

- Organise your list in **alphabetical order** on authors' surnames. (In numerical systems, this will be done in your bibliography.)

- Put titles of **articles, chapters from books, essays, speeches, songs, poems, etc.**, in single quote marks (double in the MLA system).

- Insert all **punctuation** as shown in the tables below.

- **Indent the second and subsequent lines** of individual references so that authors' names stand out and the list is easier to read. (In numerical systems, this will be in your bibliography.)

- The **date required** is the publication date, not the printing date.

- For an **article (or a chapter in a book by several authors)** give the first and last pages of the article or chapter.

- Refer to **books published by the same author** in the same year, as 2010a, 2010b, 2010c, etc.

- If you have a source where **no date** is showing, put No date *or* n.d.

- For **a quote from one source that you found in another**, give the reference for the earlier one followed by the words *cited in* or *in* and then the reference for the source you actually looked at.

- Include the **date you accessed an Internet site**. This is essential because sources on the Internet can be changed or updated at any time and even URLs themselves can change. Write it like this at the end of the reference: Accessed 2.3.12.

- **If there's no author for the article on a website**, try the site's Home Page and use the site author.

- **If author and title aren't available on a site**, use the URL.

HARVARD REFERENCING

Find your query in the left-hand column, then find the answer in the corresponding right-hand column. (See also the note following: 'Your references list'.)

▶ **The body of your essay**

Item to be referenced	How to cite an item in the body of your essay in the Harvard system
A quote when you've already used the author's name	Gill states: 'The English are not so much a cocktail of mongrel blood … they are a state of self-belief, an idea of bombastic arrogance that begins in the last half of the fifteenth century' (2005, p. 30).
A quote without first mentioning the author's name	It has been said that 'The English are not so much a cocktail of mongrel blood … they are a state of self-belief, an idea of bombastic arrogance that begins in the last half of the fifteenth century' (Gill 2005, p. 30).
An author's *idea* when you've already mentioned his/her name	Linley demonstrates that an individual's particular strengths, if made use of at work, will add to the success of a company while using his or her weak aspects will diminish it. (2008, p. 151)
An author's *idea* without first mentioning his/her name	An individual's particular strengths, if made use of at work, will add to the success of a company while using his or her weak aspects will diminish it. (Linley, 2008 p. 151).

► Your references list

The order for each entry in your Harvard references list is as follows: author's name (last name first, followed by initials), date in round brackets, title of the work (books in italics/articles in single quote marks), place of publication followed by a colon, publisher, and then first and last page numbers if referencing an article.

Titles of articles and chapters should be placed within single quote marks.

Item to be referenced	How to set out an item in your references list in the Harvard system
A book	Gill, A. A. (2005) *The Angry Island,* London: Weidenfeld & Nicolson.
A chapter in a book that is a collection of work by different writers	Wood, L. (1998) 'Participation and Learning in Early Childhood' in Holden C. and Clough N. (eds), *Children as Citizens*, London: Jessica Kingsley Publishers Ltd, pp. 31–45.
An article in a printed journal	Holmes, B. (2006) 'Turning Back the Years', *New Scientist*, vol. 189, no. 2534, pp. 42–45.
A report or article in a newspaper	Fisk, R. (2010) 'Stay out of trouble by not speaking to Western spies', *The Independent*, 18 December, p. 40.
An article from an Internet site	Wolfe, R. L. (2011) 'The Stalinization of Post-Revolutionary Art and Architecture', *Public Philosophy Network* [Online]. Available at: http://publicphilosophynetwork.ning.com/profiles/blogs/the-stalinization-of (Accessed 6 September 2011).
A CD or DVD	*Dvorak Tone Poems* (2005) [CD], Berliner Philharmoniker, conducted by Simon Rattle, EMI Records Ltd.
A radio or TV programme	*Today* (2011) BBC Radio 4, 6 September.

Notes for Harvard Referencing

- In your **references list**, all items (author's name, title of publication etc.) are separated here by commas. Sometimes, however, you'll find that full stops are used. The most important thing is to put items in the right order and use italics and quote marks accurately.
- Your **bibliography**: Occasionally, you will be asked to provide a full bibliography that includes items you've consulted but that don't appear in your list of references because you've not actually referred to them. Like the list of references, a bibliography will be in alphabetical order by the surnames of authors. It will generally include all the items in your references list as well as those you've not quoted from.

MHRA REFERENCING (Modern Humanities Research Association) – a numeric system

In the MHRA system, each quote or mention of a writer's ideas, theories, and so on is followed by a number. This number will correspond to the full reference, which will be either in a footnote at the bottom of the relevant page or in a list of endnotes following your essay (check with your tutors which layout you will need). Number chronologically throughout your essay, whether for direct quotes or mention of someone's ideas. The numbers generally go in superscript (i.e. just above the level of the last character of your quote, etc.) but some tutors will accept them in round or square brackets.

Find your query in the left-hand column, then find the answer in the corresponding right-hand column. (See also the notes following: 'Your references list'.)

▶ The body of your essay

Item to be referenced	How to cite an item in the body of your essay in the MHRA system
A quote, a mention of an author's idea, or a brief	'The English are not so much a cocktail of mongrel blood ... they are a state of self-

summary of part of an author's work is followed by a number.	belief, an idea of bombastic arrogance that begins in the last half of the fifteenth century.'[1]

▶ Your references list

The following items are numbered as if they were a full list of endnotes.

The order for each item in the list is: initials or first name, last name, title of the work (books in italics/articles and chapters in books in single quote marks). Then place, publisher, date (all those three in brackets with a colon after the place), first and last page numbers for articles and chapters and/or single page number for a quote.

Item to be referenced	How to set out your footnote or endnote in the MHRA system
A quote from a book	1 A. A. Gill, *The Angry Island* (London: Weidenfeld & Nicolson, 2005) p. 30.
A chapter in a book that is a collection of work by different writers	2 Liz Wood, 'Participation and Learning in Early Childhood'. In *Children as Citizens* ed. by Cathie Holden and Nick Clough (London: Jessica Kingsley Publishers Ltd, 1998) pp. 31–45.
A quote from an article in a printed journal	3 Bob Holmes, 'Turning Back the Years', *New Scientist*, 189.2534 (2006) 42–45 (44).
A report or article in a newspaper	4 Robert Fisk, 'Stay out of trouble by not speaking to Western spies', *The Independent*, 18 December 2010, 40.
An article from an Internet site	5 Ross Lawrence Wolfe, 'The Stalinization of Post-Revolutionary Art and Architecture'. In *Public Philosophy Network* (2011) <http://publicphilosophynetwork.ning.com/profiles/blogs/the-stalinization-of> [accessed 6 September 2011]

| A CD or DVD | 8 *Dvorak Tone poems*. Berliner Philharmoniker, conducted by Simon Rattle (EMI Records Ltd., 2005) on CD. |
| A radio or TV programme | 9 *Today* BBC Radio 4, 6 September, 2011. |

Notes for MHRA Referencing

Page numbering:

- One **chapter in a book by several authors**: give first and last page numbers of the chapter at the end of the reference, preceded by 'pp.' (note the full stop there).
- Where a **specific page reference** is needed for either a chapter in a book or a journal article, put it in brackets after the first and last page numbers at the end of the relevant footnote or endnote. In your bibliography, omit all *specific* page numbers, using only the first & last page numbers of the chapter or article.

Online journals: For articles where the information is available, give the volume and issue numbers before the year date which itself should be followed by page numbers. Put the URL in angled brackets (<>).

Multiple citations of a source:

When you first cite a source in this system, you will need full details in your note. When you refer to that source on subsequent occasions, give just the author's surname and the first few words of the title, plus a page number if relevant. For example:

2 Stephen R Covey, *The 7 Habits of Highly Effective People* (London: Simon & Schuster UK Ltd, 1989)
11 Covey, *The 7 Habits* ... p. 74

Consecutive references:

If you have two or more *consecutive* references from the same source, you don't even need to have the shortened title, you can just use the Latin word *ibid.,* which means 'in the same place' (with a page number, if it's relevant). For example:

1 A. A. Gill, *The Angry Island* (London: Weidenfeld & Nicolson, 2005) p. 30.
2 ibid. p. 43

Your Bibliography:
In addition to a numbered list of references, you will usually be expected to provide a Bibliography. As well as containing details of all the items in your numbered list, it will include any books, journals, etc., that you have read (at least, in part) but not actually used in your essay. Each item in your bibliography will have the same format as in the relevant footnote or endnote except that an author's surname will come before his or her first name or initial so that the bibliography can be set out in alphabetical order. Items will not be numbered.

Capital letters:
Capitalise the first letter of all key words in titles.

Names:
Give first names in full unless initials only are shown on a publication.

Punctuation:
All items in both notes and bibliographies are written in one sentence. Full stops, however, will appear after initials, e.g. p. & pp.

MLA REFERENCING (Modern Language Association) (frequently used in humanities subjects)

Find your query in the left-hand column, then find the answer in the corresponding right-hand column. (See also the notes following 'Your Works Cited List'.)

▶ **The body of your essay**

Item to be referenced	How to cite an item in the body of your essay in the MLA system
A quote when you've already mentioned the author's name	A. A. Gill states: 'The English are not so much a cocktail of mongrel blood ... they are a state of self-belief, an idea of bombastic arrogance that begins in the last half of the fifteenth century.' (30)

A quote without first mentioning the author's name	'The English are not so much a cocktail of mongrel blood ... they are a state of self-belief, an idea of bombastic arrogance that begins in the last half of the fifteenth century.' (Gill 30)
An author's idea when you've already mentioned his/her name	Linley demonstrates that an individual's particular strengths, if made use of at work, will add to the success of a company while using his or her weak aspects will diminish it. (151)
An author's idea without first mentioning his/her name	An individual's particular strengths, if made use of at work, will add to the success of a company while using his or her weak aspects will diminish it. (Linley 151)

▶ Your Works Cited List

The order for each item is: last name, initials or first name, title, place, publisher, date, (first & last pages if an article or chapter)
Titles of articles and chapters are in double quote marks.

Item to be referenced	How to set out an item in your Works Cited list in the MLA system
A book	Gill, A. A. *The Angry Island*. London: Weidenfeld and Nicolson, 2005.
A chapter in a book that is a collection of work by different writers	Wood, Liz. "Participation and Learning in Early Childhood." *Children as Citizens*. Ed. Cathie Holden and Nick Clough. London: Jessica Kingsley Publishers Ltd, 1998, 31–45.
An article in a printed journal	Holmes, Bob. "Turning Back the Years." *New Scientist* 189.2534 (2006): 42–45. Print.
A report or article in a newspaper	Fisk, Robert. "Stay out of Trouble by not Speaking to Western Spies." *Independent* 18 December 2010, 40. Print.

An article from an Internet site	Wolfe, Ross Lawrence. "The Stalinization of Post-Revolutionary Art and Architecture." *Public Philosophy Network.* (2011). Web. [accessed 6 September 2011] <http://publicphilosophynetwork.ning.com/profiles/blogs/the-stalinization-of >
A CD or DVD	*Dvorak Tone poems.* Berliner Philharmoniker, conducted by Simon Rattle, EMI Records Ltd., 2005. CD
A radio or TV programme	*Today. BBC* Radio 4. 6 September. 2011.

Notes for MLA Referencing

- In the MLA system, **titles of articles** are put in double quote marks.
- In an item in your cited works list, **full stops** come after the author and after the title as well as at the end.
- When giving **page numbers**, state the numbers only. (The letters p and pp are not used.)
- **Sources that you don't actually cite** in your text can be shown in footnotes and endnotes to give extra information where necessary.
- Your **works cited list** goes in alphabetical order according to authors' surnames.
- Setting-out **dates of publication**:
  scholarly journals: volume and part numbers + year date in round brackets
  newspapers and magazines: day/month/year (as available)
- For **printed** (as opposed to online) **journals**: end the entry with the word Print.
- In **titles**, capitalise the first letter in each word (apart from *a, the, for* etc.).
- For **articles in online journals** (where the information is available) give the volume and issue numbers before the year date which itself should be followed by the page numbers.
- Use **authors' names** as shown on title pages of books, articles, etc.

URLs

- When citing sites from the Internet, put the word *Web* immediately before the date you accessed the site. The URL can go in angled brackets at the end of the citation, but is not essential for easily-found sites although your tutors might prefer you to include it.
- For chapters of books where you give the editor's name, his or her first name precedes the surname or last name.

SUMMARY

This chapter has covered:

- quoting:
    direct quotes
    indenting
    quoting from literature
- using people's ideas
- plagiarism and how to avoid it
- citing sources in the body of your essay
- citing sources in a referencing list or bibliography
- the Harvard referencing system
- the MHRA referencing system
- the MLA referencing system

Part Two
Writing for Different Purposes

Part Two
Writing for Different Purposes

4 Style

This chapter shows you
how to:

► improve the general
  style of your writing
► vary your writing for
  different purposes
► write persuasively

INTRODUCTION

As a student, you'll be writing other assignments
besides essays. You might be asked to write summaries, reports, articles, letters, and even to do some creative writing. This section of the book covers various types of assignment that you might be given, and this particular chapter forms a basis for each of the others. It shows you how to make improvements to the general *texture* of your writing and how you can write in different ways to suit the purpose of a particular piece of work.

The word *style* has different meanings. It can refer to a person's own way of writing, to the type of writing needed for a particular piece of work, or to writing well. Some very effective ways of making improvements to your personal style are to check out punctuation (see Chapter 14), paragraphing (see Chapter 2) and sentence construction (see Chapter 13). Accurate punctuation will make your work easier to read, helpful paragraphing will make the structure easier to follow and good sentence construction will make what you say easier to understand.

* key points for good style are: paragraphing, punctuation and sentence
  construction

Reading well-written material will also have a beneficial effect on your style. If you haven't been much of a reader up till now, aim to try some of the following: novels, travel writing, histories, biographies, broadsheet newspapers and academic journals. From time to time, challenge yourself with some difficult reading material. Wider reading will gradually have a spin-off effect on your own work. You'll begin to absorb aspects of good style without even realising that you're doing it.

STYLE BASICS

▶ Sentence length

If you're having serious difficulties with your writing, you might like to start by sticking to a rule of writing only short sentences. This will help keep you on the straight and narrow and prevent you from writing sentences in which various parts become confused. It's a really good ploy to get you out of immediate trouble.

As time goes on, however, you'll want to progress from this, and you'll find that varying the length of your sentences will enhance your style. Have a look at the short sections on **main clauses** and **subordinate clauses** in Chapter 14 to see how to extend your sentences easily and accurately. To give impact, you can occasionally follow a long sentence with a short one. For example:

> Problems over the Norwark virus (that has killed a number of hospital patients) have highlighted the need to return to basic standards of cleanliness as advocated as far back as the nineteenth century by Florence Nightingale. Hand-washing saves lives.

▶ Simplicity and clarity

The best writing is easy to read and uses contemporary (rather than out-of-date) vocabulary. Sometimes, students feel that they are expected to aim for language that sounds important or very formal. This isn't the case. Of course, the writing in some textbooks can seem really dense and difficult, but that doesn't mean that it's written in a style that's worth copying. Don't call a spade 'an implement for turning earth'.

Writing in simple language doesn't mean leaving things out or omitting to use technical words when they're essential. It means avoiding all unnecessary jargon and giving sufficient explanation in order to be clearly understood. It also means that we must use punctuation and paragraphing to help the reader along.

Checklist for simplicity

- *use a short word* rather than a long one
- *check your logic*: have you said what you mean, and does your writing make sense?

- *be as brief as possible* without omitting essential points
- *omit clichés* (e.g. 'in this day and age', 'the bottom line')
- *use helpful paragraphing and punctuation* (see Chapters 2 and 15)
- *use active verbs* rather than passive ones (see Chapter 13)
- *use concrete nouns* rather than abstract ones whenever possible (see Chapter 13)

Look at this example of long-winded writing:

> Many of the somewhat extended psychoanalytic case notes written and published by Sigmund Freud have become the subject of castigation by feminist writers.

There's absolutely no need to say that Freud's work was *psychoanalytic* because everyone knows that. The phrase 'somewhat extended' is sheer padding. There's certainly no need to say that it was 'written' *and* 'published'. That's obvious. The phrase *the subject of castigation* can be reduced considerably, and we only need one word for *feminist writers*. The piece would be much more readable like this:

> Freud's work has been attacked by feminists.

This new sentence gets straight to the point and won't send a reader to sleep.

▶ Finding the right word

While you're writing your first draft of an essay, it's best not to spend time worrying about individual words or phrases. Concentrate on getting the whole thing on paper first. My own method is to put brackets round anything that doesn't sound right. Then I can attend to it later.

Finding the right word for what you want to say can be a bit time-consuming, but it will pay dividends. If you have a good dictionary and a thesaurus you'll have the right tools for the job. Get the best dictionary you can afford. A pocket dictionary won't do as it won't contain all the information you'll need, so get a good-sized thick one. A thesaurus – which will give you a choice of words for non-technical items – can be very handy for avoiding repetition and for searching out a word that says *exactly* what you mean. *Roget's Thesaurus* is the one most people use.

* a thesaurus will give you a choice of words so you can avoid repetition

The dictionary will help you not just with spelling but with accuracy. People often use a word that means more or less what they intend, but not quite. Every now and then, you might try checking the definition of a word you think you're quite sure of. This can be quite an eye-opener. It's surprising how many times a dictionary definition turns out to be not quite what we expect.

Here's an example of the wrong word used from Susan's essay – 'Discuss the proposition that education is wasted on the young':

> A reason why this proposition may be feasible is the way in which attending school is enforced.

The word 'feasible' relates to possibility. It is perfectly possible to make *any* proposition. A word that would fit much better here is 'valid'. What Susan meant was that the proposition could be shown to be in some ways accurate and convincing.

In the following example from an essay on Shakespeare's *Hamlet,* Christine is clearly trying to sound formal:

> Hamlet shows his love for Ophelia on many occasions and it appears more obvious than the ways in which Ophelia's love towards Hamlet is discerned.

The word 'discerned' – that is, perceived – must relate to the responses of the audience. It is *they* who perceive what is going on. But that sentence actually focuses on the behaviour of the characters themselves. Maybe Christine actually meant 'displayed', which relates to what Ophelia was doing and would fit much better. Perhaps the problem came about because Christine didn't want to use the word 'shown' as she'd already used 'shows', and so she got a bit confused.

You can see from this that finding the right word can sometimes take a little time, but it's time well spent because your work will have greater strength and your command of language will be constantly improving.

* using the right word can give your writing strength and authority

▶ Tone

Using an appropriate tone is important for all types of writing. Tone is easiest to spot in spoken language. We know at once if someone sounds friendly, upset, impatient, formal, serious or humorous. We often react strongly to tone. You may at one time or another have said to someone, 'I don't like your tone.'

Tone relates in part to how a person feels towards the subject-matter of his or her writing, but especially to the way in which he or she 'speaks' to the reader. An ironic tone, for example, is sometimes used to poke fun in a sarcastic way at the topic or person being written about. It can signal to the reader that the writer's words mean the opposite of what they appear to state. An ironic tone can also be used to point up something that is irrational or incongruous. Political journalists frequently use irony.

Tone generally comes from the combination of the particular items mentioned and the kind of words used (see *diction* below). Notice how I've tried to give a sensuous tone to the following restaurant review to help sell the restaurant to readers and make them want to eat there:

> 'Ooh, that's good!' This was from my friend, Anne, as she took her first bite of oak-smoked salmon with a dill crème fraîche and pink peppercorns. From that moment on, a happy smile occupied her face for the entire evening.

If you've been asked to write an article (see Chapter 9) or produce a piece of creative writing (see Chapter 7), you'll need to be able to vary the tone of what you write. But for essays and reports, your tone will generally need to be formal and serious, and you won't want to show any emotion.

* tone can introduce emotion – so a formal tone is best in essays

▶ Diction

The example of tone (above) relies very much on the kind of words used – that is, the diction of the writing. In that example, the words 'oak-smoked salmon', 'crème fraîche' and 'pink peppercorns' work together to suggest a luxurious eating experience. With the addition of the words 'Ooh', 'good' and 'happy smile', the effect is strengthened further.

The section on simplicity (above) showed that it's a good idea to use a short word rather than a long one whenever appropriate. This can sometimes come down to preferring to use words derived from Anglo-Saxon rather than from Latin. In English, the longer and more formal words frequently have Latin (or sometimes, Greek) roots, whereas shorter words are more likely to have Anglo-Saxon (or Old English) roots. Any good dictionary will show the derivation of each word as well as its definition.

The offer of employment (see below, section C) contains no fewer than 12 words that are derived either directly or indirectly from Latin: *offer, employment, subject, receipt, references, entirely, satisfactory, medical, include, require, provision, circular.* These are the kind of words that frequently crop up in bureaucratic writing, and they help make the job offer specific. Abstract nouns (see Chapter 13), such as words like education, philosophy and structure, frequently have Latin or Greek roots, and they fit with the specific diction needed in essays.

> * abstract words, often derived from Latin or Greek, can give essays a formal tone

▶ Register

When we talk to someone, we generally adjust our language automatically for the needs of that person. This is called changing register. When talking to a baby, we'll use short, simple words with frequent repetition. When we speak to a priest or other religious person, we might use semi-formal language and would probably take care not to use words that might offend. At a cricket ground, the talk is likely to be full of cricket terminology. There are many situations where traditional language is used. In religious services, for instance, many of the words have remained unchanged for hundreds of years.

If I turn from talking to a baby to making a phone call about my gas bill, you can be pretty certain that I'll be changing register. When we write, too, we need to adjust our language to the particular task in hand. A change of register involves a change of diction and frequently of tone, as well.

> * register is the type of language that fits a particular situation or subject

Look at the four extracts below and then at the discussion of each that follows:

A Refer to the programme guide for details of how to select programmes.

1 Turn on the water supply and check for leaks from fill hoses.
2 Switch on the electricity supply.
3 Select a spin programme and then press the on/off button to start the machine.

B Congratulations to you both
And warmest wishes, too,
For nothing less than happiness
That lasts a lifetime through.

C This offer of employment is subject to one or all of the following:

(a) The receipt of references which we find entirely satisfactory
(b) The LEA's Occupational Health Physician being satisfied as to your medical fitness for the post
(c) Satisfactory LEA checks including those required under the Provisions of the Home Office Circular 47/93 (Protection of Children)

D David Cameron last night launched his groovy new non-alcoholic cocktail at Vinopolis, a wine-tasting emporium under some railway arches in south London.

Mr Cameron's team of Old Etonian chemists, who have been working 24 hours a day round a kitchen table in Notting Hill to develop the drink, say they left alcohol out of the mix in order to make it more compassionate.

But right-wing drinkers ... fear the Cameron, as the new drink is to be known, could turn out to be a pale imitation of the Blair, middle Britain's tipple of choice since 1997.

The Old Etonian chemists yesterday dismissed these fears. They pointed out that unlike the Iron Lady – the last Conservative cocktail that achieved market leadership – the Cameron will leave drinkers with no hangover, and will also stop people thinking the Tories are a hangover from Thatcherism.

© Telegraph Media Group Limited 2006

FEEDBACK

1 *Instructions*   The language used in the instructions for my washing machine is stark. There are no descriptions of any kind. This is the language of good instructions everywhere. It's simple, clear and gets straight to the point. The manufacturers don't want users to be in any doubt as to how to proceed.

2 *Greetings cards*   The wedding card doesn't say a great deal either, but the language it uses is very different. It focuses on feelings, and it does this very simply and in a very positive tone. It's also very traditional. It makes use of rhythm and rhyme, which are powerful devices for getting feelings across, and it focuses on 'happiness'. It also uses a superlative* – 'warmest'.

3 *Formal appointments*   The language of this job offer from a local authority is so formal and carefully worded that you might mistake it for a legal document. In fact, it's a document that could be used in a court of law (once it's been signed and accepted) if either the authority or the employee fails to stick to the agreement. The language is succinct. There must be no possibility of anyone being able to find more than one meaning in it. Notice the careful wording of the introductory statement, saying that the 'offer of employment is subject to *one or all*' (my italics) of three conditions. This allows the authority scope to demand that the employee fulfil all three criteria.

4 *Journalism*   It's not just the reference to a recent event – 'last night' – that tells us that this is a piece of journalism. This drily witty writing satirises David Cameron's Conservative party policy (while it was in Opposition) by suggesting it was a new non-alcoholic drink, and the diction mixes contemporary words such as 'groovy' with the almost extinct 'emporium' for comic effect. (Note that the piece takes a sideways swipe at Labour too.)

You can see from these examples how language can be varied for a particular purpose. So, with this in mind, you'll be able to look at your own writing with a sharper eye.

---

* *superlative: a word that denotes the highest degree of a quality. These words generally end in the letters 'est'.*

▶ Discrimination and equal opportunities

Nowadays, aspects of discrimination that once were acceptable are finally being outlawed. There's quite a wide range of issues that now need to be handled sensitively. It's important that we don't use language that can disadvantage different groups of people or cause offence by treating them differently from everyone else. The main groupings cover:

- gender
- colour
- ability
- religion

- sexual orientation
- ethnicity
- age

SPECIFIC GENDER ISSUES

Not only can discrimination be annoying or hurtful – even if displayed unconsciously – but it can imply things that are incorrect. For example, the statement

A carer needs all the support she can get

suggests that no men are carers, which is not true. We need to say:

A carer needs all the support he or she can get.

or

Carers need all the support they can get.

There's also the problem of words like *manageress* and *poetess* which both seem to imply that the work done in each case is not quite as valuable as that done by a man. *Manager* and *poet* are the job titles, and nowadays we can use these for anyone, male or female. The ending *-ess* has been consigned to the bin.

The word *he* has particular problems. In the past, it used to be used in a general sense, to stand, we were told, for persons of either sex. The problems that were eventually spotted were that:

- whatever argument we try to put forward, the word *he* is actually a reference to a male person

- through the use of the word *he*, women have been screened out of many areas of life
- children have grown up seeing maleness foregrounded

So when speaking in general terms, we need to use phrases like 'he or she', or 'persons of either sex'. Sometimes, people write 's/he', as in:

> Anyone who buys a car must tax it before s/he takes it on the road.

In conversation, of course, we generally use the word 'they':

> 'Anyone who buys a car must tax it as soon as they take it on the road.'

The trouble with that construction, however, is that it's ungrammatical. The word 'they' is plural, implying that there is more than one person involved. But the sentence began with the word 'Anyone', which is singular. Unless your main subject is English, your tutors might not worry too much about you using 'they' to refer to one person, but it's important to understand the issue. When writing informally – as in a letter to a friend – there's no problem in using 'they' to refer to one person, just as we do in everyday speech. But in academic writing, accuracy is important.

> * it's essential not to discriminate in any way against any group of people in our writing

SOME DIFFERENT TYPES OF WRITING

▶ Writing instructions

If you're given an assignment in which you have to write any kind of instructions, check carefully whether what's wanted is a set of bullet points (as in my list below) or writing done in full sentences and paragraphs. A list of bullet points gives just the bare bones of information.

There have probably been countless times when you've been baffled by instructions and have muttered dire things about the person who wrote them. The problem usually relates to one or more of the following:

- information missed out
- information not clearly explained
- language for the initiated only – i.e. a lot of jargon or abbreviations
- confusion caused by incorrect grammar and/or punctuation

Some of us complain bitterly about the instructions in computer manuals. This can happen in any field, however. When we understand a subject, we tend to forget that people without inside knowledge will need to have things spelt out for them. Here's an example of an instruction that often baffles me:

> Take three a day with a main meal.

Now how many times a day would I actually be taking those tablets? Three times? Or all in one go? And should I take them during the meal, or can they be swallowed before or after it?

Let's improve the instruction:

> Take one tablet after a main meal three times a day.

That's a bit better. But I eat only one main meal a day. I wouldn't call my breakfast cornflakes or my lunchtime sandwich a main meal. Does this mean that I must increase my food intake while I'm on those pills? As you can see, writing clear instructions is not necessarily a straight-forward business.

If you have to write instructions, aim to visualise the process that someone must follow as you write each stage; and if these instructions are to be used, have several people test them and give you feedback before you put them into general use.

* instructions need to be checked carefully: there must be no chance for misunderstanding

▶ Describing a process

This is very similar to writing instructions (see above), except that it generally relates to something that has already taken place – like a scientific experiment. As with instructions on a bottle of pills, accuracy is essential. Whatever your subject, aim to make your descriptions so clear that they could be understood by someone who knows practically nothing about the topic. Below is a simple example – putting oil in my car:

> Before I begin, I must make sure that the car is on level ground and that it has been stationary for a little while. First, I unhook the catch on the car's bonnet. Then I raise the bonnet, pull out the attached rod that will support it while I work, and clip the end of the rod in place. Next, I take the dipstick out of its socket. The dipstick is a long rod that can usually be spotted by its curved handle. I then wipe the oily end of the dipstick with a rag or tissue and replace it in its socket.
>
> Then I remove the dipstick again and check the level of oil on the lower end of it. There are maximum and minimum marks. If the oil level is below maximum, I replace the stick, remove the oil-filler cap which is situated on the top of the engine, close to the dipstick socket, and pour in a little oil. I wait a couple of minutes for the oil to settle, and then re-check the level using the dipstick again. I add more oil until the level is close to maximum.
>
> Finally, I replace the filler cap and make sure that it is fully tightened. Then I release the bonnet rod from its catch, clip it back into place, and carefully close the bonnet, making sure (with a final push) that it is securely fixed.

The first thing to notice here is the amount of detail included that will appear superfluous to anyone who is used to changing oil. The second thing you might look at is how often I reuse a noun (the name of a thing – see Chapter 12) in places where we might normally use a pronoun – in this case, 'it'. For example, in the third sentence, I used the word 'rod' twice instead of using the word 'it' on the second occasion. The reason for this is that this sentence already contains the word 'it' which refers to 'bonnet'. If I'd used 'it' again, the unsuspecting reader might assume that this, too, referred to 'bonnet'.

When doing this kind of writing, as with writing instructions, it can help considerably if you can visualise the process. This will help you to incorporate minor items that might otherwise be overlooked. But if you are someone who doesn't visualise things easily, you might find that it helps to rely on your sense of touch or your ability to arrange things in a clear, logical order.

---

* every single stage in a process needs to be explained in detail

▶ Persuasive writing

The object of persuasive writing is, obviously, to get readers on your side. You'll want to stress your main points, but it's important not to overdo things or to appear belligerent. This kind of writing is slightly different from essay-writing where it's important to show all sides of an argument and to take a very logical approach.

Persuasive writing is really very simple. If you want to get someone to agree with your point of view or to take a particular action, you need to:

- show the positive features of your idea
- play down any negative aspects
- push your points strongly
- show that you are committed to your views
- take care not to offend

Of course, all this is in addition to writing simply and clearly. What follows is some work by Joan. Her assignment was to write a 750-word paper for the governors of her local college with the title 'The need for an Access building on the main college site' because the students on the College's Access to Higher Education course were having to spend a great deal of time travelling between two sites. Here's an extract from what she wrote:

> With thorough planning, costs can be kept to a minimum – but it's not all about spending money. The local area abounds with different groups that need space in order to function, so the building can be made to pay for its own upkeep by being hired out for local activities: evening classes, day classes, local drama and music groups.

Joan's final paragraph pushes hard to get her points across:

> None of this can happen with the present arrangement. With only three subjects on offer and basic facilities too far away, the current Access course is undermined and disadvantaged. It cannot become fully effective for the community it serves or for the college.

Joan leaves the reader in no doubt of her views, but she makes a compelling case by sticking to the facts and presenting her ideas in a level-headed manner.

SUMMARY

This chapter has covered:

- sentence length
- simplicity and clarity
- finding the right word
- tone
- diction
- register
- discrimination and equal opportunities
- writing instructions
- describing a process
- persuasive writing

5 Summaries

This chapter will show
you how to write:

► a detailed summary of
  an article or chapter
► an overall summary of
  a book

INTRODUCTION

There are different ways of making summaries.
You might be asked to write a careful summary of
a short text in a hundred words or so where the aim would be to keep
as much of the original information as possible. You might, however,
be asked to summarise just the main ideas in a longer piece – perhaps
a book. This chapter will first set out the basic method for writing a
summary of a short text and then give information on how to proceed
with something longer.

DETAILED SUMMARIES: SHORT TEXT

You might be asked to produce a summary of an article or, perhaps, a
short section from a textbook. A good summary of this type will include
everything of any importance from the original. There are distinct
stages in the process for this:

1 a first quick read
2 note-making during a second read
3 first draft, using your notes
4 a check on the word-count, followed by editing
5 final draft

► A first quick read

Your first reading will familiarise you with the material and so make
you a little more comfortable about the task ahead. You'll begin to get
a feel for the central issues. Skimming will probably be sufficient – that
is, reading just the first and last paragraphs followed by the first and
last sentences of every paragraph in between.

  * start by skim-reading the text

▶ **Note-making**

Make detailed notes during a second read. These will form the basis of your summary (see Chapter 1 for note-taking). You'll need to copy out any technical terms and phrases that seem particularly important, but in general, aim to translate the original material into your own words. Let's assume you've been asked to make a summary in no more than 100 words of A. C. Grayling's article in Chapter 1. Here are my notes for the task (numbers refer to paragraphs):

1 Soc. where all drugs legal = gd. because: freedom of individual.
2 Grayling believes: a) life shd. not depend on 'substances which ... distort reality' b) hard drugs shd. be legal.
3 Legal/illegal drugs used for: pleasure, stress relief, escapism. Both = 'dangerous to health'
   The law shd. treat both groups the same.
4 Only practices that harm soc. or 'unwilling third parties' shd. be illegal. Allowing those who 'claim to know better' than others to make law = wrong.
5 Children more at risk when drugs illegal.
6 Drug-taking not prevented by laws. Relaxation of law doesn't change no. of users.
7 Prohibition in USA caused increase in crime.
8 Organised crime = serious threat to society: money-laundering, terrorism, vice rings, buying political influence. Ans. = controlled sale of drugs in chemists.
9 If addicts got safe supplies, petty crime would lessen.
10 Dangers of overdose = small.
11 If a practice isn't dangerous to soc. it shd. not be illegal. A 'good society' restricts 'interfere[nce] in private behaviour'.
12 Some people will suffer from misuse, but hist. shows little damage to society as a whole from drug use.
13 The freedom of individuals to choose lifestyles = essential in 'good society'.

▶ **Writing a first draft**

Your first draft should be written from your notes. Try not to look back at the original while you're writing it so that this draft really will have your stamp on it and you won't sound as though you're merely parroting the original text. Obviously, you'll aim to keep this draft short, but don't worry too much about the word-count at this stage. The mind can't cope with two complex processes at the same time. When you've written it, check the original for errors. Here's my first draft:

> Grayling feels that people shouldn't need to 'distort reality' for pleasure. He says that all drugs have health risks and wants consistency in the law. He sees the only justification for law is protection of third parties, and feels that those laws that coerce on moral grounds are 'bad'. They give no protection to children since all who want to use drugs will do so anyway. Relaxation of drug laws brings no change in user statistics, but organised crime is a threat. The danger of overdose is small and addicts could be treated on prescription. A 'good society' is not directive. Legal availability would reduce both serious and petty crime, and has been seen in the past to have no adverse effect on society. It is essential that individuals have the right to choose their lifestyles. (136 words)

* write your first draft from your notes without looking at the text

▶ Checking your word-count and editing

Editing will depend partly on the instructions you've been given and you might need to write another couple of drafts before you get down to the required word count. If your summary is well over the word limit you've been given, look first at cutting facts and opinions that are secondary to the text's central issues. Then, think about saying things in different ways and cutting words and phrases that aren't absolutely essential.

Your writing might just need tidying up a little; but if, by any chance, your summary is *much shorter* than the word limit, it's almost certainly the case that you've omitted too much. Check your notes against the original, look for the next most important points after the ones you've already noted, and add these to your draft. You might find that you need to write your summary out more than once at this stage if it gets too messy to follow clearly.

▶ Writing your final draft

If you faithfully follow the five steps, you can't go far wrong. Problems with summary-writing are nearly always the result of rushing stage 2 –

the note-making. It really is essential to get down *the key points* and to get them down in *your own words* as far as possible.

Here's the final draft of my summary of the Grayling article. You'll see that I've chipped away at nearly every sentence in order to cut a few words here and a few words there:

> People shouldn't need reality 'distort[ion]' for pleasure. All drugs have health risks and the law is inconsistent. The only justification for laws against hard drugs is protection of society and 'unwilling third parties'. Laws that coerce on moral grounds are 'bad'. They give no protection to children. All who want to use do so, and relaxation of drug law brings no increase in use. Legal availability would reduce organised and petty crime and has been seen historically to have no adverse effect on society. Addicts, under this system, could be treated on prescription. A 'good society' promotes individual freedom. (99 words)

The trick with summary-writing is to disentangle the key points from explanations, examples, jokes and blatant diversions. Note that I've omitted all the following items:

- explanations
- the statement on the writer's own lack of drug-taking
- the example of Prohibition in the USA
- the example of paracetamol

BROAD SUMMARIES: LONG TEXT

You might be asked to summarise just the main ideas of a longer text on one side of A4, so the exact word count won't be important. You can take a slightly more relaxed approach here and the method is different. You're likely to need just a general grasp of what is contained. Detail won't be wanted in a summary of a long work.

What you'll be looking for are the main themes of the book and key conclusions. First of all, read the contents list and any blurb on the cover. You might scan the index too. This will give you a good general idea of the material covered. If you've time to read the book from cover to cover, next jot down the main ideas in each chapter as you finish it. Then it's a good idea to decide which are the three or four key aspects of the book: what ground does it cover? what key ideas does it put forward? what conclusions does it come to? Write these down as headings on a sheet of A4 and sum up each aspect under the relevant heading using the notes you've made on the chapters.

If you're pushed for time, try this: after you've looked at contents, blurb and index, scan the book for diagrams, graphs, etc., and then skim-read. That means taking one chapter at a time and reading the first and last paragraph followed by the first and last sentence of every paragraph. After each chapter, write up what you can remember. Then proceed as above, deciding on the three or four main aspects of the book and so on. You won't do as good a job this way, but you're likely to keep your head above water.

Either way, write up a page of A4 without headings (unless you've been asked to include them). The main things to bear in mind are as you work are:

- Check: contents, blurb and index
- Do a quick: scan and skim
- Make brief notes on each chapter
- Decide on the three or four main aspects
- Write up your notes under those headings
- Do a final smart draft

SUMMARY

This chapter has covered:

writing a summary: general notes for a short text
1 a first quick read
2 note-making
3 writing a first draft
4 checking your word-count and editing
5 writing your final draft

summarising a book: long text
1 scanning and skimming
2 making notes a chapter at a time
3 deciding on key aspects
4 writing-up your notes

6 Letters and Emails

This chapter will show
you how to approach:

▶ informal letters
▶ formal letters
▶ emails

INTRODUCTION

This chapter will look at the differences between formal and informal letters, at the accepted ways for setting these out in Britain, and at some of the different types of letter that you might be required to write. (You'll find further information in Chapter 18).

There can be confusion over knowing whether a letter is formal or informal. A formal letter is sometimes said to be one that begins *Dear Sir/Madam*. Sometimes, it's thought to be any letter with the name and address of the recipient at the top left-hand side. These are letters written at work or from home to a business or a government department. Sometimes, letters are divided into informal and formal according to how they begin. A letter beginning *Dear Mrs Smith* would be said to be informal, and a letter to the same person beginning *Dear Madam* would be formal. Each of these types of letter will be discussed below.

As far as structure is concerned, it's as well to use the rules of good essay writing. Stick to one topic per paragraph and, in any kind of formal letter, use your first paragraph as an introduction that sets out what the letter will be about and your last to sum up what you've said.

If you've worked in a business capacity, you may have been using an in-house system for the layout of letters. There is, however, a generally accepted layout in Britain for letters from private individuals, so that will be followed here.

INFORMAL LETTERS

Informal letters are often thought to be those written to friends. When we write to close friends, we can do exactly as we like. We can break all the rules of grammar, draw pictures and even write letters of only one or two words if we want to:

Dear Alex
  Yes!
  Luv,
  Chris xxx

These two people clearly know each other well, so Alex will be in no doubt over what this letter means. In fact, the shortness of the letter gives impact. So with letters to friends, just continue to be yourself and don't worry about doing things right or wrong. You may find, however, that, as your skills develop, some of your letters to friends become increasingly complex. Letters can be a literary form in their own right, as is clear from the number of books published containing collections of letters.

The term *informal letters* can be rather confusing. The letter to Alex is certainly informal, but it is definitely not what tutors want to see if they ask you to write informally. In terms of your course, it's best to think of informal letters as those that are friendly and helpful but that also give full information and adhere to the rules of grammar and letter-writing.

There are four important items that you will need to include in an informal letter:

- your address
- the date
- the salutation (saying *Hello*)
- the valediction (saying *Goodbye*)

If you're asked to write a letter to a friend, the layout expected is this (the blocks represent paragraphs):

                                               [your address]
                                             [line space]
                                             [date]

Dear Bob
[line space]

[line space]

[line space]

```

```

[line space]
Best wishes
[2 or 3 line spaces]
your first name (or nickname)

Note that, when writing a letter to a friend (even if it's for course-work), your friend's address must *not* be included. If you type or word-process, always sign your name by hand.

You might, however, want to write to someone who is not a friend but to whom you will need to write a friendly letter. For example, you might write a letter to a local celebrity, asking if he or she would agree to open a fête or give a talk. The layout of your letter would be similar to the one to a friend except for the salutation and valediction, and the inclusion of the recipient's name and address, like this:

[your address]
[line space]
[date]

[addressee's title, initial and last name]
[address]
[line space]
Dear [addressee's title and last name]
[line space]

```

```

[line space]

```

```

[line space]

```

```

[line space]
Yours sincerely
[2 line spaces]
[your signature]
[2 line spaces]
[your full name – in capitals if you write by hand]

There are variations on this. If you were to write to someone like the pop star Robbie Williams, who would almost certainly expect you to be reasonably chatty, you could put *Dear Robbie* without causing offence. Above his address, you could put: *Robbie Williams*.

You might, of course, need to write to someone in their business capacity. In this case, the shape of your letter will be the same as the one above, but you might use their full name above their address. Then either *Dear Mr Smith* or *Dear David Smith* would be OK as a salutation. If they reply using just your first name, you can do the same for them if you need to write again.

When you sign off, you'll need to marry up your valediction with whichever salutation you've used:

Salutations	Valedictions
Dear Lord Winston Dear Mr Smith Dear David Smith	Yours sincerely
Dear Sir Dear Madam Dear Sir/Madam	Yours faithfully
Dear Robbie	Best wishes
Dear Pat (a friend of yours)	Love

In most cases, you'll include your first name in your signature as well as your last name, and it's important to print your name underneath. The person reading your letter could easily make a spelling mistake when writing back to you if there's only your signature to go on. It's also important to use a capital Y for *Yours,* a small s for *sincerely* and a small f for *faithfully*. Incidentally, notice how *sincerely* is spelt. People very often get it wrong. You might find this easier to remember if you note that the word *sincerely* contains the word '*ere* (i.e. *here* without the *h*) in the middle.

In most businesses, it's the practice to put the name of the business at the top of the page. As a private individual, however, your name goes only after your signature.

Let's suppose that you need to write to John Fleming, the manager of Fergus Electronics, to complain about a faulty computer purchased from his company. You'll set out your letter like this:

14 Lucius Street
Maxford
Nutshire
A4 7RP

15 March 2012

John Fleming
Manager
Fergus Electronics
Bat Lane
Wallopford
Nutshire
WP14 6RF

Dear Mr Fleming

Purchase of a fault-ridden computer

Three weeks ago, I took the decision to buy a new computer. I run a small translating business from my home and an increase in my workload has meant that I need a new, up-to-date, reliable PC.

I was persuaded by your advertising, both in the local press and on television, to visit your premises for an analysis of my office needs. Once I was there, a salesman was adamant that he knew the make and model best suited to my work.

If you check your records, you will find that I have already had to return twice to have minor faults on this computer corrected. Now the machine is malfunctioning yet again.

You may imagine my exasperation. My business is suffering and I am losing custom. Will you please arrange to have this PC replaced with a more efficient model without delay and inform me of the delivery date.

Yours sincerely

R. Long

ROBERT LONG

As well as using the name of the person he's writing to, Robert also includes the recipient's job title between the name and address. This is usual in business letters of any kind. The subject of the letter is then given in bold type. If you write a letter by hand, the subject must be underlined. Although he's polite here, Robert hasn't wanted to be particularly friendly in this letter and he's not included his first name in his signature.

Two other things might have struck you: there are no indentations – either for paragraphs or in the lines of the addresses, and there's no punctuation in the addresses. This layout has been in use for a number of years now in business and government documents. It's the simplest method of setting out letters. Just as with an essay, however, leave a line between paragraphs as this makes a letter much easier to read as well as making it look smart.

▶ Titles

There tends to be a bit of disagreement nowadays on what to do about your title at the end of a letter. If you leave it out, you may find that you don't get the right one on your reply. There are not likely to be any problems for a man who uses the title *Mr*. If you sign yourself *John Brown,* you'll get addressed as *Mr Brown.* If, however, you're a man and your name is Alex Brown, the person who writes back to you will have to guess at whether you're male or female if you omit your title. If you are the Reverend John Brown, you won't get addressed as such unless you give your title or your letter itself makes your situation obvious – that is, unless it contains such things as a reference to your parish duties.

Women can have particular problems. When writing a letter to a woman whose preferred title is not known, it's usual nowadays to use *Ms*. If you sign yourself *Sally Brown,* you are likely to be addressed as either *Ms Brown* or possibly *Mrs Brown.* Government offices will call you *Ms Brown,* which is fine if you don't want to let on whether you're married or not. You'll have the best chance of getting the title you want by using it yourself, like this:

Yours sincerely

Beth Parkes

BETH PARKES (Mrs)

Put your title *after* your name, and always put it in *brackets.* Some people, however are now cutting out titles altogether. You might or might not like this, but it's as well to be aware of what's going on. Sometimes, you'll find yourself addressed in the salutation with your full name (and no title) whatever you do.

FORMAL LETTERS

If you haven't yet read the section on informal letters, you might like to look at it now, as it contains a good deal of essential information on setting out various different types of letter.

▶ Salutations and valedictions

The letter to J. Fleming at Fergus Electronics begins *Dear Mr Fleming* and ends *Yours sincerely.* Whenever you know a person's name, do use it. A classic formal letter is the one that begins either *Dear Sir* or *Dear Madam* (or *Dear Sir/Madam*) and ends with *Yours faithfully.* We generally use this form of address nowadays, however, *only* when we don't know the name of the person to whom we're writing. So we close with *Yours sincerely* even if the tone of the letter is very serious and formal. If you don't know the recipient's name, you'll have to put *Dear Sir/Madam* and close with *Yours faithfully.* It's OK to put *Dear Sir* by itself *only* if you happen to know for certain that the recipient of your letter is male. If you're sure it's a woman, then you can put *Dear Madam.*

As far as the valediction is concerned, all you have to do here is to remember to use a capital *Y* for *Yours* and a small *s* for sincerely or a small *f* for faithfully. Yes, it does all seem a bit fussy, but it's rather like knowing the accepted things to do at a wedding: everything goes more smoothly for you when you get it right.

One further bugbear can be knowing exactly who to write to. When you write a letter, you *must* address it to a particular person. This can be especially difficult when, for example, you need to write to a company and you don't know anyone's name or job title. You can phone or try the Internet to check, but it's quicker to write to *The Manager*. So if Robert Long didn't know the name of the manager at Fergus Electronics, he'd have written a formal letter, set out like this:

14 Lucius Street
Maxford
Nutshire
A4 7RP

15 February 2012

The Manager
Fergus Electronics
Bat Lane
Wallopford
Nutshire
WP14 6RF

Dear Sir/Madam

Purchase of a fault-ridden computer

Three weeks ago, I took the decision to buy a new computer *[etc. etc.]*

Yours faithfully

R. Long

ROBERT LONG

▶ Letters of complaint

Robert Long's letter is clearly a letter of complaint. If you need to write one of these, it's important to remember to control any feelings of anger. It's a good idea, however, to be forceful. Robert stated the problem very clearly and demanded a replacement, but at no point was he abusive. It's also OK to be gently humorous, but aiming for belly laughs can suggest that you don't take the situation very seriously. Robert has contented himself with injecting a little mild sarcasm into the letter's heading.

▶ EMAILS

When using email, we omit a home address because our email address comes up automatically. We don't need the recipient's home or business address either because we use his or her email address in the relevant box. There's also a box for the subject of the email, so you won't need to add it after the salutation. Indeed, many people omit the salutation too in brief or informal emails. Frequently, people just write, *Hi*. That's fine for friends, but it won't hit the right note in formal emails or those where we want to be polite. If in doubt, write *Dear* followed by the person's full name.

Otherwise, the conventions are fairly similar to those for letters. Use a simple font, clear paragraphing and be chatty to friends and more formal when it's necessary. Whenever you're emotionally involved in the material, however, it's always best to draft the email and leave it overnight before you send it. Things sent in the heat of the moment can't be recalled and may be regretted.

The main problem with emails is lack of information. Because they're so easy to write, people often take less care with them than with letters. Remember that the person at the other end can't see inside your head, so for anything other than chatty emails to friends, it's important to make sure that you've given every piece of information that will be needed. For any kind of business or formal email, include your full contact details after your name at the end of an email.

For layout, stick to fairly short paragraphs and be sure to leave a line between paragraphs. People frequently misread emails, so include only essential information. Make your text really clear with a simple font like Arial and never use fancy fonts.

When signing off, *Best wishes* can be a useful informal valediction, but if you're in any doubt, go for *Kind regards*. A more formal sign-off can be done by putting just *Sincerely*, but for fully formal emails, use *Yours sincerely* unless you've had to put *Dear Sir/Madam*, in which case put *Yours faithfully*.

SUMMARY

This chapter has covered:

letters to friends
your address:	top right
date:	underneath your address
salutation:	*Dear* [Bob]
valediction:	*Best wishes*

polite informal letters
your address:	top right
date:	underneath your address
recipient's name and address:	on the left, just below the level of the date
recipient's job title, if relevant:	between the name and address
salutation:	*Dear Mrs Jones*
the subject of the letter:	in bold type below the salutation
valediction:	*Yours sincerely*
your name:	in capitals underneath your signature with your preferred title in brackets afterwards

formal letters
your address	top right
date	underneath your address
recipient's name, job title and address	on the left, just below the level of the date
salutation	*Dear Sir/Madam*
the subject of the letter	in bold type below the salutation
valediction	*Yours faithfully*
your name	underneath your signature with your preferred title in brackets afterwards

email
- write clear, short paragraphs
- use a simple font
- consider the salutation and valediction carefully
- give full information
- include your contact details after your name at the end of business letters

7 Creative Writing

This chapter will give yo
ideas for writing:

► autobiography
► short stories
► poems
► fictional letters

INTRODUCTION

Creative writing assignments are sometimes given to enable people to look at topics on a syllabus from new angles and so to become more familiar with them. So you might be asked to do some autobiographical work or to write a poem, story or letter connected with the subject you're studying.

You might feel that this kind of thing isn't a serious part of your course, but imaginative work can really deepen your understanding. It can also help you to remember things. Using the imagination is a very valuable activity for developing brainpower. A brain that is used only for facts and figures is likely to function less well than one that is also used for making new and unusual connections between different topics and ideas.

Einstein valued the imagination very highly, knowing from his own experience that creativity can be a route to discovery and innovation. And as we struggle to select and describe scenes and events, we're also we're getting good practice in developing our skills with language.

AUTOBIOGRAPHICAL WRITING

I'd like to reassure you at once that private issues that you want to keep private can stay that way. Autobiographical work isn't set because tutors want to pry into students' lives. Taking a serious look at certain aspects of our past, however, can give us a very good foundation for further study. We learn to situate our own experience within a wider context, and doing this helps us to assess issues more objectively. Anyway, you're likely to be given a pretty free hand over what you decide to work on. There are sure to be some items in the following list that you'd be comfortable with:

Ideas for autobiographical writing

pre-school education	school trips
national events	evening classes
clothing	furniture/household items
Sunday School	museums and galleries
festivals/rituals	games
money	clubs and societies
life-changing events	primary school
wearing uniform	secondary school
toys	sports
teachers	school buildings
popular music	politics
jobs	rules and regulations
marriage	the 1980s (or other decade)
arts and crafts	family members/grandparents
transport	hospital, doctors and health
religious observation	birthdays and anniversaries
having children	running a home

There's one area that your tutors might be particularly keen for you to explore, and that's your educational experience. They won't want to know about failures and expulsion from school (unless you want to focus on harsh things), but they may well want you to look at:

what you were taught (or not)	how staff behaved
how classes were organised	what you enjoyed/hated
what the buildings were like	the national scene
what types of school you attended	

They'll want to know how you view these things in retrospect and in relation to what you now know of the rest of society. So you can see that both emotion and logic are vital here. It can be very illuminating to relate our own experiences to a national situation.

▶ Digging into your memory

Look at the lists below and, without stopping to think too hard, pick one item, take a sheet of notepaper, and, before reading any further, quickly do a mind map on it or jot down as many ideas as you can. (For an explanation of mind-mapping, see Chapters 1 and 2.)

teachers	sports	art	money
meals	lessons	music	discipline
friends	buildings	drama	assembly
prefects	prizes	poetry	uniform
books	pictures	break times	festivals

You're likely to find that one memory will lead to another. But it's often only by starting to write that these memories flow. So once you've got some ideas, write a couple of paragraphs about your chosen topic. This can begin to lead you into lots more memories.

A slightly different way of getting yourself started is to construct a lifeline. Many students find this particularly helpful. You'll probably need several sheets of A4 paper laid end to end on their sides (landscape) and taped together. Part of a roll of wallpaper would work well for this.

At the left-hand side, put the date you were born, and on the right put 'NOW'. Mark the whole strip off in decades, leaving more space than you think you need, and then begin to fill in key dates: starting school, moving house, starting work, meeting a partner, and so on. Putting in the obvious things will cause your mind to focus more clearly. You'll then begin to remember things you'd forgotten. This method is particularly helpful for getting an overall view of your experiences.

Another useful thing to do can be to start finding actual items that relate to your past educational experiences. You could look for:

photos	diaries	scrapbooks
school reports	cups or certificates	newspaper cuttings
badges	letters	exercise books

Then you might start talking to relatives and friends, encouraging them to dip into their own memories for you. If you live near one of your old schools, you might visit it. If it's in another part of the country, you could write to the principal. There might be photos and pamphlets that you could get copies of. Even if your old school has been razed to the ground, there are still likely to be records in the local education department and reference library. Try the internet as well. Information you locate in your searches could also be useful later for your CV.

▶ Relevance to academic study

It's inevitable that autobiographical writing will relate to both sociology and history – and probably, politics too. For example, anything you write on festivals and rituals or on clubs and societies will be relevant to social studies. In historical terms, all those photos, diaries and school badges from the past are called **primary sources**. These are things that originated in the period you're looking at. Any school records you can manage to get hold of are also primary sources, too, as are education acts and other legal documents.

A **secondary source** looks back at what happened and comments on it. This is what historians do all the time, and it's what you'll be doing when you write about the past. A secondary source is usually written sometime *after* events take place.

Once you begin to relate your own experiences to the experiences of others and to national – and possibly even international – events and situations, your work will become more and more interesting. What you write will, inevitably, depend on the structure or title you've been given by your tutor; but whatever you do, you are bound to end up with a valuable perspective on certain issues from the past.

▶ Structuring your autobiographical project

The important thing here is to have a plan (see Chapter 2). It's very easy to get so immersed in reminiscences that you end up forgetting the reason for doing this piece of work. Your tutor will almost certainly give you very clear guidelines. If not, check on exactly what's wanted.

You might refer to events chronologically, or you might section your material by topic. If you make a good plan, you'll be able to keep focused and prevent yourself from putting in information that's not related to the assignment you've been set. Your written work needs to be logical and easy to follow.

POETRY

Writing a poem on an event, scene, or issue about which we feel strongly forces our brains to perform new tricks. Just as with autobiographical work, our writing skills and imagination come into play but in slightly different ways. Poetry-writing can also be really valuable for getting practice in writing succinctly and for thinking hard about expressing meaning accurately. Poets nearly always *condense* what they want to tell us. So if you've been asked to write a poem, one of the things you'll be practising is the valuable skill of getting your ideas across in a few words.

One of the best ways to get yourself going on writing poems is to read some poetry. You might get a couple of books out of the library. If you're not used to reading poetry, don't feel you have to read from cover to cover. Just flick through and read whatever takes your fancy. Or you might pop into a large bookshop where you can browse for ages without being pressured to buy anything.

It's sometimes thought that poetry comes wholly from the imagination, but this is rarely the case. A good poem is usually rooted firmly in facts – and will have had a good deal of editing. Notice how, in the following poem by Carol Ann Duffy, much of the emotion is evoked through the speaker's response to everyday items in their relation to the beloved. If you read the poem aloud, you're likely to get a stronger sense of it.

Tea

I like pouring your tea, lifting
the heavy pot, and tipping it up,
so the fragrant liquid steams in your china cup.

Or when you're away, or at work,
I like to think of your cupped hands as you sip,
as you sip, of the faint half-smile of your lips.

I like the questions – sugar? milk? –
and the answers I don't know by heart, yet,
for I see your soul in your eyes, and I forget.

Jasmine, Gunpowder, Assam, Earl Grey, Ceylon,
I love tea's names. Which tea would you like? I say,
but it's any tea, for you, please, any time of day,

as the women harvest the slopes,
for the sweetest leaves, on Mount Wu-Yi,
and I am your lover, smitten, straining your tea.

Poems are as different as the people who write them, and they can be on any topic under the sun. So don't feel that your poems have to conform to some set format. I'd suggest that you give yourself two rules, however: no rhyme and no humour. If you use rhyme at this stage, you might do it at the expense of thought and emotion. It's fatally easy to focus on finding a rhyme for a word you've just written, and consequently to lose track of depth of meaning. Humour can function in a similar way. The joke becomes more important than the poem itself.

You probably know the old saying that a picture's worth a thousand words. Well, poems very often contain a lot of pictures – or images. The poet uses his or her imagination to come up with images that will spark a reader's imagination. You might like to work from a photograph or to take a particular scene to base your poem on. You might choose somewhere that you can go and make notes on before you start to write. If you have to work from memory, however, try closing your eyes and visualising your subject.

You might want to have a broad picture: a park, a townscape, a beach, a railway station, a mountain view or a market. On the other hand, you might like to go for a smaller picture: one building, a single flower, a person or an animal. The important thing is to be really interested in your subject. You'll write more convincingly about a junkyard than a palace if you're fascinated by junk.

You'll need to focus on things like objects, shapes, colours, textures, light, sound and movement. If there are people around, look at their clothing and body language. Maybe one or two people stand out. Your task is to provide yourself with plenty of useful material. Include your feelings, and any phrases that suggest themselves. When you begin to write the poem, you'll want enough notes to choose from to get you going and make your pictures vibrant.

The next stage is a little bit magical. Just sit quietly, mull over your notes, reimagine the scene, and then see what turns up. What goes on in the brain at this point is something about which we know little and certainly have very little control over. You might find that two or three quite separate phrases occur to you, or that you start to describe one particular item. Whatever comes, jot it down. If by any chance you're stuck, start to describe something anyway, using your notes to help you. At this stage, don't worry if your work looks very disjointed.

It's a good idea to aim to write a poem of around twelve lines. This will give you enough space to create a strong picture while still making sure that you condense your ideas. You might arrange it in three or four verses (stanzas).When you have written as much as you can, put the whole thing away for a day or so. Other ideas might now start to suggest themselves – usually at very inconvenient times – so if you can have a jotter handy wherever you go, you'll be able to catch them. My first poem began unannounced while I was cleaning the bathroom.

The final stage is editing. At this point, you might want to move things around a bit. You'll need to use all your knowledge of grammar and punctuation to make the poem sharp and easily understood. One of the myths about poetry is that you can put anything down and that you don't have to write fully functioning sentences. Only experienced poets can get away with that kind of thing.

Here's Amanda's poem. It's followed by her background notes. There were several drafts before the poem was finished.

The Solitary Summer

Excitement and anxiety gripped me,
'Just five turns in the lane and we'll be there.'
Nature itself appeared to herald us, the flowers
swaying in the breeze like hands waving, the summer sun
bright and the sky as enticing as the sea on a hot day.
Only I saw clouds on the horizon.

They waited to greet us as we arrived.
Him, imposing but smiling, and her, ever ready with hugs for all.
The cottage, like a scene from a picture postcard,
was before us. Its stout wooden door was
framed by honeysuckle, whose aromatic scent,
although admired by the others, invaded my nostrils.

Then they were gone, and we three were left,
to be looked after and loved by those, not our parents.
'They're together, that's the main thing,' I'd heard them say,
but the three of us weren't together, only two,
and all I saw of them were their backs,
as we biked, climbed, or picnicked, 'together'.

Their time was spent on exciting adventures.
While mine was spent with she who hugged.
Our place was the kitchen all homely and warm, with its big
wooden table, and shelf upon shelf of herbs, spices, pickles, and
jams, and the big miracle milk pan which changed milk to cream.
There, without the two, I was happy, contented.

Background notes

smells	sounds
bread, apples, stewing, baking	birds, cows, horses
mothballs, summer	tractors, Simba barking
cow dung, cut grass/hedges	TV, bees in long grass meadow
lily of the valley	G & Gdad talking, cockerel
	P & S laughing

inside sights	outside sights
big wooden table	large trees towering over me
high beds in my room	gates, fields
large silvery milk pan	barns, animals, tractors
row upon row of jam jars full	backs of P & S in distance
of jam, pickles & marmalade	chickens

feelings being there
love for Gran
adventure, being on holiday
loneliness, spending much time on my own
missing home & parents
dislike for P & S for always leaving me

In this poem, the pain of the writer's isolation from her siblings is contrasted with the beauty of their surroundings at the grandparents' home. The reason for the trip is not made clear, and it hovers with some menace in the words 'They're together, that's the main thing'. We realise from this that there's been a crisis of some kind. The fact that the writer doesn't say exactly what it was actually makes the poem stronger. The imagery in the poem focuses on the natural world and on items in the kitchen, and we can see from her notes that Amanda chose carefully what to include.

SHORT STORIES

Writing a short story gives practice in logical thinking and structuring that can be useful practice for structuring essays. You'll need to spend time thinking about how to introduce your characters and get them interacting, you'll need to keep the plot going throughout body of the story, and you'll have to bring everything to a believable conclusion, with loose ends neatly tied up.

Writing a story can develop both your ability to structure a piece of writing and your skills with language itself. Character work will develop your ability to analyse. Since your imagination is crucial for each stage, you'll be developing that too, and if you've read the introduction to this chapter, you already know the value of the imagination.

▶ Choosing your topic

You might start by recalling stories you've read and considering which ones you've especially liked. You might be drawn to a particular type (genre) of fiction – historical, crime, or adventure, perhaps. Think for a minute about what you've really enjoyed. Your tutor will be looking for a good structure (beginning, middle and end), believable characters, descriptions that make the story come alive, and language that fits your particular topic.

It's probably best to avoid: personal hobby-horses, politics, sex and/or violence, horror, humour, science fiction and dreams (which are usually the ultimate cop-out). Now you're probably wondering if there's anything left. In a nutshell, what you want is some fairly simple interaction between two or three people, at least one of whom is changed – at least in some small way – by the events that you recount.

▶ Plot

People have always loved a good story. We always want to know what happens next. If you think back to stories you've read, however, you'll realise that there must be an awful lot left out. If a guy goes shark fishing, for example, we don't want to know that on the previous day he washed his socks, sent his aunt a birthday card and had a bit of indigestion. What you need are key incidents that will demonstrate character and advance the plot. If your man is to encounter danger, you can begin to indicate what's likely to happen by showing him preparing his boat and being meticulous – or negligent.

If your story is about, lost love, you might have the following plot:

A loves B
B meets C and falls in love
A is desolate

If your plot revolves around a troubled marriage, it might look like this:

>The Smiths move to a new home
>Mrs Smith hates the area
>They argue and problems in the marriage are revealed
>They separate/are reconciled/fight/go into counselling/whatever
>   you like

And here are about a hundred and twenty-five other plots:

A wants to	change jobs
	get married
	buy a particular home/car
	emigrate
	save/spend
	etc., etc.

A is blocked by	B
	lack of money
	health
	B and C together
	age
	time
	etc., etc.

The outcome is that A	wins through
	finds a new way
	commits suicide
	enlists the help of D
	accepts the situation
	cheers up
	gets angry
	etc., etc.

The crux of a good short story is conflict. Readers are interested in problems and difficulties. You don't need civil strife, but you do need to show human beings struggling to cope with life. One of the best student stories I ever read was about a tramp living rough in a local park. A teenage girl tries, briefly, to offer him some kindness, and her boyfriend turns nasty about it. That's all. But I've always remembered this story for its sensitivity and the way in which each character came alive through brief snatches of conversation.

Here are some tips on how to cope with a few of the above plot outlines:

1 LOST LOVE

Here you could keep the story short by showing one encounter between A and B, one between B and C and a little narrative in between. You'd need to show only one key point in the relationship between B and C for readers to cotton on.

2 THE TROUBLED MARRIAGE

It's not necessary to describe the house move. You could refer to it neatly in one sentence:

> Three months after the move to Suffolk, the Smiths' hall was still blocked with boxes.

Then you'd need one argument followed by its result. You don't need to accompany the couple the whole way to their changed existence.

3 OTHER POSSIBILITIES

You can take any one person and put him or her in whatever situation you like – as long as it's believable. Choose just the key points in the episode you want to cover, add some description, a snatch or two of conversation, and you've created a human drama. You can focus on two or three events that would encapsulate the whole story. Go for highlights rather than a moment-by-moment account. Readers tend to fill in the gaps themselves.

▶ The beginning

Don't spend a page recounting your characters' past lives. Remember, this is a short story, not a novel. There isn't time for long explanations. Get stuck into the action straight away. Get the characters interacting and they'll start to reveal themselves. If there's something that you *must* explain, do it as the plot moves along. (I've given a couple of examples below.)

▶ The end

This is merely the ending of the story – not a summing-up of the characters' whole lives. What you need here is a resolution of whatever issues you've raised. That just means that a reader needs to know what has changed for your main character(s). Stick to small, believable changes. There's not time for much, and a reader would probably find wholesale change unbelievable.

By the way, if you feel you absolutely must put your characters on a spaceship or in some other imaginary situation, just be sure to follow the basic rules for short-story writing. Remember that you'll have been given a creative writing assignment to practise structure and your use of language, and you'll be wanting a good mark.

▶ Theme

Your story will also need a theme. This is not quite the same as the plot. It's the general idea that your story is based around – for example:

> love of money is the root of all evil
> progress can entail loss
> we cannot fully know the mind of another person
> the best laid plans can go awry
> romance
> greed

▶ Writing about what you know

If you were writing about the Smiths and their marriage problems, stick to describing the kind of people and living quarters of which you have personal experience. You'll be convincing on what you know about – whether it's poverty, dog-racing or the Women's Institute.

▶ Descriptions

If you've read through the section on poetry, you already know what to do here. If your story is set in the local bus station, go along there and make some notes. You might write something like this:

> yellowing paint – peeling near seats
> concrete – hard, cold
> queues/crush of people
> lines of bus stops/buses – red & white/coaches
> wind
> café – plastic cups
> information boards – small print
> inspector – peaked cap – holding small board
> sound – voices/brakes/engines running
> child in pushchair – asleep
> smell of diesel

You might use only two or three items from your list when you come to write, but having plenty to choose from makes things much easier, and becoming fully aware of the place will ultimately give strength to your writing. A good way of adding description to your story is to slip some in every now and then rather than adding a whole chunk in one go. Your story might be about a couple who were once lovers and who meet by chance, after many years, while changing buses on long-distance journeys. Notice which particular items from the above list I've included in an opening paragraph for this story:

> The wind seemed to be blowing all the way from the Russian steppes. Pete held the plastic cup close to his chest, warming his fingers on the heat from the hot coffee. Suddenly he saw her – or thought he did. He caught sight of the auburn hair and the angular stance. Then a crush of people surging forward to the London coach got in the way. He grabbed his holdall and started round the back of the queue in a rush, slopped coffee burning his skin.

You can begin to see what the bus station is like from brief details. It's cold, windy and busy. You don't need to include a whole paragraph of description. That would slow things down. Incidentally, bus and train stations are very useful places for setting stories because people are there for just short periods and their emotions are often heightened as they meet, say goodbye or have arguments in the stresses and strains of travelling. There's also plenty to describe, such as cafés, news-stands, vehicles, architecture, other travellers, and so on.

▶ Characterisation

If you need a couple of characters and you've got a mental block, just go for a walk to your local shops and look around. Or go into a pub or restaurant where you can sit and watch people unobtrusively. People are everywhere. You'll need some descriptions of clothes, expressions, movement, and so on. So make a list, just as I did for the bus station. Then use individual items from this list at relevant points. If I want to describe a young woman begging, I might note:

> bedraggled hair
> old brown wool coat that hangs loosely – like a sack
> trousers tucked into very worn black boots
> thin dog on a blanket
> knitted hat – rainbow colours
> thin fingers
> pallid skin
> hunched sitting position

I might decide to write a story about a successful banker who has no understanding of the lives of those less fortunate than himself. The story could show how one day he has a mind-broadening experience. I could begin like this:

> Martin habitually rose early. He parked his car in the Home Counties, read *The Times* in first-class peace on the London train, took the tube to Waterloo and walked to his office in the Strand to improve his health. He was in the habit of keeping his mind on pleasant thoughts while travelling. He often smiled at the occasional beggars in the underground to demonstrate to them that a better world lay within reach if only they would open their eyes to it.
>
> Why he looked more closely at Carla he was never quite sure. Maybe the bright rainbow colours of her knitted hat reminded him of his younger sister in childhood. Perhaps it was those blue

eyes staring from the pallid face like a saint in a Renaissance painting. Or maybe the long, slim fingers that stroked the half-starved dog made him think of his mother. Whatever it was that had arrested him, Martin's defences had been breached.

Carla had learnt to spot indecision. Her voice was thin but her stare acted on Martin like a tap on the shoulder from the Almighty. Without shifting from her hunched position, she asked, "Spare something for a hot meal, sir?"

You can see again that I've not given a straight description, but have started to weave items from my list into the plot as it moves along. I'll need only the briefest snatches of conversation to make the characters come alive.

► Speech

We have to make a character sound 'real'. So we need to choose speech that's appropriate for the type of person who's speaking and for the situation in which we've put him or her.

There are two main issues to remember when you're writing dialogue in a short story:

- Real people don't often speak in carefully thought-out sentences.
- Only the key items are necessary.

You want to get the *feel* of your character on the page. The following examples will explain what I mean:

(a) I've had enough. I can't stand it. I'm going."

This is a character in some kind of difficulty. Notice how the short sentences demonstrate frustration followed by decision. The repetition of the word 'I' puts the focus on the view from one person's angle.

(b) "Puss, puss, puss. Who's a lovely pussy-cat, then?"

This language is gentle and very simple. If your story is about a lonely person, you might underline that loneliness by demonstrating love for an animal. If those were the only words your character spoke in the whole story, this could demonstrate how he or she is cut off from society.

(c) "Where's Darren?"
"He had to go early. He sees his mother Sundays."

In this story by Suzie, we see a girl trying to cover up the real reason her boyfriend has departed. Look carefully at the wording. If the writer had been aiming to write grammatically, that last sentence would be likely to read, "He always sees his mother on Sundays."

You seldom need to write much speech. You just need enough to give a flavour of a character and to heighten the reader's awareness of tensions in a particular situation. Listen to people chatting, or having an argument. You'll notice that we often speak in short bursts.

WHO SAYS WHAT

There's nothing worse than an account which keeps repeating *he said* or *she said*. That kind of boring repetition can be avoided quite easily, as you'll see in the exchange between Jim and Dick below:

"Give me the loot, Jim." Dick held out his hand.
"What for?"
"Just hand it over and I'll stash it away." It was getting late, and
  Dick was beginning to get angry.
"I'm not sure," said Jim slowly, "that I like the arrangements."
"You flippin' idiot! Either we stash it or we're done for!"

The words *Dick held out his hand* let the reader know that it is Dick who is speaking. It's obvious, since he spoke to Jim, that it is Jim who replies. So I didn't need to put *said Jim*. Another comment on Dick's behaviour – that he was getting *angry* – again shows clearly who is speaking. The word *said* occurs once only, and, because of the build-up, it's clear that it's Dick who loses his temper in the end.

Another useful way of steering clear of repetition and keeping your reader awake is to use words that are more specific than said. In certain circumstances, you might find something that fits just right from the following list:

replied	shouted
whispered	giggled
moaned	snorted
spat	cooed

You can find lots more. Don't overdo the variations, however. Too much change can look contrived. But the occasional new word can be wonderfully evocative of a particular character.

LETTERS

You might have been given an assignment in which the task is to write some correspondence between two people who feature on your course. If so, the aim will be to show your understanding of the issues or theories concerned. It would probably be a good idea to set up a reasoned argument between the writers. You might, for example, be writing letters between Freud and Jung on their theories of psycho-analysis, between two Impressionist painters discussing techniques, or between Mrs Pankhurst and someone disagreeing with her views on women's right to vote.

It's important here to stick to the facts and to identify as closely as you can with each party to the correspondence. Instead of aiming to write conversational speech (see above) you'll almost certainly be writing in a sophisticated manner that's appropriate to the educational level of the people concerned, showing how they think and how they explain the ideas that drive them. It's a case of putting yourself in each person's shoes. Obviously, you'll need appropriate paragraphing, plus good grammar and punctuation.

SUMMARY

This chapter has covered:

autobiography	your memory
	sources
	planning
	relevance to other studies
poetry	using the imagination
	observation and note-making
	imagery
	drafting

short stories	plot
	theme
	description
	characterisation
	speech
letters	facts
	argument
	sophisticated writing

8 Reports

This chapter will explain:

▶ the function of each section of a formal report
▶ how to prepare an action plan for your work
▶ a traditional way of constructing a full report

INTRODUCTION

Report-writing involves the gathering of information, usually to show what's been done or is happening in a particular area. The requirements for particular subject areas are likely to be different, however, so it will be very important that you check with your tutor on exactly what's expected for the task you've been given. In particular, the requirements for certain science subjects can be substantially different. Once you're clued-up on the general nature of a report, however, it should be relatively easy to adjust to whatever is wanted.

The first section here, *Preparation*, shows you how to organise the initial stages of information-gathering and gives a guide to the items you'll need to include if you're required to produce a full and comprehensive report. This is followed by some information on the language needed for report-writing.

Working from scratch on a report is likely to entail a good deal more legwork than writing an essay. Here you're likely to be doing a good deal of fact-finding and, possibly, interviewing. Depending on the topic, you might have less to worry about in terms of understanding complex concepts, but you're likely to need to cover more ground.

Once you've got the hang of it, writing reports isn't difficult, but people often find it confusing at first because of the number of sections. So it would be a good idea to read right through this chapter before beginning any work for your report. This will ensure that you have an overall grasp of the method before you start to work out what goes where. The examples given here are deliberately straightforward so that you'll find report-writing easy to understand.

There's one exception to all this. In some cases, you might be asked to write a report on a particular event – perhaps a conference. This will be shorter than the formal reports and won't use the formal sections. You'd probably just need a heading for each topic and then you'd summarise the main points for each.

PREPARATION

It's a good idea to begin any piece of work with a mind map to get your ideas flowing (see Chapter 2). Let's suppose you've been asked to report on the Castle Centre – a local centre for adults with learning difficulties. Your task is to look at the value of the Centre to its users. Your mind map might look something like this:

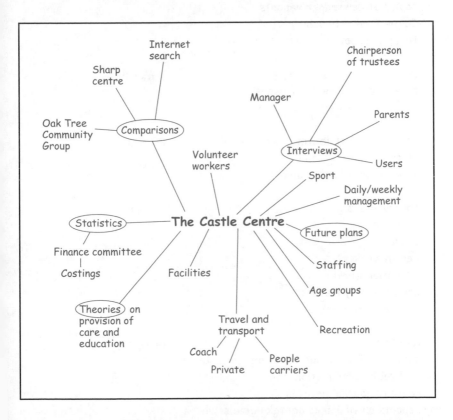

Bear in mind that your map is likely to be wide-ranging. You then choose the most relevant ideas from it. Once you've decided on the key areas, you need to work out an action plan showing all the things you need to do. If you've worked in commerce or industry, you may be thoroughly familiar with action plans. Let's suppose you need to have your report in by 30th April and it's now early February. You might decide to plan your work like this:

ACTION PLAN

TASK	DATE FOR COMPLETION
Materials to be acquired copies of committee minutes photographs of building & site plan initial surveys of need in the area copies of newspaper reports Castle Centre brochure Internal reports	28 February
Data figures on: number of users costs	7 March
Writing & distributing questionnaires staff – views/practice adult users – likes/dislikes	20 March
Interviews manager users health worker education worker carers/family members voluntary workers	7 April
Reading sections of academic texts on learning disability/education relevant journal articles reports on similar undertakings elsewhere	14 April
Writing up report	24 April

▶ Organising your materials

Keeping your notes and other materials well organised will be really valuable for the writing stage. Any or all of the following can be useful for recording your findings:

- A4 paper (in a hardback binder with dividers)
- cards (sorted alphabetically by topic)
- a memory stick (in case your computer malfunctions)
- digital voice recorder (if you do interviews)

Devise a method of sorting at the outset, and you'll save yourself hours of trouble later. Label everything clearly and cross-reference wherever possible. While you're collecting your materials, it's best to ignore all the different headings of a report. The mind can't cope with several new processes at the same time. You'll be ready to think about the structure of the report when you've completed the fact-finding.

▶ The structure of a report

What follows is an explanation of each section of a traditional report. You might find that you're given an assignment which requires only *a few* of these sections; or you might find that you are given some headings that are slightly different from what you will see below.

The sections of a full-blooded report are as follows:

Title-page
Abstract (sometimes called the 'Summary')
Contents
Terms of reference
Procedure (sometimes called 'Method')
Findings
Conclusions
Recommendations
Glossary
References
Bibliography
Appendices
Illustrations
Index

In essence, however, any report will contain the following in one form or another:

- a brief note on what's in it – the *Abstract*
- an explanation of why and how it was set up and how you went about it – *Terms of reference* and *Procedure*
- a description of the things you found out – *Findings*
- an analysis of what you found out – *Conclusions*
- your suggestions for how things might be improved in the future – *Recommendations*

One of the keys to good report-writing is clear separation of those last three sections – description, analysis and suggestions.

The following is an explanation of each section of a traditional report:

▶ Title-page

This is a separate page containing just three things:

- the title or subject of the report
- the author's name
- the date the written report was completed

▶ Abstract

This is a *very brief* summary of what's contained in the report. It will usually be no longer than one paragraph. An abstract enables anyone to find out, without having to plough through the whole thing, whether or not the report is applicable to his or her field of work and therefore worth reading.

For example, imagine that you're a solicitor dealing with a client who is claiming that she was unfairly made redundant from her job with a large company. You want to find out something about that company's staffing policy, and you've managed to get hold of two reports. The titles of both are 'Staffing'. They are written by different authors on different dates. You turn to the page in the first that is labelled 'Abstract'. Here you find that this report describes a survey that catalogued numbers of employees by job title and geographical location. You look at the abstract for the second report and find that this one deals with revised staffing policy and redundancies. Clearly, this is the one you want to read.

An abstract is always written *after* the main body of the report has been completed. You won't be sure exactly what should go in your abstract until you've set out your findings, conclusions and recommendations.

► Contents

You will include this section only for reports that have a great many subsections. It's just a list of headings with appropriate page numbers. The section on findings, for example, might have a number of subsections, each on a slightly different topic. The contents enable anyone to turn directly to what he or she needs to read. This section should also list any illustrations, photographs, tables and graphs, with relevant page numbers.

► Terms of reference

In just a few lines, you'll explain here the reason why the report was undertaken, who asked for it, and any guidelines that were given for conducting it. This can all seem like stating the obvious, but remember that the person who reads a report months or even years after it was written might need to understand how and why it came to be written.

It can be very useful to know whether a report was put together by an unbiased outsider or someone connected directly with the items covered. Knowing the reason why a report was written can also give readers valuable insight on the situation; and knowing the guidelines used for gathering the data will also help people to assess whether the report is likely to contain material relevant to their particular interests.

► Procedure

Here you explain how you went about gathering the information – who you interviewed and why, what types of question you asked, what you decided to include or exclude, and the places from which information was gathered. Somebody glancing at your report might decide whether to read further solely on the basis of what you say here.

▶ Findings

This is likely to be your longest section. It will contain everything you have found out – everything, that is, specifically related to the task you've been given. Your findings will be what you've seen, heard and read (and sometimes even what you've smelt and touched). As with an essay, however, you must leave out anything that doesn't really fit the criteria that were set for the report.

Unlike essays, however, reports benefit from being split up into sections. You don't need to worry about links here as you would in an essay; your task is just to make things crystal clear. So headings and subheadings will be valuable tools in making your work easily readable.

It's crucial to remember that this section must contain *nothing* of your own ideas or opinions. Here you must act like a robot and record things exactly as you have found them. Your task is to describe very clearly what you have found out *without* commenting on any of it in any way.

Your findings are likely to contain *some* of the following:

- information from any source you've consulted: things you've seen, heard or read
- numerical data or results from questionnaires, experiments, published statistics, etc.
- details from letters and/or interviews, together with quotes

Numbering can be an important aid to organizing your information. If I were writing up my report on the Castle Centre, my findings might fall into four main categories:

1 views of users	2 views of staff
3 activities provided	4 other centres

Each of these sections would be likely to have subsections, and these subsections might themselves have further subdivisions. Good headings and a clear system of numbering will keep sections clearly organised and easy to read. The *structure* of my findings might be something like this:

1 <u>Views of users</u>
   1.1 results of questionnaire
   1.2 information from interviews

2 <u>Views of staff</u>
   2.1 salaried staff on site
      2.1.1 manager
      2.1.2 other site staff
   2.2 visiting health workers

3 <u>Activities provided</u>
   3.1 vocational & educational classes
   3.2 leisure classes
   3.3 social activities
   3.4 figures on attendance

4 <u>Comparison with other centres</u>
   4.1 The Oak Tree Community Group
   4.2 The Sharp Centre
      4.2.1 mission statement
      4.2.2 summary of first annual report

► Conclusions

This section will, in some ways, be similar to the end of an essay. Here you look at the facts you've found and weigh up what they mean and what consequences are likely to follow from them. You must be totally ruthless with yourself here, however, and continue to keep to yourself your opinion on what changes should be made.

In essence, the core of your conclusions will say something like this:

The findings demonstrate that:

   a is the case
   b is the case
   c is the case
   d might occur

If it seems helpful, you can re-use here the headings you've used in your findings. My conclusions on the Castle Centre – given here briefly – might look something like this:

Conclusions

1 Views of users
The Centre is, in most respects, coming up to expectations. The facts that responses from questionnaires to users showed an 87% satisfaction rate and that responses from families seem to back this up demonstrate evidence of quality provision. Information from interviews was also extremely positive.

2 Views of staff
These are also positive in the main. The views of visiting health workers are broadly similar to those of the manager. Views of other site staff give insight into areas such as the provision of lunches and other refreshments, however, and certain issues here could lead to dissatisfaction if not addressed.

3 Activities provided
Weekly timetables demonstrate a wide variety of facilities for users. The lack of take-up on some opportunities might seem to be a result of over-provision in general. Figures on attendance at vocational classes showed a high take-up. Sports activities achieved a lower-than-expected score in many cases, so this area would seem to need some attention.

4 Other centres
The Castle Centre has had the benefit of both Lottery funding and the consequent design by prize-winning architects. Its facilities are of a far higher standard than those of the Oak Tree Community Group. The Sharp Centre, however, also has first-class premises and has been able to develop a particularly good system of individual client care.

▶ Recommendations

Ah, at last. It is here – and only here – that you can finally say something of what you think should be done about the situation. This is where you make suggestions on how you think things might be changed for the future. You will be focusing on making *improvements*. There is still one constraint, however. Your views *must* be based clearly on your findings themselves.

Here are my recommendations for the Castle Centre:

Recommendations

- Discuss wider choice of lunches with caterers.
- Set up a user group to provide regular feedback on curriculum.
- Reconsider policy on sports activities, negotiate links with local fitness centre to provide coaching and research possibility of visits from local sports personalities.
- Arrange for the manager from the Sharp Centre to give a presentation on excellence in client care to all staff at the Castle Centre.

Notice that each of the points above begins with a verb (an action word – see Chapter 13). They all show that a particular action is necessary.

▶ Glossary

You might have had to include some technical terms in your report. A glossary lists these, giving definitions. This will be especially useful if the report is likely to be read by people who are not experts in your particular field. They are sure to need explanations.

▶ References

These are brief notes on texts where you found particular information or from which you've quoted. References can appear either individually at the bottom of the relevant pages or in the form of a list in this section (see Chapter 3 for information on referencing).

▶ Bibliography

This is a list of books, journals, other reports, and so on that you have consulted while preparing your report. The purpose of a bibliography is to give readers some indication of the kind of ideas *behind* your work as well as to direct them to further reading on the subject (see Chapter 3).

▶ Appendices

You will place here any material which you feel is important but perhaps not essential. An appendix gives extra information. This is likely to include lengthy items such as tables, and correspondence that is too long and/or detailed to be included in the findings. You might like to think of an appendix as an overspill area. You may need more than one appendix in order to accommodate different issues.

▶ Illustrations

Items such as maps, tables, graphs, photographs, and so on can appear here.

▶ Index

Include an index only in a very detailed report. As in any book, it's an alphabetical list, with page numbers, of all topics, names and technical terms that have appeared in the piece of work.

THE LANGUAGE OF REPORTS

Decisions we make on the language we use in a report are just as important as those we make when writing essays. So focus on making things easy for whoever is going to be reading your report. Keep your sentences short and aim to be very specific. You might like to look back at how I described putting oil in my car in the section *Describing a process* (see Chapter 4). I concentrated there on making things easy for someone who was new to the process. I showed every single step of the job, used simple language as much as possible, and kept my sentences fairly short. That style of writing is ideal for reports.

I suggested earlier that you write like a robot. I wasn't joking. Your language should be:

- clear and concise
- objective
- unemotional
- jargon-free (wherever possible)
- impersonal

You'll have found that in writing essays, you need to put your emotions in cold storage. When writing reports, you need to bury your feelings six feet down in solid ice. It is only in *Recommendations* that you can make any suggestions on what you've found out, and you must still aim to be unbiased.

▶ Active versus passive verbs (see also Chapter 13)

Some tutors might accept assignments that include comments in the first person – that is, using the word *I*. Reports, however, have traditionally been written impersonally. The reasons for this are to help prevent emotion creeping in and to enable the reader to concentrate on the facts. This means that a statement such as

I interviewed employees in three different occupations

is better if changed to:

Employees in three different occupations were interviewed

A statement in your **recommendations**, such as

I feel that further training is essential for operators of machines

is better as:

Operators of machines should be given further training

In these examples I've changed the verbs from active to passive ones.

▶ Reported speech

If you've carried out interviews, you're likely to want to report what one or two people said. Use Chapter 16, pp. 265–8 to help you here.

▶ Tense

Reports are written largely in the past simple tense (see Chapter 13). Obviously, since you are describing what you found out, you are bound to use the past tense a great deal. When you talk about processes that are still taking place, however, you are going to need to use the present tense.

SUMMARY

This chapter has covered:

Your action plan

Organising your material

The sections of a full report:
- Title-page
- Abstract (sometimes called the 'Summary')
- Contents
- Terms of reference
- Procedure (sometimes called 'Method')
- Findings
- Conclusions
- Recommendations
- Glossary
- References
- Bibliography
- Appendices
- Illustrations
- Index

The key items
- *Abstract:* a brief note on what's in the report
- *Terms of Reference* and *Procedure*: an explanation of why and how it was set up and how you went about it
- *Findings:* a description of the things you found out in numbered points
- *Conclusions:* an analysis of what you found out
- *Recommendations*: your suggestions for how things might be improved in the future

The language of reports:
- clear, concise, objective, unemotional and impersonal
- jargon-free (wherever possible)
- interviews in reported speech
- past simple tense (except when referring to something still happening)

9 Articles

This chapter will explain:

▶ the differences between articles and essays
▶ the basics of interviewing
▶ the key issues involved inputting an article together

INTRODUCTION

Some courses nowadays require you to write one or more articles as part of your coursework because this can deepen your understanding. As well as giving you practice in structuring your work, it can allow you to follow a personal interest, give you a little more freedom than you have when writing an essay, and enable you to look at a topic in a broader context than usual. It's also great for practising to communicate an aspect of your subject to a wide audience.

Article-writing can be a lot of fun. You'll get the most out of it if you proceed as if you intended to submit your article to a magazine. The important thing is to make sure that you choose a topic you're interested in. Your enthusiasm will then show in your finished piece. You might even produce something that you really could get published.

The way you write your article will depend on the course you're taking and the guidelines you've been given. If you want to write for children, do check this out with your tutor before beginning. In some cases, writing for children would be acceptable because doing this requires particular skills. For most assignments, however, it would be important to write for adults.

This chapter is not concerned with articles written for academic journals. These need to be longer than those for mainstream journalism and as tightly-constructed as a good essay. Generally speaking, writing for academic journals is something associated with postgraduate work because it involves a good deal of research together with very detailed referencing.

PLANNING AND RESEARCHING

▶ Starting from scratch

The first thing to do, of course, is to make a broad decision on your topic. If you've been given a general subject area, you'll need to narrow this down to something quite specific. As with all assignments, the best thing is to start with a mind map or a similarly random spread of ideas. Let's suppose that you're studying child development and that you've been asked to write a magazine article on any aspect of development of the under-fives. Your initial mind map might look something like this:

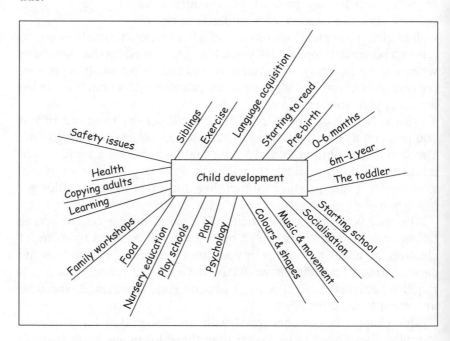

At this stage, it's useful to throw down absolutely everything you can think of without worrying whether or not your ideas seem sensible. You might leave this map around for a day or two so that you can add any new ideas that come to you. From this you'll narrow down your topic.

You might feel that you don't know enough about *any* of the areas you've come up with, but we all often feel that about any assignment. It's a perfectly normal initial response to the task. Look at the topics about which you already know *something* (from lectures, reading, experience, and so on) and just choose the one you're most interested in. Then you'll enjoy your research. And don't ignore everything else on your map; notice other items that will be relevant and can be used as parts of your article.

* choose a topic you're keen on

▶ Choosing the type of article to write

Your first job will be to decide what kind of article you'd like to write. It's a good idea to base your work on a real publication as this will help to keep you focused. Have a look at magazines in your college library or in large newsagents. When you find a magazine you like – and in which you think your topic would fit – you'll need to look at the kind of material printed:

* How long are the articles?
* How much detail is included?
* How long are paragraphs in the articles?
* How do the articles help readers to understand the topics?

If I were to write an article on language acquisition in the under-fives, the facts would remain constant whatever magazine I aimed my piece at, but the number and type of facts I included and the style and language I used would be specific to the magazine. Before going any further, you might check with your tutor that the kind of piece you want to write will be suitable for your assignment.

* find a magazine that suits your style and interests

▶ Researching the topic

Your research will be very similar to research done for an essay: you need to find out facts, ideas and opinions. Your tutor might suggest relevant material. Librarians, too, are usually happy to point you in the right direction. Here's a selection of items that might prove useful:

* magazines – especially those catering for your topic area
* books and journals

- maps
- videos,CDs, etc.
- minutes of Local Authority proceedings
- publications by societies
- journals of statistics
- autobiographies and letters

▶ Interviewing

Talking to someone involved in the field you're writing about can be a real eye-opener and can provide very valuable material for your article. A quote from the horse's mouth can add strength to your own explanations and considerably enliven your piece. So where do you find a willing victim? There might be someone in a local college or university who works in the field you're covering. Failing that, a librarian might be able to suggest local companies or societies that you could contact. Once you begin a search, one link generally leads to another.

When you've located a possible interviewee, all you have to do is ring them up, explain that you have to write an article for an assignment, mention the subject matter, and ask if s/he could spare you half an hour. If the person refuses, just thank them and go on to someone else.

Always take a prepared question sheet to an interview. You'll need to appear professional and it's hard to remember everything you want to ask when you're under pressure. Here are some suggestions for the type of questions you might ask:

- What areas of *a* do you cover?
- What is your specific interest?
- How often does *b* happen?
- What is your view on c?
- Can you explain x for me?
- Can you suggest where I might find out more about y?
- What is the strangest thing that's happened?
- What would you like to do that you've not yet done?
- What are you most proud of having done?

Preparing a question sheet will help to get your mind in gear. Do some hard thinking before you meet someone. If the interview takes a completely different turn, your question sheet will still have been useful preparation. You could record the interview – if your interviewee is willing – but this can end up being more trouble than it's worth. You'll have a great deal of work to do in going through the recording.

You might be told that you'll have to conduct your interview on the phone. If this happens, you'll find prepared questions especially helpful. Face-to-face interviewing is generally easier, however, so try to arrange a meeting. By the way, be sure to have more pens, pencils and paper than you think you'll need.

* prepare a question sheet before you contact your interviewee

WRITING-UP YOUR WORK

▶ Angling your topic

If I were to write that article on language acquisition, I'd need to look very carefully at the level of complexity required by the magazine I'd chosen. I'd do this before writing a single word. If I wanted to write for a general magazine, I'd probably need to limit the number of facts I mentioned, keep analysis quite short, steer clear of jargon and make sure that I gave explanations for any technical terms. I'd also probably need to give examples from everyday life. Many magazines use the trick of relating issues directly to individual people in order to get complex issues across. If you've not yet looked at the sections on *register* and *tone* in Chapter 4, it would be a good idea to do that before starting to write.

Whatever kind of magazine you choose, facts will be crucial (as in an essay) but any analysis needs to be especially clear. What you write needs to be related to the expectations of readers. If I were writing the language-acquisition article for a nursing magazine, it would be important to relate my comments directly to a nurse's experience of children within a hospital setting. So I might decide to talk to one or two nurses to get some inside information.

When writing for members of a particular profession or for people with knowledge of a specific subject area, you need to think about what might be new to them or what might raise useful ideas for discussion. You'll want to take care not to bore them with things they learnt at 'A' level.

Once you've got your material together and decided on a magazine, it's time to make a rough plan. Planning is a vital part of the process, just as with an essay. So make a working plan to get yourself going (see Chapter 2).

* write in the style that readers of a magazine will expect

▶ Openings

As with essays, it's sometimes easier to leave the actual writing of your opening paragraph until last. This is because you might not know how to introduce your article when you're not yet sure exactly what you'll put into it. When you're ready to write your opening paragraph, aim to begin with an arresting topic or idea. Here's the opening of an article I wrote about hemp farming (after someone had alerted me to the need for a sharp opening):

> The hemp plant grows at 6cm a day and is ready to harvest in just 20 weeks. It's GMO-free and needs no pesticides, herbicides or fertilisers. Its uses range from food to building materials, and it's a crop that can add value for the small farmer.

That gets straight to the point, with some statistics that will probably surprise and interest readers.

Another way to 'hook' your readers is to focus on a real person. Here's the opening to an article I wrote on allotments:

> When Roy Southcott was 10 years old in 1929, he was set to work on his first allotment to help feed the family of twelve. His plot was on the railway embankment at Whitchurch, near Tavistock, and Roy had to shield his face from the sparks from passing trains.

And here's the opening of an article called 'Sustainable Rural Development' by Mark, a student. The article is aimed at *Resurgence,* a magazine that covers, in a serious fashion, environmental issues, alternative lifestyles and New Age theories and ideas. Mark's second paragraph leads really smoothly from his introduction and he hits just the right note for *Resurgence* by referring to legend. In the third paragraph, he's getting down to basics:

> Vortigern the Tyrant wanted to build a Great Tower, but every time he tried, the tower fell down. Even his wisest counsellors were unable to tell him what was wrong. Then Merlin was brought before him.
> Merlin at once saw the problem, which was not only in the fabric of the tower, but more so in its very foundation. For beneath the tower was a deep pool, and beneath the pool were two hollow stones, and within the stones lay two dragons.
> Now if this fable were to be applied to development today, especially rural development, then one of the two dragons would represent the relentless pursuit of a false economy which in turn is used to prove the standard of 'good' living. And the other dragon would be the increasing erosion of social life and well-being.

The allusion to a story is a very clever trick to get readers 'hooked'. Few of us can resist the urge to know what happens next. The link to the subject of rural development is then made very neatly in Mark's third paragraph. He goes on to examine his topic in detail, suggesting some innovative ideas.

* your opening needs to grab readers immediately

▶ Paragraphs and sentences

When checking on the style suitable for a particular magazine, one of the first things to do is to look at the length of paragraphs and sentences. The more serious the magazine, the more its readers want to have ideas analysed in depth. That is likely to result in longer sentences and longer paragraphs. If, on the other hand, you're writing in the style of a very popular magazine, both your paragraphs and your sentences will need to be kept quite short and you'll need to get your ideas down in very few words. (For more information on paragraphing, see Chapter 2.)

▶ Structure and links

Linking your paragraphs and topics will be especially important. Readers need to know where they are at all times. Your structure will need to make your material clear and easy to follow. Group your facts in the most straightforward way possible (see the sections on *Linking* and *Planning and structuring* in Chapter 2). A good rule of thumb for articles is to cover the most important issues first and work down to the less important.

▶ Language and style (see also Chapter 4)

The type of words you use and the way you construct your sentences are both crucial for ensuring that your article is suitable for the magazine you've chosen. This is easier than it sounds. You may already have a good 'feel' for the magazine you've chosen and be able to imitate the way its contributors write. Here's a checklist that might come in handy for assessing it:

- verbs   How lively are they?
- nouns   Do many of them fall into any particular category?
- register   Is it formal, journalistic, technical, etc.?
- tone   Is it serious, persuasive, friendly, helpful, conversational, etc.?

▶ Quoting

If you've interviewed someone and you want to quote something they've said, keep it brief and follow the rules for setting out direct speech in Chapter 16. Including brief snippets of speech always makes an article more lively and can give it authenticity. It's important to keep to the speaker's original words, but it's OK to include the occasional connecting word to make the sense clear.

▶ Endings

Like openings, these can be tricky. An ending should tie things up neatly, but it also needs to be lively – perhaps with an engaging idea.

You might consider how you'd like your readers to *feel* after reading your article. Here are some possibilities:

- fired with enthusiasm
- calm
- aware of new facts
- keen to join a special interest group, etc., etc.

It can be a good idea to relate your closing remarks to the central ideas of your article – or perhaps to the beginning. Look at how Mark managed it in his article on rural development by referring to people he's discussed and linking all this back to his opening:

> These ... innovators of the future would ... be those people with special skills ... Because of their new relationship with nature and indeed their sense of belonging within nature they will bring about their own deep feelings of worthiness and trust in the future. Then the dragons of the past can be put to rest forever.

Problem solved!

SUMMARY

This chapter has covered:

- choosing a magazine on which to base your work
- researching your topic
- planning
- interviewing
- angling your topic to the magazine
- paragraphing
- structuring and linking
- using the appropriate language and style
- managing openings and endings

10 Oral Presentations

This chapter will show you how to:

► plan a talk using memory cards
► give a PowerPoint presentation
► prepare a poster presentation
► cope with presentir

INTRODUCTION

Having to give your first oral presentation at a seminar is something that people often dread. If you follow a careful plan of action, however, you'll be able to give a creditable performance first time. The methods outlined below really do work – for everyone. They can be adapted for any circumstances – including the world of work, where the ability to give presentations is becoming more and more important.

People who're scared of giving presentations sometimes feel that the best thing to do is just to write an essay that they can then read out. Not only is this method not acceptable, but it has considerable disadvantages:

- essays take longer to prepare
- they're less useful for group discussions
- they frequently bore the listeners
- they prevent you from learning how to give a talk
- they'll result in a low mark

Obviously, if you've never spoken in public before, it's going to take a bit of practice before you feel wholly at ease, but if you follow the instructions below, nerves will be kept to a minimum and your audience will probably have no idea of your fears. It is, however, essential that you follow the instructions carefully. You'll need to think about the three aspects of giving a talk:

1 the subject matter
2 the medium – using cards, PowerPoint or posters
3 the audience

GETTING STARTED

Despite what I've said above, you'll need to begin *as though* you were going to write an essay (see Chapter 2). You'll probably have been given – or chosen – a topic. So first of all, it's a good idea to draw a mind map so that you can be clear on what you already know and can then work out what reading and note-taking you're likely to need to do.

Next, it's often useful to construct a question to cover your topic (if you've not been given one). This will focus your mind and help you to organise your material because you'll be working out how to answer it. Then you can underline the key words, just as you would if you were writing an essay, so that you'll stay focused as you prepare your presentation.

If, for example, you're an English literature student and you're going to talk about social life at the beginning of the nineteenth century as shown in Jane Austen's *Pride and Prejudice*, you might construct the question:

> What does *Pride and Prejudice* tell us about middle-class life in the early nineteenth century?

Then you might decide to look at inheritance, housing, social etiquette and careers as described in the novel.

If you're studying criminology and you were to give a presentation on problems in prisons, you might construct the question:

> What changes in government policy would be necessary to improve prison conditions?

or

> What are the main issues that have an adverse effect on re-offending?

Getting your facts right will, of course, be crucial but, because you'll be speaking, you'll have a bit more leeway for expressing your personal opinions. Any presentation is considerably enlivened by a presenter who comes across as a real human being with his or her own ideas and feelings. If you give any handouts, however, or circulate material by email, be sure that this material is fully accurate.

---

* formulating a question can keep you clearly focused on your topic

STRUCTURE

The plan for your presentation is going to be vital – whichever type of presentation you prepare. Most people, when listening, aren't able to remember more than three or four key points. You might like to play safe and work on three. This doesn't mean that you can only say three things. It means that all your points must fit under one of three headings. As with an essay, you'll need facts and examples as well as a convincing argument.

It can be a good idea to sort your notes and materials into three lots. By doing this at an early stage, you'll have a clearer sense of where you're going. You'll also need to think very carefully about links (see Chapter 2). Your listeners will come to your presentation cold, so to speak, with little or no idea of what you'll put before them. They need as much help as possible to understand how different aspects of your talk fit together.

Your introduction is going to be especially important. It needs to be clear and simple. Simplicity at this stage in no way precludes you from giving detailed descriptions and penetrating analysis as you progress. If I were to give a presentation on snakes, for example, I might decide to introduce my talk by remarking on the widespread fear of snakes and on their appearance in myths and stories. I could then pick up on the topic of fear to let my listeners know that I'll be dealing with three types of reptile:

- harmless snakes
- poisonous snakes
- snakes that kill by constriction

You might begin each section with a brief reference to things that most of your listeners will already have heard of. That will make them feel comfortable and you can then move on to new and complex information in each section. A little (I stress, *little*) humour in the early stages is likely to put your audience in a relaxed and positive frame of mind for listening to what else you have to say.

* devise a good structure that will be clear to your audience

THE AUDIENCE

Think about presentations you yourself have attended. What kind of things have made a lecture or talk come alive for you? You'll probably have noticed that the best talks have been those where the presenter has:

- shown enthusiasm for his or her topic
- had a very good knowledge of that topic
- explained the material well
- included something that surprised you
- spoken clearly and not too fast
- appeared relaxed and included the occasional joke

Aim to speak about something you feel passionate about. If you've been given a topic that doesn't excite you, find an angle on it that you can get your teeth into. Whatever gives you a buzz is what you'll talk about best. If your own interest level is low, this will affect (or probably infect) your audience. One way to raise your own level of interest is to find out more about a topic.

An audience almost always begins by being favourably disposed towards a speaker. People nearly always want you to do well and will generally ignore small slips. Frowns may have nothing at all to do with you anyway. So if your audience looks hostile in any way, assume it's had a bad morning and aim to cheer it up.

The success of your presentation will depend in part on pitching it at the right level. So ask yourself three questions:

1 Who am I talking to?
2 What do they already know?
3 What will interest or excite them?

Although it's important to begin with simple ideas, it's essential not to bore people. You need to show respect for their expertise and opinions. If you're aware that some people know more than you do on a particular aspect of your talk (apart, of course, from your tutor) you can acknowledge that. It's easy enough to say something like, 'Of course, I'm aware that some of you know a good deal about x.' Be careful, however, over encouraging contributions from the audience. It's very easy to lose control of a presentation. You don't want the group taking over or chatting among themselves. So it's usually safest to wait until the end of your talk before opening up a discussion.

There's absolutely no need to appear to know everything. Indeed, it can be useful to point people in the right direction for further reading. If you can suggest where someone is likely to find the answer to an awkward question, you'll have covered yourself.

> * focus on giving your audience an interesting time

SPEAKING FROM CARDS

Constructing a good 'route map' is your key to navigating your way through the presentation. So be sure to draw up a good plan with clear headings and sub-points under them. Then, instead of writing sentences, you're going to write down only key terms and topics plus the occasional phrase. This is so that you'll be able to glance down quickly to see what comes next and then look at your audience and talk directly to them. Each sub-point from your plan might need one card. For a twenty-minute talk, you might end up with anything from ten to twenty cards.

Your route map must be *easily readable when you are under stress*. Use plain white cards, size 8 x 5 inches (203 mm x 127 mm), writing on one side only. This is a tried-and-tested method that will ensure success. Smaller cards force you to squash up your writing, so when you're under pressure, it's very hard to pick out the information you need. White space is essential.

Everything must be done to make things easy on yourself. Your cards are going to carry all the essential info. you'll need. People who've never done this before often think they'll never remember what they want to say without a full script in front of them. But with a careful layout and a little practice (see below) you'll find this will work like magic. As you work on preparation, you'll begin to commit your topic to memory, and after a few practice runs, you'll be able to deliver your material confidently. (Well, at least you'll appear confident.)

Cards are much easier to handle than sheets of paper and they don't rustle. The fact that there's much less space on them than on a page of A4 is an advantage. When you're standing in front of an audience, the less writing you have to look at in one go the better. As long as your layout is clear and simple, your eyes won't get lost wandering around looking for a vital piece of information. Losing your place in a talk is one of the main hazards for speakers. Number your cards so that if the worst should happen and you drop the lot, you'll quickly get them back into sequence.

* put only headings, key words and brief phrases on your cards

The most important words on each card can be put in capitals, and you can use colour to highlight different sections. Bullet points and lists are useful. Aim to have plenty of white space on each card. When you're giving your presentation, you need to be able to glance down and pick out just the topic word you're looking for. If there's a lot on a card, you won't be able to do this. You might decide to put key points on the left and evidence on the right. Use clear headings, but beware of highlighting, as in some lights this can make words difficult to read. Your layout can be helped by most of the following:

sections	colour-coding
headings	underlining
key words	boxes
columns	symbols
numbering	brackets
capitals	

It's also possible to add instructions to yourself on the cards – perhaps in a different colour. For example:

- pause
- point to diagram
- emphasise

Speaking from notes on cards allows you to look at the audience and speak naturally. If you have sentences in front of you, there is no way forward other than to read them, and that can be very boring for your listeners. Here's a copy of the cards Judith used for her first presentation.

①

NEO-NAZISM
WHAT IS IT?

SOCIAL POLITICAL MOVEMENT

FORM OF FASCISM

POST-DATE WWII

②

IDEALS

ADOLF HITLER & SYMBOLISM

RACISM, ANTI-SEMITISM,
XENOPHOBIA

NATIONALISM, MILITARISM,
HOMOPHOBIA

③

MEMBERS

DISINTEGRATION OF
NATIONALISM & CULTURE

MULTICULTURAL FRICTION

NON-WHITE IMMIGRANTS
JEWISH WORLD CONSPIRACY

④

HOLOCAUST
REVISIONISM

DENIAL - EXAGGERATED?
(STIGMA, MASS GENOCIDE)

IMMORAL EQUIVALENCIES →
DRESDEN, ETHNIC CLEANSING

JUSIFICATIONS →
TERRORISTS, SABOTAGE,
SUBVERSION

---

⑤

THE LAW

OPERATE LIKE MAFIA

TOP COMPANIES - PROFESSIONAL
& RESPECTABLE

CULPRITS CAUGHT - OF NO USE,
CANNOT TALK BACK

---

⑥

HOW MANY?

PUBLIC OPINION - ALD, SPLC

UNDERGROUND - FUNDRAISE,
ORGANISE, RECRUIT

GLOBAL PHENOMENON

---

⑦

STRENGTH

GLOBAL NETWORK

STRONGEST SINCE FALL

STRONGER THAN WHEN CAME
INTO POWER

---

⑧

NOVEMBER 9TH
SOCIETY

1977 - TERRY FLYNN
INACTIVE

KEVIN QUINN -
ONLY ONE, LEAFLETS, STICKERS

PRESSURE GROUP
2004 POLITICAL PARTY

⑨

IDEALS	AGAINST IMMIGRATION, ABORTION, COMMUNISM
	AGAINST HOMOSEXUALITY
	SUPPORTS HIERARCHICAL SYSTEM, REPATRIATION, BRITISH OWNERSHIP OF INDUSTRY, CENTRAL GOVMT. BANK

⑩

NAME	DATE IN 1923, 16 MARTYRS BEER HALL PUTSCH
	OPPONENTS – KRISTALLNACHT – ANTI-SEMITIC
	N9s OPPOSE THIS – JEWS: DEADLY ENEMY

⑪

POLICIES	CRITICISE BNP – SOFT
	'TRUTH FOR EVERYONE⎕ – MAGAZINE ON WEBSITE
	ILLEGAL IMMIGRANTS → SWIM

⑫

ACTIVITY	SUPPORT IRVING 17.12.05
	SPORADIC ACTIVITIES 120 MEMBERS
	DEMONSTRATIONS

Judith's first attempt at giving a presentation was a great success. You can see that she used a very straightforward layout with plenty of space on each card and clear print so that she was able to see her topics easily. Her listeners found the presentation interesting because it had a logical sequence and she explained each point in a conversational style.

Judith found she was able to speak easily from her cards. It's perfectly possible, however, to include a little more detail if you need to. Here are some further suggestions:

- headings at the top – to give more space
- points on the left – brief details on the right
- references to books/journals in another colour
- more cards – to allow space for more information

POWERPOINT PRESENTATIONS

A PowerPoint presentation, like the oral presentation with cards, has two aspects: the key points on separate slides (which you can think of as very similar in their form to the cards above) and the spoken commentary (again similar to the basic card presentation). The bonus is that you don't need cards since your basic material will all be on the screen so you only have to glance at it to see what you need to talk about next.

If you've not used PowerPoint before, you'll find it's not difficult to master. You'll just need to get someone to show you how to prepare the slides. Do that before you do anything else.

The idea of putting material on screen is to give your listeners a clear idea of the bones of your talk. You then give plenty of spoken explanation. It's really important that you put just the essential points on each slide. If you put too much, your listeners will be reading and not listening. When that happens, you can lose control of a presentation.

Just as with a card presentation, when you're planning what will go on the slides, you might like to think back to how you prepare an essay plan (see Chapter 2). Think first of the main sections that will be important for your presentation and then the items that will be important under each main heading. The number of slides will be up to you. The average is probably 10–12. The student whose work you'll see below used 16.

The slides are a visual aid. If you can, put some very brief statistics on them and/or some relevant diagrams or pictures that will make them more useful and attractive. A diagram that you then explain bit by bit can be especially good because your audience will be engaged both visually and aurally.

* your slides are visual aids for the audience, not detailed explanations

By the way, you might need to pre-book equipment with your college's resources centre. Finding out at the last minute that you can't get hold of what you need could scupper your whole performance. You'll also need to check the location of electrical sockets in the room you'll use and whether the flex for the PowerPoint button will reach to where you'll be standing.

Below you can see two slides from the middle of a presentation by Elizabeth on *Community Research and the Early Years Worker*. She was studying part-time for a degree in early-years education which relates to children from birth to the age of 5. Her studies complemented her day job in early-years education. Elizabeth's presentation resulted from research she'd done in an area close to her home. You can see that each slide – as well as giving her listeners a clear structure of points she would speak about – gave her a good route map of what she'd planned to say:

Community Research and the Early Years Worker

Community Profile

• Services and facilities in the area
• Deprivation statistics
• Housing data
• Religion statistics
• Government strategies
• Factors affecting vulnerability
• Life expectancy statistics

With this slide on the screen, Elizabeth explained that the bulleted items were key to understanding early-years' needs in any area and that developing a community profile by researching these topics had given her a deeper understanding of the community's needs. She then commented on each one.

Elizabeth went on to explain that the geographical area she'd researched ranks highly in terms of social deprivation and so is a priority neighbourhood. She then read a quote that stressed how low income can link to low educational attainment and poor health and even to low-income households becoming victims of crime. Reading a short quote can add to and enliven your presentation.

Elizabeth's next slide takes a closer look at issues that signal where problems can occur:

Community Research and the Early Years Worker

Indicators to vulnerability

- Low income and dependency on benefits
- Main wage earner unemployed
- One or more parents that smoked
- Lone-parent families
- Behavioural problems in children
- Depressed and/or mentally ill parents

With this slide on screen, Elizabeth explained that families throughout this particular geographical area are classed as vulnerable if those visited by a health visitor had shown least four of these indicators. She then went on to give some of her conclusions, explaining that she found she'd needed to challenge statistics in order that she and those she line-managed in her day job could change the way they related to families.

Whatever is put on a slide will be merely the bones of a talk. It's how the material is interpreted by the speaker that makes the presentation come alive. Elizabeth received a high grade for her work, but she wasn't wholly satisfied with her slides. She wished she'd had more time to reduce the text on them. Below is my suggestion for some reduction on the second of the two shown here. You'll see that I also like to omit capitals wherever possible as I feel this makes things easier on both the eye and the brain:

Community Research and the Early Years Worker

Indicators to vulnerability

• low income/benefits
• unemployment
• smoking
• lone-parent families
• behavioural problems
• depression/mental illness

POSTER PRESENTATIONS

Posters are used for various purposes. You might have to produce a poster for information, for use at a conference where you might be required to stand beside it to explain it to anyone who's interested, or for an oral presentation. Here, we'll think about oral presentations. A poster you design for an oral presentation can, however, also be used for any of those other purposes.

Contrary to what you might at first think, the best posters are generally those that don't say very much. You'll need to prepare a large poster (A2, perhaps) and your talk will consist of explaining what's on it. Sometimes, two or three linked posters are necessary. You might like to begin preparation just as you would for either of the other types of presentation, by planning the general structure of your talk. From this, you'll get ideas for the poster.

Your poster will need to be visually arresting and professionally prepared. (Hand-drawn posters won't do.) The best way forward is to design it on computer (or rough it out by hand and get a computer whiz to do the design for you). Then you can get it printed poster size or, if your tutor is happy, you can show it via computer on a PowerPoint screen.

The most important things to remember for the poster itself are to keep your wordage down, to use large print that can be seen from a distance and to leave plenty of empty space on your poster. It's fatally easy to put too much on a poster so that it's only of any use if people go right up to it and stand there for ages reading what you've put. A poster for a presentation is there to whet people's appetites and to give a visual focus for those who see it. And paragraphs are a no-no.

The bulk of the information will be in what you say, not in what you write (unless you are preparing an information poster that is to be left in position to give instructions). The idea is to spark interest without giving your audience all the answers on the poster. Your poster should generate more feedback from your audience than a card or PowerPoint presentation, so be prepared for interaction with your listeners. You might also need to be especially open-minded and accepting of others' points of view. There's some advice on how to conduct yourself under *Performance* below.

* interact with your poster: point things out as you go along

Choose print that is large enough to be easily read by your audience. You'll need to build a set of useful words and/or phrases which are key terms in the topic you're presenting. You'll discover the best words to use as you do your preparation. They're likely to come from your section headings and bullet points. It's hard to generalise, but a total of 100 words on a poster is likely to be too many. If you look at the PowerPoint slide above, you can see how I've reduced the original screen by almost half. Cutting down wordage is a very easy job once you've got your main items in place.

Many presentations rely on diagrams or flow charts, and these work well. The need, of course, is for great clarity. If your topic is scientific, for example, you can show progression of a process. If it's from history, you can show change over time. With almost any topic, you could have a central hub with linked areas leading off it. Sometimes, people use headings with bullet points underneath. But if you do that, you'll need to be sure that there are very few words in each point, that the print is large enough to read and that there's plenty of space between the individual points.

You might decide to give extra details on a handout – such as the aims and methods of an experiment. It's fine to do that with any complex information. But always wait until the end of your presentation before giving handouts (see below).

* keep your word count down and leave plenty of space

On p. 162 is a useful example produced by Melanie, a student on a degree course in child-health nursing. The original is in full colour. The poster is dynamic so keeps viewers' eyes moving around the subject matter, it's set out in an interesting way, and it shows links between

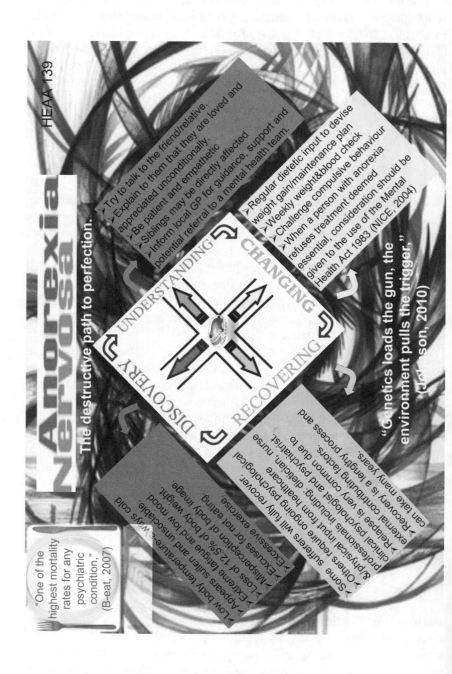

HEAA 139

Anorexia Nervosa

The destructive path to perfection.

> Try to talk to the friend/relative.
> Explain to them that they are loved and appreciated unconditionally.
> Be patient and empathetic.
> Siblings may be directly affected
> Inform local GP for guidance, support and potential referral to a mental health team.

> Regular dietetic input to devise weight gain/maintenance plan
> Weekly weight&blood check
> Challenge compulsive behaviour
> When a person with anorexia refuses treatment deemed essential, consideration should be given to the use of the Mental Health Act 1983 (NICE, 2004)

UNDERSTANDING

CHANGING

DISCOVERY

RECOVERING

"Genetics loads the gun, the environment pulls the trigger," (Johnson, 2010)

> Some sufferers will fully recover.
> Others require ongoing psychological &physical input from healthcare professionals including: dietician, nurse clinical psychologist and psychiatrist.
> Relapse is very common due to external contributing factors.
> Recovery is a lengthy process and can take many years.

> Low body temperature-always cold
> Appears sullen and unsociable.
> Extreme fatigue and low mood.
> Loss of 12.5% of body weight.
> Misperception of body image.
> Excuses for not eating.
> Excessive exercise.

"One of the highest mortality rates for any psychiatric condition," (B-eat, 2007) different topics. It would have been even better if the wordage in the bullet points had been reduced. Less is almost always more where posters for presentation are concerned.

If you're giving a poster for an oral presentation, be sure to interact with it as you talk. Point to the items on it, explain them fully and encourage your listeners to join in a discussion of them as you go along.

ADVICE FOR ALL PRESENTATION TYPES

▶ Checklist

In order to make things easy on yourself, check out the room where you'll be speaking well in advance. You need to know things like where people will be sitting, where you'll be standing, and the position of lighting, electrical sockets, and so on. Then make a list of all the items you'll need to have with you, and have these ready the day before. You might want Sellotape, Blu-Tack, pins, boards, items for a display, and your memory stick (for PowerPoint), and so on. Leave nothing to chance.

▶ Visual aids

Sometimes, a small display is useful. Setting out some books on a table can lend a professional air to the proceedings. You can include pamphlets and articles from newspapers and magazines. You'll need to plan this carefully, too. Check where any illustrations can be fixed. But don't let people get their hands on anything until after you've finished speaking.

▶ Handouts

If you're going to provide handouts, it's best to give them out at the end of the proceedings. If you give your audience something to hold, they will look at it immediately and will stop listening to you. Don't be fooled into thinking that this would take the pressure off you. It can make things harder. Everyone reads at different rates and people will ask you to repeat what you've said while they were busy reading. They can also start asking questions about the handouts at inconvenient moments, and it's very easy to lose the thread of your talk altogether.

▶ Practising

Without practice, it's almost impossible to know how long a piece will last. So first, find out how long you'll be given, and then have at least two practice sessions in complete privacy. Perform your presentation exactly as if you had an audience in front of you. Speak aloud, pausing where necessary, adding any jokes in full, speaking slowly and including gestures and any movements you'll need to make towards or away from your visual aids. If you're giving a poster presentation, it's a bit harder to estimate time because your listeners will, hopefully, be joining in. Just be sure you can cover the essential ground.

If you need to cut, keep just the best bits and your talk will sparkle. If you find you've not prepared enough material, go back to your collection of notes, articles, etc., to see what else might fit. Or it might be the case that you need to slow down your delivery. If you speak fast, no one gets a chance to take in what you are saying. Or you might decide to include a personal experience. If your piece is seriously short on what you need, go on a voyage of discovery for new material. There's no knowing what nuggets you might unearth at the last minute.

▶ Performance

There's a study that shows that 38 per cent of what an audience remembers from a talk depends on the sound of your voice. That means you have to think about tone, about how loudly you speak, and about pauses and speed. A dramatic pause before an important point, for example, can be invaluable. But 55 per cent of the message is said to be delivered by what the audience sees, so your enthusiasm is essential. A convincing speaker shows that he or she is totally involved with the material. The remaining 7 per cent, it has been said, is for the words themselves.

As far as your language is concerned, don't be too formal. Use the appropriate language code for the people you are speaking to, and in an academic situation, this will mean using appropriate technical terms wherever necessary; but otherwise, be fairly chatty. Aim to create an informal atmosphere.

Obviously, if you were giving a presentation for a job interview, you'd need to look especially smart. On a college or university course, however, you won't need to dress up. But there are a few tips worth remembering. Don't wear anything that makes you feel uncomfortable, that is revealing, makes a noise or keeps slipping. Make sure your hair won't get in your eyes, and check buttons and other fastenings are secure before you get to the presentation room. When you speak, don't fiddle with pens or investigate problem areas on your person.

Do, however, allow the audience to know that there's a real human being out there. Audiences usually love it when speakers reveal something about themselves. Don't overdo this, but a brief anecdote can relax people and lighten the atmosphere. Use gesture occasionally to reinforce what you're saying, and smile when it's appropriate.

Look around and aim to make a connection with everyone in the room, and allow your tone of voice and your facial expression to fit your words. If you feel nervous, pretend that you don't, and your listeners will probably have no idea of your fears. Just speak clearly and go a little more slowly than seems necessary.

You might consider what you think are your best qualities. If you don't know, ask a friend. A practised speaker accentuates his or her good points. This might be your gift for explaining things clearly, your kindliness, your skill at making people feel at ease, or your sharp mind. Prepare your material carefully, be the best you can possibly be, and you can't fail.

SUMMARY

This chapter has shown ways for:

- devising a question
- structuring your talk
- considering your audience
- preparing: cards with key words and phrases
              slides for a PowerPoint presentation
              poster presentations
- using visual aids and handouts
- practising and performing your work

11 Exam Essays

This chapter will explain how to:

► revise for an examination
► write within the time allowed
► plan and write your answers

INTRODUCTION

The best time to read this chapter is when you are within two or three months of your exams – possibly less. It's unlikely to be much use to you a year before you sit them. You'll only depress yourself if you start worrying about exams too early when there will still be a lot of new material to cover. Even when you are at the end of your course, you may feel incapable of tackling an exam. It's only when you've completed the revision process that you are likely to begin to feel confident.

Ignoring exams at an early stage in the course is not to be confused with finding out what the course itself will cover. You really do need to know that. It's also a good idea to find out what general areas you'll be tested on. You can then make sure that you cover these thoroughly during the year.

This chapter will first look briefly at how to revise for exam essays. It will then give an example of a student's exam answer, showing how she went about tackling the essay. So once you've done some revision, it's a good idea to give yourself some practice in writing exam answers so that you can get a feel for how much data you can get down in the time available.

What this chapter won't do is prepare you for writing short answers or coping with multiple-choice questions. For these, you'll need explanation and help from your tutor.

THE REVISION PROCESS

The best way of coping with revision is to make yourself a weekly timetable, setting out what you'll do and when. Cover only topics you're likely to be tested on. For each area, you'll need to go through all your lecture notes, class notes, handouts and any photocopied material you possess. Take these items one at a time, and each time you come to a key point, either circle or highlight it. Sometimes, a tutor will have written one or more useful points on your essay, so highlight these too. Work as fast as you can.

Next, list the points you've ringed or highlighted on a fresh sheet of paper in as few words as possible. Do this with everything, and read nothing twice. Fit in a short session of this work whenever you have a spare 15 minutes.

* list the main points from all your notes, essays, handouts, etc.

All you have to do after that (as they say on children's TV) is to condense all your lists into as few sheets of paper as possible and to colour-code the main areas. Stick to key points and key words. If you need to remember formulae, include these on the lists. Aim to note ideas and trends, where possible, rather than overloading yourself with too many facts. Draw mind maps or diagrams whenever you can. These are often easier to remember than lists because they're more strongly visual. If you're able to add drawings, these will be even better memory aids.

When you've done all this, you'll be getting well prepared for your exams. Keep going over your master lists, and practise trying to write them out from memory. If you've any spare time at this stage, have a go at writing answers to past papers – or make up questions of your own to answer.

* make master lists that you can carry with you and keep going over

BUDGETING YOUR TIME IN AN EXAM

If your exam lasts three hours and consists of three essay questions, expect to write approximately three to five sides of A4 for each answer. It's only common sense, of course, to spend longest on questions that carry the most marks. The following is a well-known fact:

> The combined marks for one really good answer and one poor answer are generally less than the combined marks for two average answers.

So don't make the mistake of spending extra time on your best topic. It really is essential to manage your time carefully and to give each question your best attention if you're to maximise your chance of success.

A STUDENT'S EXAM ANSWER

Here's one of Sandy's essays on a sociology paper. It's followed by some explanation of how the essay has approached various essential features of an exam answer. I've added headings for the introduction and conclusion and I've numbered the paragraphs in between so that you'll be able to refer to them easily when you read my comments.

'Our bondage to society is not so much established by conquest as by collusion.' Explore this statement in the light of the relationship between culture and identity.

Introduction Culture is all things that affect mankind in the society we live in. It is the way we live and work, and all the things we achieve. Culture only exists in our heads and only concerns our relationships and interactions with other people. It is a changing, adapting mechanism which governs our behaviour patterns. Society is the organism that displays the behaviour. So culture and society are not the same thing, although they are intrinsically linked.

1 Culture can be seen as made up of three layers. Tradition is made up of values and beliefs passed from one generation to the next, and commonly held within a society. Subcultures are commonly held beliefs, values and behaviours among like people in a society – for example, there could be people from one culture who live in another culture but still keep the characteristics of their common primary culture, and identify with each other because of the primary culture. Cultural universals are characteristics which are common to all known culture. They include systems of meaning (communication), hierarchy and leadership, a form of family, privacy and rules governing good and bad behaviour and sexual behaviour. Universal qualities may be practised differently within different cultures, but they are still a part of all culture. So every individual is exposed to these 'cultural rules' in some form or another.

---

2 Culture (as evident within the universals) ensures the survival of society, and its rules ensure a level of conformity and control amongst the individuals within it. For example, the rearing and nurturing of children are accepted amongst all cultures, whereas generally (except in war situations) killing others is not.

3 All cultures change, but their change is normally slow and gradual. Individuals within society get stability from the culture they identify as their own. This stability arises from the reinforcement of culture through repetition. Individuals collude with culture as they can enjoy the boundaries it provides (not wanting to be killed, and wanting children raised safely within a family).

4 Forces that affect culture are natural forces and human forces. Human forces include technological advancement, economic and political dominance, war and victory over others (conquest).

5 Culture itself can affect the inquisitiveness of society. This can affect the rates of change and willingness to change of individuals and societies as a whole. Our bondage to society and evidence of our collusion is displayed in ethnocentricity. Ethnocentrism is the means by which we seek to protect our own culture and feel superior to others. It can be viewed as promotion of racism and yet it is also an individual's and society's attempt to prevent the infusion of values and beliefs from one culture to another, thus preserving culture and minimising change.

6 Technological advancement and media are the largest influences on cultural change. The rate of change is different between cultures and yet we often adapt readily to change and collude with advancement over which, as individuals, there is little control.

7 Often, culture and its relationship with individuals can only be explained through history. People do not have an instinct for a predetermined culture when they are born. Babies are only born with an instinct to eat and drink. A baby born in one culture and placed in another would accept it as its own (McDonald Mason 1999). America has traditions which can be dated back to 1782. They are still practised today which, as America is a country made up of immigrants since that time, also shows clearly that culture is learned by individuals.

8 Different individuals within the same culture may hold different beliefs and values. Things that can affect different individuals within the same society are age, generation and *Zeitgeist*. Age can affect values held by individuals as youths and children are more likely to absorb modernity and changes in culture, and the older people become the less receptive they are to change. It may also be that a particular generation has absorbed certain beliefs and values in youth which have stayed for life. *Zeitgeist* is when something so profound, large, different or impacting happens to a society it affects the culture of society and the beliefs and values of everyone in that society, regardless of age, generation or socio-economic background.

9 However, study conducted over a period of time showed the most impact upon culture came from individuals (H. E. Hofstede) and individualism which can be viewed in two ways: as the disintegration of existing culture which makes the concepts of social class, gender roles and status fragile, or as the breakdown of state-sanctioned normality, role models and traditions (as sanctioned by religion, the state and tradition). It can be seen as a fight against cultural norms.

10 In the past, individuals had little opportunity to express their identity either in work or social situations. Now, people are expected to make choices and be responsible for their own lives. Individuals may see this as control by themselves, only taking from culture what they choose.

11 If an individual does not like the cultural norms of a situation they are in, they can seek to make a change – e.g. from one social class to another or from poverty to wealth. Yet they are merely swapping the cultural norms of one situation for the cultural norms of another. Individuals do not have 'free will' to break away from culture per se. They just move to different parts of a culture. They may be making changes to culture or it's possible they are merely adapting to new culture as it arrives.

12 Individuals get much of their identity from the views of others within their culture. There are trends amongst individuals to better each other and seek progression while shaking off old culture. They 'plunge into modernity' and enjoy 'precarious freedom' (U. Beck 2002) and yet modern culture places an abundance of constraints and provisos on people, ranging from the rules on pension entitlement to a need to MOT the car. All individuals must plan for and take into account all constraints and provisos of modern culture as they live their lives. They cannot merely live subjectively: 'Under the surface of modern society is a highly efficient, densely woven institutional culture' (U. Beck, 2002).

Conclusion In the past, culture's control over societies, and the individuals within those societies, was obvious. Evidence now suggests that although we believe we have the choice to opt out of a culture, it is in fact the case that culture is as controlling as ever, but less obvious. Hence rather than individuals controlling culture, culture has adapted to control, maintain and ensure the survival of modern society. It seems in modern society we accept the overarching values of our culture and even its constraints.

▶ Analysing the question

The best way to start is to underline the *key words and phrases* in the question. This is essential. In an exam, most of us are under stress, so underlining key words is a good way to focus on what's necessary. It breaks the question down into its separate parts and prevents us from missing anything. We're then able to plan the essay around these key items. Here are my underlinings for the question Sandy answered:

> Our bondage to society is not so much established by conquest as by collusion.' Explore this statement in the light of the relationship between culture and identity.

▶ Planning

It's essential to make a quick plan. If you launch into writing without a plan, you'll have less chance of working to a clear structure and you may well forget things. If you have a plan, you can add any new ideas as they strike you. There's a further advantage: if by any chance you don't have time to finish your answer, whatever is in your plan might get you another mark or two. It might just make the difference between passing and failing the entire paper.

Aim to:

- write a quick *list or mind map* of the main areas or issues you'll need to cover
- note the order in which you'll deal with the issues
- note any comments you might make (i.e. the argument – see below and Chapter 2)

Selection is crucial. You're not likely to gain many marks by just writing down everything you know on a topic. Choose just those issues that relate specifically to the question. Argument will be essential, so concentrate on what you've learned of the possible angles on each issue. If a question asks for your views, what's wanted is your carefully considered opinion after taking into account the relevant facts and the writings of experts in the area.

* a good plan will help you write an essay easily and quickly

Once you've got a rough plan, you can begin to write. It's a good idea to tick off the points on your list as you cover them. This will give you a feeling of being in control. Sandy's plan might have looked something like this:

Intro   explain terms

culture
3 layers
universals are control
change – slow

change
forces affecting culture
inquisitiveness/ethnocentrism
technology & media – rate of change/collusion

the individual
culture is learned (McDonald Mason)
values & beliefs – age, etc.

freedom & the individual
biggest change = individualism (Hofstede)
people think – control own lives
moves within culture – no free will
identity, constraints, institutions (U. Beck)

<u>Conc</u>   personal freedom = mirage. Culture controls.

If you look at Sandy's essay against the plan, you'll see that the four sections work out like this:

	Paragraphs
role of culture:	1, 2, 3
change	4 ,5, 6
the individual	7, 8
freedom	9, 10, 11, 12

▶ Introduction

In an exam, there's no time for carefully thought-out introductions. If you can set the scene with a *little* explanation of the main topic or some background information, that's good. But if nothing occurs to you, just leave a few lines and launch into your first issue. If there's time, you can come back after you've written the rest of the essay and fill in some introductory material. Sandy has begun by defining the word 'culture', showing that she understands that there are clear differences in sociological terms between this and the word 'society'.

* Don't lose time worrying about your introduction

▶ The main body of the essay

FACTS, THEORIES AND EXAMPLES

Facts, theories and examples are what give credibility to your work. You might find it helps to note briefly in your plan those specific items and examples that you want to include in your answer.

The kind of data you use will vary according to your subject, of course. Sandy's essay includes plenty of factual material, starting with a breakdown of the three layers of culture (paragraph 1). Almost every paragraph mentions theories that have become accepted aspects of sociological studies. There are also specific examples of recent studies and writings – for example, the statement on a baby's relationship to culture by McDonald Mason (7) and the study on change noted by Hofstede (9). You won't need to give referencing details in an exam, but you'll need to get key names right.

* include plenty of relevant facts and theories

QUOTES

Long quotes are never needed in an exam and would, in any case, be seen as padding. But if you can memorise an important phrase or two that relates to each of the main areas you've studied, these can give further strength to your answers. Sandy has given two quotes from Beck that underline points on the institutional base of contemporary culture (12).

* quoting a brief phrase from a respected source can give an answer credibility

THE ARGUMENT

It's important to explain how what you say relates to an exam question. In fact, a good clear argument can be the key to getting a high mark, just as in term-time essays. So show how relevant facts affect the topic, and give what seems to you to be the most sensible view of it all.

It's fatally easy to assume that because you've written down the relevant facts, an argument is implicit. It isn't. You *must* spell out the implications and add comment. Different students often have very different views on the same set of facts. So make your argument clear and, as you write, look back at the question every now and then in order to check that you're still on track.

* it's good argument that racks up the marks

It's interesting to note how many times Sandy has used terms from the first half of the question in her essay (the numbers relate to paragraphs):

collude [3]
bondage to society [5]
collude [5]

Including terms from the question demonstrates forcibly to whoever is marking that you are addressing the question. Sandy also uses the terms *individuals* and *individualism* (to relate to the question's term *identity*) and *culture* throughout the essay, showing that she is focusing clearly on the question's key topics. By doing this, she also makes it clear why she has included particular facts and theories. The following statement concludes her explanation of the three layers of culture:

> So every individual is exposed to these 'cultural rules' in some form or another. [1]

Just by including brief sentences like this one you can demonstrate your ability to make judgements. Here's a point on cultural stability (again using terms from the question):

> Individuals collude with culture as they can enjoy the boundaries it provides ... [3]

And here's her summing-up of change brought about by individualism:

> It can be seen as a fight against cultural norms. [9]

Every time you use facts and theories, show clearly how you want them to be viewed. Here's how the essay argues for contemporary culture's controlling base, supported by a quote from another sociologist:

> All individuals must plan for and take into account all constraints and provisos of modern culture as they live their lives. They cannot merely live subjectively: 'Under the surface of modern society is a highly efficient, densely woven institutional culture' (U. Beck, 2002). [12]

CONCLUSION

It's important to sum up in your conclusion whatever you've argued on each main issue from the question. It's also important to show clearly how your conclusion demonstrates that you've addressed the question. As with term-time essays, there must be no new material in your conclusion.

Sandy's conclusion sums up the essay's points, keeping closely to the question which had asked candidates to look at how far we collude with our place in society and to relate this to culture and identity. After commenting on the historical situation, Sandy ties up her points on the contemporary situation. Her final sentence underlines her position neatly:

> It seems in modern society we accept the overarching values of our culture and even its constraints.

LANGUAGE AND PARAGRAPHING

Sandy has made points clearly and succinctly. Unless your subject is English, no one's going to worry about a few spelling mistakes or grammatical errors. (Key names and terms, however, do need to be accurately spelt.) Some of Sandy's paragraphs are rather short, but again this kind of thing will generally be forgiven in an exam if the essay includes plenty of facts and a strong argument.

The best language is clear and simple. If you've been working on improving the way you write, this will certainly pay dividends in the exam. If you've not had a chance to do this, and your exams are due soon, aim to keep your sentences fairly short so that there's less chance of getting into difficulties. Be sure to split your answers into paragraphs and, as with any piece of work, leaving a line between paragraphs will help make your answers look clear and well organised.

SUMMARY

This chapter has covered:

- **revision**
  work in bite-sized chunks
  highlight key points from your notes, essays, hand-outs, etc.
  make master lists/mind maps

- **planning your exam essay**
  underline key words
  make a list or mind map
  plan the order of your main points
  budget your time

- **writing your exam essay**
  write a *very brief* introduction
  give *at least* one paragraph for each main issue
  include: facts, theories and examples
             argument
             brief quotes where possible
  tie things up in a neat conclusion

12 The Proposal for Your Undergraduate Dissertation

This chapter will help y
to:

- ► decide on the area (
  your research
- ► understand the shap
  of a dissertation
- ► cover the essential
  sections in your
  proposal
- ► understand the
  requirements of a
  literature review
- ► plan your work load

INTRODUCTION

This chapter will get you started on preparing your proposal. In order to give you an idea of what a dissertation entails, it lists the main sections you'll need to include. You'll find below explanations of each of these areas together with some suggestions of how to address them briefly in your proposal (before you start work on the dissertation itself).

A dissertation uses certain skills that are covered in Chapters 2 and 8 on essays and reports, so you might want to check these out. This book doesn't, however, explain research methods in detail. For that, you'll need other material.

Working on your dissertation will be a process of discovery. By the time you finish, you'll have a really good grasp of your topic. Actually beginning, however, can feel daunting because, until you've done some work, you might well feel you're in the dark. So the topic you decide to write on needs to be something you're going to be really interested in. And ideally, your dissertation will demand expertise in the kind of things you do best.

Once you've decided on the general area you're going to look at, you'll need to think about how you can keep it small. You'll probably be expected to produce about 10,000 words. When you consider the number of issues you're going to have to cover (see *Structure* below) and the fact that you're going to have to deal with most of them in some depth, you'll see that there isn't scope for taking on wide areas of research.

* choose a small topic that fascinates you so you'll cope and stay enthusiastic

You'll have a supervisor to help you, and if there's the possibility of choice, choose someone who you know you'll get on with. This person will be discussing your drafts with you and giving general advice. If they already know your work, they can often suggest areas for you to consider that they think you'll be comfortable with.

The point at which you have your first meeting with your supervisor will vary from one college to another. This chapter is based on the assumption that you'll need to submit your proposal before that first meeting. It's likely that you'll be required to submit something like 500 words setting out your main ideas.

It will be essential to work on a computer so that you can easily add items as you go along and re-draft with ease. You'll also be able to work on just the section that interests you at any particular time. Back up everything on disk or a memory stick since losing material from a project like this could be disastrous. And save your work every few minutes. I speak from bitter experience with an unruly computer.

FIRST THOUGHTS

Before you begin work on your dissertation, you'll need to do some hard thinking about your topic – its scope, your reasons for choosing it, and the angle you intend to take. It's a good idea to rough this out on paper straight away. It's fine to scribble and tear things up. The act of writing something down forces us to be explicit. That way, problem areas are likely to show up and you can avoid getting yourself into areas that might cause difficulties.

Start by constructing a working title. It can be useful to form a question. So think about the ground you hope to cover and write down a question for which your dissertation could provide the answer. Then turn that question into a statement. You might find that you have to change your title as you discover things you weren't expecting, but don't worry, you have to start somewhere, and that title will give you a bedrock for your first investigations. In science subjects, you might need to construct a working hypothesis.

* start with a working title

THE STRUCTURE OF A DISSERTATION

In order to write your proposal, you'll need to have some understanding of the shape your dissertation itself will take. Then you can refer briefly to relevant aspects of it in your proposal even though you'll be unlikely to have a clear idea of the finished product at this stage. You'll want to show you're aware of what's needed so that a supervisor can check that you're going in the right direction. The following are the accepted sections of a dissertation, but bear in mind that the way you'll treat them will vary according to your subject area:

The sections of a dissertation

Introduction
Literature review
Methodology
Findings
Discussion
Conclusions and recommendations
Bibliography

If you've read Chapter 8, *Reports*, you'll see that the shape of a dissertation is rather similar to that of a report. Dissertations need to be structured according to the requirements of individual universities and colleges, however. In **scientific, sociological and technical subjects**, you'll probably include each section of the above list in that order. In **humanities subjects**, however, you're more likely to be asked to submit three main chapters, each of which will contain your findings, discussion and conclusions on separate aspects of your research. Each section below ends with a tip for your proposal.

> * understanding the components of a dissertation will help you write your proposal

▶ Introduction

In your dissertation itself, your introduction will need to give some background information and state clearly what your research aimed to do. You'll need to explain your title, the line your research takes, the methods you've used, the scope of your work and your reasons for doing it. So **in your proposal**, aim to give some indication of these aspects.

▶ Literature review

A literature review looks at work that's already been done in the field you're going to work on. It performs three functions: it demonstrates to examiners that you've carried out an overview of the particular field, it puts you in good position for going forward and it helps to situate your work and give it strength and credence. Your job here will be to analyse and evaluate what's out there.

Working on the actual review for your dissertation can help you generate some ideas and prevent you from reinventing the wheel. You might decide to build on something that someone else has started. Don't overload yourself, however. You have a limited time for this task, so skim-read whenever you can and aim to use articles and chapters rather than whole books. A rough rule of thumb is to cover no more than twenty titles. According to the area you're working in, ten – or even five – might do. A good practice is to organise your literature review in topic sections. Below is a list of some possible headings:

- historical background
- specific approaches: empirical, philosophical, historical, post-modernist, etc.
- current research and discoveries
- principal questions being asked
- methodologies in use

And here are some questions to consider when reading a text:

- does it involve an empirical or theoretical study?
- what methods and types of data are used?
- what conclusions does it reach?

For your proposal, you just need to show that you've got some idea of what's around – not necessarily what's in it. Aim to note one or two key writers or pieces of research that will be important for your work and give some idea of the areas you intend to cover and the kind of items you'll be looking at.

▶ Methodology

You'll need to start by setting out the questions or hypotheses that you've investigated. Then you can give details of the way you've done this and why. What you do here will depend, in part, on whether you're working in the sciences or humanities:

> In this section, you will need to explain the methods, tools, and procedures used (if you are a student in the sciences) while conducting the research. If you are a humanities student, explain the structure you will use for your dissertation by stating the core argument of each chapter, the links between chapters and how this will help prove the point you wish to make. For humanities students, this section could be part of the dissertation's introduction. (The Writing Centre, London Metropolitan University, n.d.)

There are two main types of methodology: quantitative and qualitative. Quantitative methods are used for things that can be accurately measured where results can be put in numbers such as percentages. Qualitative methods are used for things such as ideas, opinions and feelings where it's not possible to give exact results. In the main, you'll be using one or the other method – quantitative for science subjects, for example, and qualitative for assessing novels, plays and poems. It's possible, however, that you'll want to use a combination of the two.

> * the main research methods are quantitative (numbers) and qualitative (ideas)

In your proposal, aim to give some idea of the type of research methods you expect to use.

▶ Findings

Obviously, you'll set out here what you have discovered and the results of any surveys, questionnaires or experiments you've undertaken. You could also include a note on any difficulties you've encountered in collecting and/or analysing data. Some departments will be happy for you to combine this section with the *Discussion* section – or even require that you do that. Note, however, particularly if you are doing empirical work, that it will be very important to make a clear distinction between your findings and your critical evaluation of what you've found.

For your proposal, just explain the kind of things you'll be looking for and mention anything you expect to find.

▶ Discussion

The purpose of a discussion section is to set out your interpretation of your findings – in other words, to make sense of the results of each aspect of your study. You'll need to show in some detail their relevance and their application to further study. Don't skimp on this section because it's here that you have the opportunity to demonstrate your skills of analysis and synthesis. Make connections between your findings and the various trends you've discovered in your literature review.

You also need to comment on how successful your research has been. If, for example, you discovered at the eleventh hour a further path you needed to explore but just didn't have time to follow, explain this clearly. Far from being a negative comment, it could be a very useful pointer to further research – particularly if you can show that it was only by doing what you've done that it was possible to see this new path. Demonstrating that you can stand back and take a hard look at your work will go down well with an assessor.

Obviously, you won't be able to include any discussion of findings **in your proposal**, but if you have any tentative suggestions to make, add them in.

▶ Conclusions/recommendations

Your conclusion can be brief, but you need to link it up to the topic and area of your study as set out in your introduction. As in an essay, your conclusion needs to show that the dissertation has done what it said on the tin. You'll need to sum up your work clearly and show what opportunities there are for further research. Remember that whoever assesses your dissertation can't see inside your head, so you'll need to spell things out and show the overall value of your work.

In your proposal, aim to give some idea of the area of your conclusion, but this needs to be kept very loose. You don't want to give the impression that you've decided on the results before doing the research.

▶ Bibliography

You're going to be looking at a range of books and articles, so it's going to be important to record full bibliographic details as you go along. You'll need to provide a bibliography or list of references (see below) and you might well need to revisit texts you at first thought unhelpful, so don't delete any notes until you've submitted your dissertation.

Your **Bibliography** will cover all the items you've referred to and/or quoted from in the body of your dissertation – including all items in your literature review – together with items you've looked at but not used. If, however, your department wants a list of **References**, you'll omit items you've looked at but not used. (See Chapter 3 for further details of how to set out references.)

You can start your bibliography as soon as you begin work on **your proposal**.

PRESENTATION

The rules for presentation of both **your proposal** and the dissertation itself are very similar to those for essays:

- organise your material carefully
- write clearly and with good paragraphing
- check your grammar and punctuation
- type or word-process your material
- use double line-spacing
- leave an extra line between paragraphs
- number your pages
- put indented quotes in single line-spacing
- use one side of the paper only

You'll need to include with your dissertation itself:

- a title page
- a table of contents
- your bibliography on a separate sheet

YOUR ACTION PLAN

An action plan with dates is crucial because you're going to have to develop your dissertation alongside other work. Getting behind would be stressful and could put your other grades at risk. It's possible that you'll need to submit an action plan with **your proposal**. In any case, writing a plan at an early stage will show a prospective supervisor that you mean business and will also help you to feel that you've got control of the process. You need to write your plan in detail, showing exactly what you're going to be doing at each point.

You'll also need to check with your supervisor when he or she will want to see drafts of the different stages of your work. Meetings with your supervisor need to be on the plan, together with time slots for acting on his/her recommendations while they're fresh in your mind. Build in plenty of research time and writing-up time. Always assume that things will take longer than you expect. They will.

Below is an example of an action plan. It's Alice's plan for her dissertation that focused on pre-school children. She gave it the working title: 'Is there a gender difference in computer use in an early years setting?'

Alice has focused here on her empirical research. By the time she wrote this plan, she'd already completed her literature review and a draft of her introduction.

The timetable of events for the research project: September 2011 to May 2012.

- Initial Planning Sept 2011 – 2 weeks
- Initial Research and obtaining consent for research to be undertaken Mid Sept–Mid Oct 2011 – 4 weeks
- Create Questionnaire Oct 2011 – 2 weeks
- Pilot Questionnaire Nov 2011 – 2 weeks
- Undertake Questionnaire Mid Nov 2011– Jan 2012 – 6 weeks (allowing for school holidays)
- Analyse Data Jan 2012 – 2 weeks
- Create Interview Feb 2012 – 2 weeks
- Pilot Interview Mid Feb 2012 – 2 weeks
- Undertake Interviews March–Mid Apr 2012 – 6 weeks
- Analyse Data Apr 2012 – 2 weeks
- Write Report May 2012 – 4 weeks

SUMMARY

This chapter has included:

Some thoughts on your choice of topic

The structure of a dissertation (with some ideas on how to refer to these sections in your proposal:
- introduction
- literature review
- methodology
- findings
- discussion
- conclusions/recommendations
- bibliography and references

Notes on presentation of your proposal and dissertation

An example of an action plan to start you off

Part Three
The Nuts and Bolts of Good Writing

13 Verbs and Other Parts of Speech

This chapter will explain the eight different parts of speech, especially:

▶ The big five – verbs, nouns, pronouns, adjectives and adverbs
▶ The way that each of them works

INTRODUCTION

In traditional grammar, all the words we ever use (well, very nearly all) fall into one of eight groups. These groups are called parts of speech – or, sometimes, word classes. Some grammarians now define extra categories, but you needn't worry about those in order to have a good basic understanding of how parts of speech function.

The most important parts of speech for your purposes are verbs. Of the other seven, four are important and worth learning about: nouns, pronouns, adjectives and adverbs. But unless you're really keen or you plan to study linguistics, you can probably ignore the other three: conjunctions, prepositions and interjections.

VERBS

If you're having trouble writing grammatical sentences, it's ten to one that the key to the problem is your use of verbs. Once you've an understanding of how they work, you'll be able to write well-formed sentences without too much trouble.

You may have terrible memories of having been unable to learn verbs at school, but fear not. Like all other aspects of written English, there's no mystique to verbs. We all use them expertly when we speak. You might like to think of a verb as being the spark that gets a sentence's engine going. A verb is the central key to every well-formed sentence.

▶ Doing

If your school used to teach verbs, you might remember that verbs are often called 'doing' words. Most verbs show us some kind of *action*. Here are some examples:

run	drink
swim	breathe
blink	work
walk	drive
eat	talk

It's easy to imagine somebody (or perhaps some animal) doing some of those things, isn't it? They are all actions. Let's put some of them into sentences. We may have to alter some of them very slightly to make them sound right:

Jenny **runs** for her school in league fixtures.
We usually **blink** several times a minute.
Both my children **walk** to school.
Most of the time, we **breathe** very quietly.
Carl **works** on the shop floor.
Many people **drive** to work.
Politicians **talk** a lot.

There are other things we do that may not show up quite so clearly as actions, but which still count as verbs. They're all to do with thinking or feeling – like these:

like	remember
love	plan
hate	want
wonder	think
calculate	imagine

And here are some of them in sentences:

Jamie **loves** curry.
Cindy **hates** cabbage.
My grandfather **remembers** the Second World War.
I **want** lots of money.
Ben **likes** jazz and **loves** the blues.

You've probably noticed that there are actually *two* verbs in the last sentence. If we wanted, we could put more in:

Ben **likes** jazz, **loves** the blues, **buys** CDs, and **goes** to concerts every month.

ACTIVITY 1

See if you can pick out the verbs in the following sentences. There is just one in each. Remember that you are looking for words which tell you what somebody or something *does, thinks* or *feels.*

1 I wash the car on Saturdays.
2 Horoscopes foretell the future.
3 The farmers long for rain.
4 Before winter, many birds migrate to warmer lands.
5 Marco sends faxes to America.
6 We all desire happiness.

▶ Being

The verb *to be* is a one-off. It has nothing at all to do with 'doing'. You might have heard of this verb because it's in a very famous speech from William Shakespeare's *Hamlet*:

To be or not to be: that is the question ...

If you're interested in New Age ideas, you may have heard of the idea of just 'being'. Some people, exhausted with what they see as the 'rat race' of modern life, have decided that they no longer want to rush around 'doing' things but that they prefer just quietly existing – or 'being'.

The verb *to be* may look rather insignificant, but it does some very important work. It's the verb we use when we want to describe things, and probably gets more use than any other verb.

▶ Describing people, animals and things using the verb 'to be'

The words in bold in the following sentences are all parts of the verb *to be*: *am*, *is*, *are*, *was*, *were*, and *will be*. We use one or another of them whenever we describe anything, or when we give a brief explanation about it. Here they are in some sentences:

> I **am** Nigerian.
> You **are** wonderful.
> Alan **will be** an architect.
> The model's dress **was** raspberry red.
> The kangaroo **is** an ihabitant of Australia.
> The chidren **were** noisy.

THE VERB 'TO BE' AS AN AUXILIARY (HELPING) VERB

The verb 'to be' can be used as what's called an **auxiliary** verb – that is, it helps other verbs. Here it's used as an auxiliary verb in **continuous** tenses (see below):

> Brad **was swimming** strongly.
> John **is swimming** in the shallow end of the pool.
> Charlie Blunt **will be swimming** in the championships.

▶ Having

Altogether, verbs are about three things – doing, being or having. We've looked at the first two of these, so all we have left now is a very small group of words that tell us about owning things – words such as *have* and *possess.* Here are some examples of them in use:

> Joe **has** a cupboard full of cricket gear.
> Chris **owns** a pub.
> Aladdin **possesses** a magic lamp.

THE VERB 'TO HAVE' AS AN AUXILIARY (HELPING) VERB

Like the verb 'to be', the verb 'to have' can be used to help other verbs. Here it's used as an auxiliary verb in **perfect** tenses (see below):

Marco and Monique **have lived** in Britain for ten years.
Sue **has lived** on a houseboat since last March.
Michelle **will have lived** in Ireland for three years in July.

ACTIVITY 2

Underline the verbs in the following sentences and note down whether each is a 'doing', 'being' or 'having' verb. There is only one verb in each sentence.

1 Mary is six years old.
2 Max has six fossils.
3 We cross the border at six tonight.
4 The earth goes round the sun.
5 The lions are very hungry.
6 The view from the mountain is beautiful.
7 The dog has fleas.
8 Terry owns a racehorse.
9 Flies buzz round meat.
10 The calculation is tricky.

► Time

When we speak, we all use verbs expertly to show *when* something happens. Let's imagine that the mother of a teenager called Jenny is speaking to a friend. She might say:

'Jenny **runs** for her school in league fixtures.'

She means that whenever there's a league race, Jenny is in it. This is the current state of affairs – it tells us about what is happening in the **present**.

Let's suppose that Jenny has now grown up, and that her mother is recalling her schooldays in a letter to a friend. She might write:

Jenny **ran** for her school in league fixtures.

She's now talking about what Jenny did in the past.
Now let's suppose that Jenny has only just been picked to run for the

school, and that her mother is explaining what this means in a letter to Jenny's grandmother:

> Jenny **will run** for the school in league fixtures.

Here, Jenny's mother is talking about the **future**.

The verbs in those three sentences are written to show whether something happens in the **present** (*runs*), the **past** (*ran*) or the **future** (*will run*). There's a word for this: **tense**. We can say that those three sentences are written in different **tenses**: the **present tense**, the **past tense** and the **future tense**.

ACTIVITY 3

Look at the following sentences, and write down past, present or future for each one:

1 Margaret Thatcher led Britain's Conservative party for many years.
2 America's President lives at the White House.
3 Napoleon won many battles.
4 Denise will sit her final exams in June.
5 I go to my guitar lesson once a week.
6 At 10 p.m., the supermarket will close.
7 Some animals hibernate in winter.
8 Mark will get redundancy pay from his employer.

▶ **Perfect tenses**

Let's suppose that Jenny's mother is talking to a neighbour. We've seen that if she says:

> 'Jenny **runs** for her school in league fixtures'

she's obviously talking about what is going on now. She's talking in the **present tense**. But she might put this slightly differently. She might say:

> 'Jenny **has run** for her school in league fixtures.'

Here she means that *up until this point* Jenny has run in the school's league fixtures. If she puts it this way, she's probably implying that the situation might not continue – Jenny might not get picked next time. When we want to show that something has happened up till now or that the action is now finished, it's done in the **present perfect** tense – in this case, *has run*.

There's also a **past perfect** tense. We often use this when we want to show that two things happened at different times in the past. If Jenny's mother says:

> 'Before she **won** the cup, Jenny **had run** in league fixtures for two years'

we can see that running in league fixtures had *preceded* winning the cup (which itself is in the past). This is what had happened up to the point when Jenny won the cup. The clue to the past perfect tense is in the use of the word *had* along with a verb in the past tense. It implies that something happened a long way back or prior to something else.

Now if Jenny's mother says:

> 'By the time she's eighteen, Jenny **will have run** for her school for four years'

she'll be explaining *what will have happened* up to a particular point in the future. She'll be using the **future perfect** tense.

ACTIVITY 4

See if you can say which of the following sentences are in the **present perfect**, which are in the **past perfect** and which are in the **future perfect**.

1 All the members of the club had attended the previous meeting.
2 Cindy has been to the theatre three times this week.
3 We had worked on the boat all morning.
4 Palab will have played in every match this season.
5 The children have put away their football things.
6 The dog had eaten his dinner.
7 By this evening, Tracy will have finished painting her bedroom.

> 8 I have found the map.
> 9 It will have stopped raining by the afternoon.
> 10 Sean has given his mother a watch for her birthday.

▶ Continuous action (sometimes called progressive)

We show when an action is continuing to happen by adding '-ing' to a verb and preceding it with a part of the verb *to be*. This is called **continuous** action:

Last week, Martin **was thinking** about a holiday.	**past continuous**
John **is thinking** about a holiday.	**present continuous**
Soon, Cherie **will be thinking** about a holiday.	**future continuous**

In each sentence, the person doing the thinking is spending quite a bit of time at it – the action is *continuing* over a period.

We can also talk about continuous actions that were over and done with at a point in the past or have been happening up to a point in the present or in the future:

> Martin **had been thinking** about a holiday all last year.
> John **has been thinking** about a holiday all day today.
> Cherie **will have been thinking** about a holiday for a whole year next month.

Below is a table that you can use as a checklist for all the different tenses:

Checklist for tenses

I wash the car every week.	**present simple**
I am washing the car now.	**present continuous**
I have washed the car this morning.	**present perfect**
I have been washing the car all morning.	**present perfect continuous**

I washed the car last week.	**past simple**
I was washing the car with a new shampoo.	**past continuous**
I had washed the car by six o'clock.	**past perfect**
I had been washing the car on Thursday.	**past perfect continuous**
I will wash the car this afternoon.	**future simple**
I will be washing the car this afternoon.	**future continuous**
I will have washed the car by six o'clock.	**future perfect**
I will soon have been washing the car for two hours.	**future perfect continuous**

Use the above list to help you as you work on the next activity:

ACTIVITY 5

Write down the tense for each verb in the following sentences:

1 I want a drink.
2 Jane broke her coffee mug.
3 Mark will laugh at the photo.
4 After the exams, the students will be celebrating.
5 Marie had been eating her breakfast.
6 Stan had considered the problem.
7 Kirsty will have been cooking all evening.
8 We were enjoying Disneyland this time last year.
9 We're having a wonderful time.
10 Stan will have considered the problem.
11 The cat has washed itself.
12 The cat has been washing itself for half an hour.

▶ Actives and passives

In a simple sentence, the person at the beginning can usually be seen to be *doing* the verb, so to speak. We call this type of verb **active**. But sometimes, the verb is being done *to* him or her. The verb in this case is called a **passive** verb. The difference between active and passive verbs shows up in the following two sentences:

I was bitten by the dog.   **passive**
The dog bit me.   **active**

The meaning is those sentences is the same, but in the first, the focus is on 'I' and in the second on the dog. Notice that the second sentence seems much more lively. It's simpler and more informal too.

In passive verbs, as explained above, the person *preceding* the verb (whom you'd normally expect to be 'doing' it) is having it done *to* him or her. These days, we don't use the passive much because it often seems rather cold and dead.

Below are some active and passive verbs. You can see that sentences that use active verbs are generally sharper and punchier.

ACTIVE	PASSIVE
Present	
Maisie **is watching** the parrot.	The parrot **is being watched** by Maisie.
Hazel **likes** everyone.	Everyone **is liked** by Hazel.
Past	
I **bit** the dog.	The dog **was bitten** by me.
Sue **phoned** the TV company.	The TV company **was phoned** by Sue.
Future	
Tim **will give** a vote of thanks.	A vote of thanks **will be given** by Tim.
The President of the United States **will meet** the Russian envoy.	The Russian envoy **will be met** by the President of the United States.

Unless you're an English-language student, the only time you're likely to need to know much about passive verbs is if a tutor comments that you are using too many of them. A piece of writing filled with passives can sound rather lifeless. Sometimes, however, it *is* necessary to use a passive verb.

▶ When to use passive verbs

Sometimes, it's necessary to use a passive verb when:

- focusing on the *receiver* of an action
- writing up *reports* and scientific *experiments*
- showing that the *doer* of the action is *unknown*

Here's an example of that last item:

> The baby was abandoned in the church.

Because we don't know who did the abandoning, the only way we could make that sentence active would be to say:

> Someone abandoned the baby in the church.

Try your hand at the following activity.

ACTIVITY 6

Note down A or P (active or passive) for each of the following sentences:

1 The priest tripped over the bridesmaid's foot.
2 Food was provided by the bride's sister and her husband.
3 The couple's friends were greeted by the bride's parents.
4 The bride wore a beautiful dress.
5 All the speeches were brief.
6 The bride was given a kiss by the groom.
7 The little bridesmaid was looked after by her mother.
8 The wedding guests were served by catering students.
9 A journalist reported on the wedding in the local paper.
10 The day will be remembered for a long time.

You can read a little more on passives in the section 'The subject of a passive verb' in chapter 14.

▶ Conditional and subjunctive verbs

The rules for both these types of verb are rather involved, and unless you're studying grammar, you're unlikely to need to understand how they work. You'll probably get them right anyway when you write them down. If your first language isn't English, however, or if you want to know more about them for any other reason, you'll need a specialist grammar book. I'll just touch on them here.

Instead of telling us about things that have happened, are happening or will happen, **conditionals** tell us what might or could happen, or have happened, i.e. they tell us about things that aren't certain. For example:

> It <u>might</u> rain tomorrow.
> If I'd taken the car instead of going by train, I <u>could</u> have stopped off to see you.

The **subjunctive** deals with things that we perhaps wish for, suppose, doubt or fear. For example:

> I wish that Mike <u>would</u> stop smoking.
> If I went to the gym three times a week, I <u>would</u> be a lot fitter.

NOUNS

Nouns are words for **people, places and things** – everyone and everything, in fact, that does the doing, being and having (see VERBS, above):

People	Places	Things
Boy	New York	table
girl	Adelaide	car
Mrs Thatcher	Japan	clock
Buddha	Nigeria	milk
Mick Jagger	Machu Picchu	computer
Bill Gates	the French Riviera	grass
Susie	South West England	newspaper

The **names of animals, birds, insects and sea creatures** are also nouns:

dog	eagle	beetle	whale
cat	sparrow	bee	seal
lion	duck	moth	octopus

The **names of government departments, companies, corporations and shops** are nouns too; and so are **brand names**:

Berkshire County Council	Marks and Spencer	Coca-Cola
the Church of England	The National Gallery	Nescafé
Microsoft	McDonald's	Ford
Toshiba	Debenhams	Porsche
Barclays Bank	Macy's	Persil
Oxfam	the Foreign Office	Tesco

Seasons, periods of time and words relating to **weather** are also nouns:

spring	hour	snow
summer	minute	sunshine
autumn	month	wind
winter	century	rain

Here are some sentences with the nouns highlighted in bold:

Joan threw the **ball** across the **garden**.
Toshiba is building a new **factory** in **Wales**.
The French are known for good **food**.
The **moon** and **stars** shine brightly on a clear **night**.

One way of understanding nouns is to remember that it's usually possible to see and/or touch them. You can put some nouns in your pocket, eat some for breakfast, meet some for a drink, read about them in a newspaper, or look at pictures of them.

The next activity focuses solely on nouns:

ACTIVITY 7

Underline all the nouns in the following sentences:

1 Mrs Steele sent a letter to the Queen.
2 Bees make honey.

> 3 Carlos has been living in France for six years.
> 4 Mary wanted a bike.
> 5 Julius Caesar ruled in Rome.

The whole category of nouns can be divided into two groups – into what are known as **concrete nouns** and **abstract nouns**. Concrete nouns are the ones we have already been looking at. These are the ones that can be seen, touched, or found in some form. Abstract nouns, as the name suggests, are things that it's not possible to find. Below are some examples of the two types. Notice that each concrete noun is related to a corresponding abstract noun on its left:

Abstract	Concrete
beauty	flower
education	book
war	gun
kindness	gift
love	ring
crime	burglar
sadness	tears
religion	church

Abstract nouns are things that we often talk about but we wouldn't be able to see or touch. They're usually generalised ideas or emotions. Concrete nouns, on the other hand, can be found somewhere – even if it takes some searching.

So things like the heart and lungs are concrete rather than abstract because, in an operation, they are visible. Ghosts, too, surprisingly, are concrete. If they exist, they are visible and very specific. On the day that I see one, I shall be able to describe it in detail. Air and other gases are concrete too, because they can be measured. We could obtain a jar of hydrogen, so it's not abstract – it's not a mere idea, it exists.

Abstract nouns can only be talked about – never found. We can see a beautiful painting or person, but we can't find a piece of beauty; we can find students, lecturers, books and universities, but we can't get hold of a piece of education.

See if you can pick out the concrete and abstract nouns in the next activity:

ACTIVITY 8

Underline the concrete nouns and put a ring round the abstract nouns in the following:

1 Water is essential for life.
2 Fruit is good for our health.
3 The atmosphere in the bar was dense with smoke.
4 The monk had great understanding.
5 The members talked endlessly about strategy.
6 Paul was studying philosophy.

PRONOUNS

Pronouns save an awful lot of time. They're used in place of nouns. It would be both boring and time-consuming to have to write the following:

Jack was born in Toronto, but soon Jack's parents moved to Britain. Jack went to school in Huddersfield. Jack has now started Jack's own business, making greetings cards.

We'd actually write:

Jack was born in Toronto, but soon his parents move to Britain. He went to school in Huddersfield, and he has now started his own business, making greetings cards.

Obviously, we all use pronouns a great deal. Here are some of them:

I/me	we/us
you	you
he/him/she/her/it	they/them

There are also some other types of pronoun, but it's not necessary for most people to worry about remembering these. You'll almost certainly use them correctly. They are *relative, possessive* and *demonstrative pronouns*:

relative pronouns
who, whom, that, which

possessive pronouns
my/mine, your/yours, his, her/hers, its, our/ours, their/theirs

demonstrative pronouns
this, these, that, those

One of the most important things to remember about pronouns is that they stand for nouns. So when you write essays it's essential to use the appropriate noun *before* you go on to use a pronoun so that the pronoun has something specific to stand for.

ADJECTIVES

Adjectives are words that describe something. Look at the following sentence:

The old lady owned a beautiful red necklace.

There are three describing words in that sentence: *old, beautiful* and *red.* The first one tells us something about the lady. The other two tell us what the necklace looked like. You might start to wonder what it was made of – coral, perhaps, or rubies.

Did you spot that *lady* and *necklace* are nouns? The rule is: *adjectives describe nouns.* In the following sentences, I've underlined the adjectives:

There was an <u>enormous</u> dog in the office.
John's <u>crazy</u> mother brought a <u>large, fat</u> hen to church.
Pat Patch owned a <u>noisy</u> parrot.

Adjectives are also used to describe pronouns:

He was <u>hot</u>.
They are <u>happy</u>.

You can see from the last two examples that adjectives can be used in a simple way with parts of the verb *to be.* Here are some more examples:

The children are <u>hungry</u>.
The dress was <u>expensive</u>.
The sun is <u>hot</u>.

ADVERBS

Since adjectives describe nouns, you might have guessed that *adverbs are used to describe verbs.* They show us how things are done. The good news here is that the vast majority of adverbs end in *-ly* so they're usually very easy to spot and they're formed by putting *-ly* on the end of an adjective. Look at the following sentence:

Sarah walked home <u>slowly</u>.

You'll remember that most verbs are action words. The verb here is *walked.* The word *slowly* tells us *how* Sarah walked, and gives us the beginning of a visual picture. While you are practising spotting the difference between adjectives and adverbs, always ask yourself which word is being described.

You might say, 'Which word does *slowly* describe? Is it *Sarah?* Well, she is going slowly. But that doesn't quite seem quite right. I can't say that Sarah is *slowly.* Let's try *walked.* Ah yes, that fits.' If I ask myself the question, 'How did Sarah walk?', I'm bound to come up with the answer '*slowly*'.

You can see the difference between adjectives and adverbs in these two sentences:

My room is tidy.
I have arranged my room tidily.

In the first sentence, the word *tidy* describes the word *room,* which is a noun. So *tidy* must be an adjective. In the second sentence, the word *tidily* tells you how I *arranged* the place. The word *arranged* is a verb. It tells us about an action. So *tidily* must be an adverb because it describes a verb.

There are a few adverbs that are not quite so easy to spot, but they work in just the same way as the *–ly* ones. For example:

The boy ran <u>fast</u>.
We worked <u>hard</u>.

The word *fast* tells us how the boy *ran*. The word *hard* tells how we *worked*. The words *ran* and *worked* are both verbs, of course.

If we want to be a bit more academic about this, we can use the term *modify* instead of *describe*. It's a little more precise because, rather than confining the job solely to describing, it implies that the effect of a particular word is *changed* slightly.

As well as modifying verbs, adverbs can also modify adjectives and other adverbs. If you want to pursue this one, take a few minutes to see if you can work out how adjectives and adverbs function in the following sentence:

> That soldier will probably easily outrun his very heavily loaded colleague.

If we start at the end of the sentence, we can see that *colleague* is a noun. The word *loaded* describes it, and so is an adjective. That word is modified by the word *heavily*, which must therefore be an adverb. This, in turn, is modified by *very*, which must then be another adverb. The verb is *will outrun* and it is modified by *easily*, which is therefore yet another adverb. Finally, the word *probably* modifies *easily* so that, too, is an adverb. Here's the list:

Nouns	*Verb*	*Adjective*	*Adverbs*
soldier	will outrun	loaded	probably
colleague			easily
			very
			heavily

There are also a few words which are adverbs although you might not, at first glance, expect them to be, for example:

> how, where, when, why

In the following sentences, each of the above words modifies a verb. The verbs are in bold type.

> How **is** John?
> Where **is** Joan's coat?
> When **did** you **buy** your car?
> Why **was** Roy **laughing**?

Notice that, in the last two sentences, the verbs have two parts but are split apart.

The words *here* and *there* are also adverbs. Again, the verbs are in bold type:

Please **put** your boots here.
I've **left** my rucksack there.

ACTIVITY 9

Underline the adverbs in the following:

1 I felt I'd managed the first essay beautifully.
2 Slowly and silently, the cat crept through the grass.
3 I finished my lunch quickly.
4 Cheetahs can run fast.
5 Jason has worked harder and harder throughout the year.
6 The athlete jumped high.
7 Josh had a green jacket that he loved dearly.
8 Dan answered the question rather rashly.

CONJUNCTIONS

A conjunction is a word that connects either two other words or whole constructions such as *phrases* or *clauses* (see Chapter 14):

and	because
but	if
or	although

Here are a couple of examples used in sentences:

I'll come down the pub **if** John gets home early.
I'll come down the pub **although** I'm short of cash.

PREPOSITIONS

Prepositions have a number of uses. The main function of a preposition is to appear before a noun or pronoun and link this word in some way to the next part of the sentence. Examples of prepositions are:

at, from, of, through, without, during, for, with

Here are some of them used in sentences:

I left my umbrella **at** the hospital.
I had a present **from** my aunt.
I've come **without** my diary.
I'll be away **during** March.

Perhaps the most common use of prepositions is to show the position of something in relation to something else. Look at the following sentence:

I put the saucepan **on** the cooker.

Other prepositions for showing position are:

in, beside, under, near

INTERJECTIONS

These are usually one-word shouts, such as:

Hey! Oops! Bother! Ouch! Ugh!

One-word greetings (or the opposite) are also interjections, such as:

Hello! Hi! Cheers! Goodbye!

MEMORY-JOGGER

You can use a very basic sentence as a way of checking out four of the five main parts of speech: nouns, verbs, adjectives and adverbs.

adjective	noun	verb	adverb		adjective	noun
The	cat	sat		on the		mat.
The black	kitten	sat		on the	white	rug.
The spotted	dog	sat	proudly	on the	red	carpet.

If you've been really alert, you might have realized that *on* is a preposition. The word 'the' is what is called a **determiner**, but it's not necessary to remember that.

SUMMARY

Verbs
Verbs tell us about: doing
                       being
                       having

- The majority are *action* words – i.e. doing
- The verb *to be* helps us to *describe* people and things – e.g. *is, are, were*
- We show *when* something happens through using different *tenses*
- Many verbs have more than one part
- *Active* verbs are more lively than *passive* ones

Nouns: words for people, places, things, brand names, shops, companies and any other observable items
   concrete nouns: all the above
   abstract nouns: concepts and feelings like *peace* and *love* (that can be spoken of but not found)

Pronouns: words that stand *instead* of nouns – e.g. *he, it, they*

Adjectives: Adjectives describe nouns – e.g. *hot, happy*

Adverbs: Adverbs (often ending in 'ly') *are words* that describe verbs – e.g. *quickly*

Conjunctions: link words that connect two other words, or two phrases or clauses – e.g. *and, but, so*

Prepositions: Prepostions often point out place – e.g. *on, at, beside, from, for*
   They also link parts of a sentence – e.g. *from, through, during*

Interjections: These are shouts – e.g. 'Bother!' And greetings – e.g. 'Hello!'

14 Writing Clear Sentences

This chapter will:

▶ help you revise the main rules for writing clear sentences
▶ explain some of the most common areas of confusion
▶ give you some information on clauses

INTRODUCTION

Everybody knows roughly what a sentence is, and this works fine when we leave notes around for people we live or work with or write simple letters to friends. It's when we start to write about complex topics that difficulties can arise. This chapter will show you the basic rules, together with a number of pitfalls and how to avoid them. It will also give you a deeper understanding of how sentences work. You might find that you need to refer to the section on verbs in Chapter 13 as you read.

You'll also find some information on clauses here. It's not always necessary to understand how clauses work in order to write well, so aim to get a broad understanding rather than trying to learn things off pat. Understanding a bit about traditional clause analysis will help you to get a sense of how sentences are composed of a number of working parts. You'll then have greater control over what you write. Your thinking will be sharpened, too, and you'll find it easier to read difficult material.

MAKING SENSE

It's not likely to be news to you that a sentence needs to start with a capital letter and end with a full stop. Beyond this, there are three basic rules for writing good sentences. A sentence must:

• make sense by itself
• contain a working verb
• contain a subject for the verb

Meaning is crucial for whoever reads what we write. Look at this sentence:

> With all his football kit.

I'm sure you can see that there's a problem here. This 'sentence' doesn't make sense, does it? I'd better improve it:

> John went to school with all his football kit.

Now you know what I mean. A sentence should always tell us something clearly. It makes some kind of *statement*. In this case, I've communicated information about John going to school with his kit. You may want to know who John is, or the name of the school, and whether John was just practising or was playing in a match, but you now have a reasonably clear idea of what was going on.

A good test of whether a sentence works is to check whether someone reading it would be able to ask a sensible question about it, or whether their likely response would be a very puzzled "Eh?" My first example was only half a sentence, and you probably found it pretty confusing.

Look at the following extract from Susan's essay on education. She has made a very common error. Most of her sentences are well formed, but while concentrating on explaining something, she suddenly forgets the rules:

> A majority of children and teenagers benefit greatly from the structure and compulsory nature of school attendance. For many from a background of poverty, school can mean a haven. A warm and stimulating place.

Susan's final sentence doesn't make sense by itself. It's actually part of her explanation in the previous sentence. We could improve what she wrote like this:

> A majority of children and teenagers benefit greatly from the structure and compulsory nature of school attendance. School can also be a haven – a warm and stimulating place in which disadvantaged children can begin to catch up with their peers.

If a tutor has written 'not a sentence' in the margin of your work, the problem may be that you've not been aware of this first crucial rule on making complete sense. You may have been writing things down exactly as you would have said them. When we speak, we frequently break the rules of written grammar, but we still easily make ourselves understood because we also use facial expressions, gesture and tone of voice to get our meaning across.

It's worth looking closely at the kind of thing that happens when we speak. In the following snatch of conversation, look carefully at what Sam's mother says:

> "Where are my pyjamas, Mum?" asked Sam.
> "On the floor," replied his mother crossly. "Where you left them!"

Sam's mother has spoken two 'sentences', but neither of them makes sense by itself. But it's OK for her to say,

> "On the floor"

because Sam knows (a) exactly what is on the floor, and (b) which floor she's referring to. He knows from the tone of her voice that she's cross, and he'll hear the sarcasm in

> "Where you left them!"

His mother will probably put heavy stress on the word *left*. Not only does his mother give lots of extra clues to her meaning, but both Sam and his mother know a good deal about those pyjamas. So when they speak to each other, they can use a kind of shorthand. When we're writing, however, our sentences must make complete sense by them-selves, because whoever reads them can't hear us or pick up clues from our expressions or body language.

If I were writing a story about Sam and his mother without includ-ing any dialogue, I'd have to explain things very carefully. I might do it like this:

> When Sam pestered his mother to find his pyjamas, she brushed him aside crossly, telling him to go and look for them on his bedroom floor where he had thrown them that morning.

You can see that I've had to give quite a bit of extra information to make things quite clear.

ACTIVITY 1

See if you can work out which of the following sentences make sense by themselves (capitals and full stops have been omitted):

1 about half-past nine
2 you don't often see kangaroos in Britain
3 I want a Coke
4 all by himself
5 whether you like it or not
6 wearing light blue trousers
7 I'm hot

WORKING VERBS (this isn't a grammatical term)

The next crucial thing for a sentence is that it must contain a **working verb**. If you're not too clear on what a verb is, have a look at the verb section in Chapter 13 before you read any further. By *working verb*, I mean one that is involved with a person or thing. The lack of a working verb is the cause of by far the greatest proportion of ungrammatical sentences that are written. In every well-written sentence, somebody or something has to be doing, being or having something or be on the receiving end of something done by someone else.

The really annoying thing is that if you are leaving out verbs, you are probably doing it only occasionally, and so it's often hard to spot just the one or two instances in a piece of work where you've made the error. Once you get a *feel*, however, for how a good sentence is constructed, you'll stop getting things wrong.

The name of a verb is called the **infinitive**. So *to talk* and *to be* are both infinitives. They are not doing any specific work, but are just hanging around, so to speak. An infinitive on its own won't be sufficient to make a clear sentence and it's easy to see why if you look at the following poorly constructed sentence:

I to walk by the sea.

This makes no sense. But if I add a working verb it will be fine:

I like to walk by the sea.

It's OK to have an infinitive in a sentence as long as there's a working verb there as well.

By the way, be careful not to confuse the two functions of the word *to*:

I went to Paris.
I like to swim.

In the first sentence, the word *to* introduces a place; in the second, it's part of an infinitive – *to swim*.

SUBJECTS

You are probably used to using the word *subject* to mean either *area of study* or *topic*. So if I ask you what subjects you're studying, the answer is likely to be "English and history", or "physics and maths", and so on. Or if I ask what was the subject of the lecture you went to yesterday, the answer might be "the poetry of John Keats", or "the French Revolution", or "recycling waste materials".

The word *subject* used in relation to grammar has a rather different meaning. It's closely linked to verbs, and verbs are about doing, being or having. A sentence always tells us about somebody (or something) doing, being or having something. That person or thing is the subject of the verb it goes with. Look at these two sentences:

Roy ate cheese sandwiches for his lunch.
Sarah sold her car last week.

Each of these sentences gives us information about a particular person. We know what Roy ate, and what Sarah did with her car. Roy is the **subject** of the verb *ate* and Sarah is the **subject** of the verb *sold*.

This rule functions in exactly the same way with animals, birds, insects and things, too:

Polar bears live in the Arctic.
Spiders have eight legs.
The church stands beside the river.
Water freezes at 0° centigrade.

The subject of a verb is the person or thing that is doing the doing, being or having. In the sentence about polar bears, the verb is *live*. So we can ask ourselves who or what is doing the living. The answer is polar bears. So the subject of the verb *live* is *polar bears*. In the second sentence, we can ask who or what is doing the having, and the answer is *spiders*. So we now know that the subject of the verb *have* in that particular sentence is spiders.

Remember that the word *subject* here means the *subject of the verb*. Any sentence will have a topic. It can't help being about *something*. The *topics* of those four sentences above are:

> the geographical habitat of polar bears
> the physiology of spiders
> the position of the church
> the properties of water

but the subjects of the *verbs* are *polar bears, spiders, the church* and *water*.

The following confusing sentence, from an essay by Susan on the topic 'Discuss the proposition that education is wasted on the young', lacks a subject and working verb:

> Pressures from their peer group, like keeping up with the latest fad, fashion, and pop sensations.

This kind of error is very common. If you look at Susan's previous sentences, you can see how the problem occurred:

> In secondary school, young people come into contact with all sorts of influences and a whole new social scene emerges. These problems include drink and drugs which, previously, young people would have been sheltered from at primary school. Pressures from their peer group, like keeping up with the latest fad, fashion, and pop sensations.

What happened was that Susan started writing as if she were speaking. She added another idea without considering how to construct the sentence. By adding a verb with a subject, it can easily be remedied:

> Teenagers encounter pressures from their peer group, like keeping up with the latest fad, fashion, and pop sensations.

ACTIVITY 2

In the following sentences, underline each working verb and then put a ring around the subject of that verb.

1 Jimi Hendrix died young.
2 Beatlemania swept Britain in the 1960s.
3 Fraser plays guitar in a folk band after work.
4 Duke Ellington is a favourite with traditional jazz musicians.
5 Perhaps surprisingly, Mick Jagger still performs to large audiences.
6 Salsa is a highly popular dance.

In any sentence that contains more than one verb, there is likely to be more than one grammatical subject. For example:

> **The kitchen** *looks* awful since **the dog** *chewed* the curtains and **the baby** *spilt* blackcurrant juice down the wall.

Here there are three verbs and three subjects: the kitchen, the dog and the baby.

▶ Subjects at different places in a sentence

You can see that each of the following sentences begins with an introductory *phrase* – that is, a group of words *without* a working verb (see below, at the end of this chapter). Then comes the subject and its verb:

> Three hours after sunrise, **Bill** *spotted* the heron.
> Despite the rain and cold, **Bill** *had waited* by the stream.
> By a roundabout route, **Bill** *returned* to the town.

In the following sentences, the usual order is reversed in order to give impact. The subject of each verb, therefore, sits right at the end of the sentences:

> Out of the cave, *crawled* **Brian**.
> Beside the motorbike, *stood* **its owner**.

▶ The subject of a passive verb (see 'Actives and passives' in Chapter 13)

Most 'doing' verbs are active. This means that the subject is the person or thing *doing* the verb. In the case of passive verbs, however, something is being done *to* the subject. Look at these sentences:

> **Ray** *was bitten* by the dog.
> **Ray** *bit* the dog.

It's easy to see that, in the second sentence, *Ray* is the subject of the verb *bit*. Biting is what he did. It's not so easy to see that *Ray* is also the subject of the first sentence. You might assume that, since the dog did the biting, it is he (or she) who is the subject. But the *focus* of the sentence is on *Ray,* and *was bitten* is a *passive* form of the past tense of the verb *to bite.*

Similarly, in *both* the next two sentences, the subject is *Polly* even though, in the second sentence, the alien wins:

> **Polly** *ate* a toffee apple.
> **Polly** *was eaten* by a creature from outer space.

In the next two sentences, the subject of the first is *Max,* and the subject of the second is *the referee*, even though the meaning is the same:

> **Max** *was shouted* at by the referee.
> **The referee** *shouted* at Max.

The verb in the first sentence is passive, and the one in the second sentence is active.

You could make the point that it is Max's experience that is more important than the referee's in both sentences here. In the second sentence, however, the verb is active: the referee is doing the shouting. It's the referee's action that is the focus of attention in this sentence.

▶ Extended subjects (this isn't a grammatical term)

It often happens that a *group* of words (rather than a single person or item) functions as the subject of the main verb in a sentence. Here are some examples:

Planning a holiday *is* fun.
To err is human.
Worrying about exams *is* a waste of time.
Collecting wood for the fire *took* a long time.
Looking after the horse *was* Sid's responsibility.
That Patrick was in two minds *was* clear from his hesitation.
That nations must co-operate in order to achieve lasting peace *is* obvious.

In each case here, we can check out the **subject** by asking ourselves a simple question. What was it, for example, that *took a long time?* It was *Collecting wood for the fire.* What was *Sid's responsibility?* It was *Looking after the horse,* of course.

ACTIVITY 3

Underline the subjects of all verbs in the following sentences:

1 Carl won the race.
2 After breakfast, Ron did the washing up.
3 Over the hill, rode the cowboy.
4 Pam was given a bonus by her boss.
5 Tomorrow, a belt of rain will cross the county and high winds will make driving difficult.
6 Every morning, Maxine was shown a different job in the greenhouses.
7 The children ate all the chocolate but the buns were left untouched.
8 To work at a satisfying job is a pleasure.

OBJECTS

You're probably used to using the word *object* to mean something like a reason for doing something, as in *The object of reading this book is to improve my writing.* In grammatical terms, an **object** is a person, animal or thing which is on the receiving end of a verb.

A very simple sentence will be composed of a subject followed by a verb. For example, *The President laughed.* Many sentences also contain an object too:

Jack hit **John**.
I threw **the ball**.
Peter owns **a Porsche**.

Just as you can ask yourself who is doing the verb when you are looking for its subject, you can ask yourself who or what is, for example, being hit, thrown or owned when you are endeavouring to find an object. The answers to those questions here are *John*, *the ball* and *a Porsche*. These are known as **direct objects** because the action by the subject is done directly to each one.

ACTIVITY 4

Put a ring around the objects in the following sentences:

1 The gangsters robbed the casino.
2 The police rounded up the suspects.
3 The gamblers clutched their winnings.
4 Rudy started a fight.
5 The newspapers reported the events.
6 The magistrate passed sentence.

Many, many sentences have this basic structure of subject, verb, object.

▶ Extended objects (this is not a grammatical term)

Extended objects function in a similar way to extended subjects (above). The objects in the following three sentences are not single items but a group of words:

Sid liked looking after the horse.
Jess wondered what the outcome of the vote would be.
The delegates agreed that nations must co-operate in order to achieve lasting peace.

The subjects here are *Sid*, *Jess* and *The delegates*; the verbs are *liked*, *wondered* and *agreed*. You can check out the object in each case by asking yourself:

What did Sid like?
What did Jess wonder?
What did the delegates agree?

The answers, of course, are:

looking after the horse
what the outcome of the vote would be
that nations must co-operate in order to achieve lasting peace

▶ Indirect objects

In a sentence that includes an **indirect object**, the relationship between it and the subject of the verb is *not quite so close* as that of subject and direct object. The indirect objects are in bold here:

Louise sent **Father Christmas** a letter.
The children gave **their teacher** a present.
Ron gave **the dog** a bone.

The *direct* objects in those sentences are: *a letter*, *a present* and *a bone*. If I write the sentences slightly differently, you can probably see things more clearly:

Louise sent a letter to Father Christmas.
The children gave a present to their teacher.
Ron gave a bone to the dog.

ACTIVITY 5

Underline the indirect objects in the following sentences:

1 Jim will show you the photographs.
2 The schoolteacher set Class IV an exercise.
3 The homoeopath gave her client some pills.
4 The Chancellor's Budget will save us money.
5 The reflexologist gave me a treatment.

▶ Problems with I, me and myself

When speaking, everyone automatically uses the words I and *me* correctly most of the time. The word *I* is always a subject and the word *me* is always a direct or indirect object. The trouble usually arises whenever we have a friend or colleague with us. Look at the following sentences:

I	went to the cinema.
John	went to the cinema.
John and I	went to the cinema.

It's incorrect to say or write: *John and me went to the cinema* because *me* can only be an object, never a subject. There's a very simple way to check whether you need to use *I* or *me* where two people are involved: mentally omit the other person. You'd never say *Me went to the cinema* or *John gave I the tickets.*

Particular problems arise when there's a business associate involved or when we want to be sure to be polite. Many people are worried about sounding pushy and will say: *Mrs Smith and myself went to the meeting.* This is *not* what's needed, though you will frequently hear things like it. The correct way to say this is:

Mrs Smith and I went to the meeting.

That is because there are two people who are both subjects of the verb *went.*

The word *myself* is used like this:

- as the object of a verb where I is the subject: *I scratched myself.*
- for putting stress on an action: *I'll take you to the station myself.*

More problems over the word *myself* occur when the word is incorrectly used as an indirect object. It's not correct to say something like: *Mr Smith gave the tickets to Jane and myself.* This is how it should be done:

Mr Smith gave the tickets to Jane and me.

MORE PROBLEM AREAS

▶ The infuriating 'ing' problem

The good news is that just as the greatest proportion of errors are caused by the lack of a working verb, the greatest proportion of working-verb difficulties are the result of one specific type of problem. This means that once you are aware of this particular issue, you can quickly learn to look out for it. I call it the *ing* problem. It generally occurs when someone is struggling to get a complex idea on paper and lapses momentarily into speech patterns. Here's a simple example: *Ken had been at the football ground all afternoon. Watching the match.*

The problem occurs because this would sound OK if it were spoken aloud. The first sentence is fine, but the second has several problems. To start with, it doesn't make sense. It also lacks both a subject and a fully working verb.

There are two ways we could sort out the problem above:

1 Instead of putting a full stop after *afternoon,* we could use a comma. Then the statement about the match becomes a small piece of information added to the first sentence:

   Ken had been at the football ground all afternoon, watching the match.

   Now we've got just *one* sentence. The working verb is *had been,* and the subject of that verb is *Ken.* We could even omit the comma.

2 We could make sure the second sentence has a subject and the *ing* verb has *at least two parts* to it (look at the **continuous verbs** in Chapter 13 and you'll see these all have more than one part):

   Ken had been at the football ground all afternoon. He **had been watching** the match.

   The second sentence now has both a subject (someone doing the *watching* – He) and a fully working verb (*had been watching*).

Most *ing* verbs must have two or more parts. Our example above has three – *had been watching* – and you'll come across instances where there are four. As long as you remember that any *ing* (continuous) verb at the start of a sentence must have *a subject and at least two parts*, you won't go far wrong. Once you've alerted yourself to the problem, your knowledge of the language will automatically supply you with what you need.

The classic place for the *ing* problem to occur is, as in the example above, just after a full stop. Here it is in a more complex piece of writing by Mark, a student on an environmental science course. This is from an article he wrote on sustainable rural development:

> Even human waste could either be composted or put through a water reed-bed purification system. Thus alleviating the need to be connected to the present archaic disposal system in place today.

His *ing* word – *alleviating* – has no subject and stands all by itself. The simplest way of sorting this one out would be to change the full stop after *system* to a comma. Otherwise, I think Mark would have to change the wording. His second sentence might read like this:

> This type of process would alleviate the need for connecting every dwelling to the archaic disposal system in place today.

The *ing* problem also occurred in Sandra's opening to her essay on *Hamlet*:

> Shakespeare ensures that nothing can be taken at face value in the play *Hamlet* by showing us many different sides to the characters. One side often contradicting another.

Again, the easiest way to sort this one out is to use a comma. With a comma after *characters,* that ungrammatical final sentence would become a phrase in the main sentence, and so the lack of a working verb in those final words would no longer be a problem. If Sandra had wanted to keep that final statement in a separate sentence so that it stands out more, she could have done it in various ways:

(i) We often see one side contradicting another.

With the addition of the working verb 'see' and its subject 'we', the fact that 'contradicting' only has one part no longer matters. Alternatively she could write:

(ii) One side often contradicts another.

In some cases, an *ing* word can appear perfectly legitimately at the start of a sentence if it's part of an **extended subject** (see above) – as in *Collecting wood for the fire was Sid's responsibility.*

Hot tip: notice whether the *ing* word looks forward or back. If it's linked to the previous sentence, it's likely to be a problem. *Collecting* (above) looks forward to *Sid's responsibility*, so it's fine.

By doing Activities 6 and 7, you'll be likely to get a really good grasp of the *ing* problem and so save yourself trouble with it in the future.

ACTIVITY 6

See if you can sort out each of the following sentences in two ways: once as one sentence and once as two. (You might find only one way of writing number 6.)

1 Lucy ran home. Crying all the way.
2 Ken's dog had been annoying the neighbours. Barking all morning.
3 Brad ran down the road with the cheque. Laughing all the way to the bank.
4 The children came home covered in mud. Looking absolutely filthy.
5 English grammar can be difficult. Causing all sorts of problems.
6 I couldn't think how to get the cork out of the bottle. Trying everything I knew.
7 The wolf set off through the forest. Looking for the cottage belonging to Little Red Riding Hood's grandmother.

ACTIVITY 7

Now see if you can sort out these problem sentences. Write two sentences each time:

1 Nursery schools are places where children learn some of the basic skills they will need for primary school. Recognising their names, making simple models, and getting along with others.

2 My local school has started a monthly newsletter. Believing this will help make local people more aware of all the activities available for children and parents.

3 This essay will look at both sides of the argument in order to show the complexity of the issues involved. Crucial issues affecting every aspect of our lives.

▶ Word order

The order in which we arrange the words in any sentence is important for making meaning clear to a reader. Problems sometimes occur when descriptive or explanatory phrases are put beside the wrong person or thing.

Here's an example: *The bride was given away by her father wearing a dress of antique lace.*

Obviously, it was not the father who was wearing the dress. So information on the dress needs to go with the person to whom it refers – the bride. The sentence should read:

> The bride, who was wearing a dress of antique lace, was given away by her father.

Here's another example: *I saw the van arrive standing beside the photocopier.*

This sentence actually states that when the van arrived, it was standing beside the photocopier. Corrected, it could read:

> I saw the van arrive when I was standing beside the photocopier.

or

> When I was standing beside the photocopier, I saw the van arrive.

Look out for this kind of thing when you are proofreading. Aim to check that what you say is logical.

Another problem can arise with the position of the word **only**. It's essential that it sits immediately beside the word or phrase it refers to.

Supposing I were to write *The sprinter decided that she would only eat healthy foods in future.* If I wrote that, I would have implied that this woman would stop socialising, showering, sleeping and everything else that we'd expect in a normal life apart from eating sensibly. This is what I should have written:

> The sprinter decided that she would eat only healthy foods in future.

In the first sentence, the word *only* is attached to what the sprinter would do in general. In the second, it's attached what she'll eat. Now It's unlikely that you misunderstood my meaning in the first sentence. When you're writing on complex topics, however, it's essential to be accurate. It's fatally easy to misuse the word *only*.

▶ Referring to the right person

There is a particularly important thing you need to know about using pronouns (see Chapter 13). Make sure that you have used the relevant noun first and that the pronoun lies fairly close to it. Can you see what's wrong with this extract from Andy's essay?

> In the Neolithic era, many tools were already in use and archaeological remains can tell us much about the undertakings of daily life. They were able to make stone tools for their agricultural needs.

The rule is that a pronoun will stand for the closest previous noun. Generally speaking, as readers, we automatically work out which noun that is without thinking. But, as writers, we need to be in the habit of making sure that we've got things correct so that there can never be any confusion.

When we read Andy's second sentence, we have to look back for a plural noun because he has used the plural pronoun *They*. The closest plural noun is *undertakings*, but that second sentence wouldn't make sense if we were to substitute *undertakings* for *They*. What he actually meant was:

> People were able to make stone tools for their agricultural needs.

The noun *People* had not appeared anywhere, however, so the pronoun *They* couldn't refer to it and shouldn't, therefore, have been used at all.

The more complex the topics you write about, the more important it is to make sure that a pronoun lies close to the noun it stands for. If I write the following, it could become quite confusing: *Education is vital for all children, and financial survival is crucial for everyone. Governments are morally bound to provide it.*

I had intended that the word *it* should refer to *Education*, but the closest singular noun is *survival.* Now *financial survival* is, of course, crucial for everyone. So anybody reading what I wrote is likely to assume that I meant that it is essential for governments to make sure that individuals are given the means for *financial survival.* Obviously, *financial survival* is likely to be partly dependent on education, but my intended focus on the importance of education itself is becoming obscured. What's happened here is that I have not fully explained what I meant. I should have written something like this:

> Education is vital for all children and governments are morally bound to provide it. Without education, a young person has less chance of a job; and without a job, he or she will find financial survival difficult.

Now the word *it* clearly refers to *Education,* which is the closest previous singular noun.

There can also be another difficulty. In the following sentence, who do you think is referred to by the word *her* in the following sentences? *Ruth is Jack's fiancée. He saw Ruth and Wendy coming up the path. He ran out and gave her a hug.*

We would assume that, since Jack is engaged to Ruth, it was Ruth that he hugged. But *Wendy* is the closest noun to *her.* So maybe, for reasons we're not aware of, he hugged Wendy. Maybe she had just suffered a blow to her financial survival and needed cheering up. The meaning just isn't clear from the way I've written the two sentences. Let's rewrite them:

> Ruth is Jack's fiancée. When he saw her coming up the path with Wendy, he ran out and gave her a hug.

Now that I've clearly used the word *her* to relate to Ruth in *he saw her coming up the path*, it must relate to Ruth again when it's used a second time.

If you're writing an essay on one person – Hitler, for example – a good rule of thumb is to use the name at or near the beginning of each new paragraph, then you can continue with *he* or *she* throughout the paragraph. Of course, once you start to include mention of different statesmen and other historical figures involved in situations with (or relating to) Hitler, you're back with the problem of having to check very carefully that any pronouns you use do actually stand for the person you'd intended.

▶ Sentences that fork

Sometimes, you'll want to make a statement that refers to more than one issue in the remainder of the sentence. For example:

> The council official suggested that I should write in with my complaint and explain exactly what happened.

You might like to think of the beginning of the sentence as the handle of a fork and of the issues related to it as prongs. In a well-written sentence, the prongs will all have a similar construction. It's easiest to see this in a diagram:

| The council official suggested that I should | write in with my complaint
and
explain exactly what happened |

Here, each of the prongs begins in exactly the same way with a doing word (a verb). Now look at an example of a fork with four prongs: *Questions on the legalisation of drugs revolve around evidence of harm to users and others, views of the public, cost, and intervention by medical authorities.*

And here it is in a diagram. You can see that each prong begins with a noun:

| Questions on the legalisation of drugs revolve around | evidence of harm to users and others
views of the public
cost
and
intervention by medical authorities |

Sometimes, just a small alteration can make an important difference. Look at Joe's sentence on committees: *For the committee to be viable, members need to understand procedure, they must make succinct contributions to discussions and get their facts right.* There are three things here that committee members must do. Using the prong method, the sentence becomes:

For the committee to be viable,   understand procedure
members need to   make succinct contributions to
                                   discussions
                                            and
                                   get their facts right

So the words 'they must' from the original need to be cut out. It's a small change, but it gives greater control over what's being written. A sentence with matching 'prongs' reads more easily and is clearer and more forceful. All you need to remember is that however you construct the first prong, you just copy that structure for subsequent prongs.

Here's another example, this time with an infinitive (the name of a verb) at the start of each prong:

If someone has a bad fall,   to leave the patient where s/he fell
it's important   to cover him or her with a blanket
                              or coat
                              to phone for an ambulance
                                       and
                              to give reassurance that help is
                              coming

▶ A note for people who like to use the correct terminology

The formal name for my term *working verb* is **finite verb**. The word *finite* means *having boundaries*. This is opposite to the *infinitive,* which is open-ended – like infinity. I also made up the term *ing* word because it's an easy way of referring to those parts of verbs ending in *ing* that can cause difficulties. The correct term is **present participle**. You'll find a present participle in any present continuous verb – for example, *barking* in the following sentence:

The dog **is barking**

The present participle here is *barking*. The infinitive of the verb is *to bark*. The *ing* form also appears in the **past continuous** tense as well as the **future continuous**. You can tell the tense of a continuous verb from the bits that precede the *ing* word. The present continuous tense uses *is* and *are*; the past continuous uses *was* and *were;* the future continuous uses *will be* (see Chapter 13).

The same type of problem as the *ing* problem can occur with a **past participle**, but this happens far less often. A past participle very often ends in *ed*. The past participle of the verb *to bark* is *barked*.

If you're happy with this formal terminology, you'll no doubt use it to think about issues discussed in this chapter. If, like many people, you find jargon a bit intimidating, stick to thinking of *ing* words and *working verbs*.

▶ Breaking the rules

There are certain times when rules can be broken. When we write conversation (see Chapters 7 and 16) there are likely to be lots of sentences without verbs. You'll also find what might appear to be ungrammatical sentences in novels and journalistic writing. This could be because the material is badly produced, but it is more likely to result from the writer having taken a conscious decision to write in a particular way in order to create a particular effect. The omission of a verb can add impact when done occasionally.

It's a good idea, however, not to do this until you are really familiar with writing correctly. It's OK to break the rules once you know what you're doing and why, but unless you're on a creative writing course, your tutors are not likely to be very happy to see sentences that lack either verbs or subjects.

TRADITIONAL CLAUSE ANALYSIS

▶ Main clauses

Ways of analysing grammar are currently undergoing change, but an understanding of traditional clause analysis can improve your ability to write well. In a nutshell, a clause is a group of words containing a working verb and its subject. Look at the following sentence:

My dog Rex fancies the cat.

The working verb is, of course, *fancies,* and the subject is *My dog Rex.* This is a simple sentence consisting of just one clause.

When a sentence contains two or more clauses, one of them will generally be more important than the others. It's called the **main clause**, and It's verb is called the **main verb**. Look at the following sentence (the verbs are in bold type):

My dog Rex **fancies** the cat who often **sleeps** in the dog basket.

Because there are two working verbs here, there are two clauses in the sentence:

1 My dog Rex fancies the cat
2 who often sleeps in the dog basket

You can probably see that the first part of the sentence is more important than the second, which just gives us some extra information about the behaviour of the cat. The main focus here is on the dog. So the main clause in that sentence is:

My dog Rex fancies the cat

A main clause can stand alone as a sentence, and we saw this clause functioning as a simple sentence above.

▶ Subordinate clauses

In any sentence, the name given to any other group of words containing a working verb is a **subordinate clause**. So the words *who often sleeps in the dog basket* form a subordinate clause.

The following sentence also contains two working verbs (which are in bold type). This means that there must be two clauses:

John **was** cross with his dog because it **had eaten** the pie.

The main clause – or statement – is:

John was cross with his dog

The second clause,

> because it had eaten the pie

is a subordinate clause because it gives us some extra information which is less important here than the main statement. The main focus of this sentence is on John's feelings towards his dog.

Now you might feel that the loss of the pie is crucial and therefore more significant than how John felt about the dog. That pie might well have been John's dinner. The issue here, however, is my intention as the writer of the sentence. I want to stress John's anger. The fact that the second clause begins with the word *because* shows that it contains an *explanation* rather than a straightforward statement of the situation, so it must be a subordinate clause.

The sentence about John and his dog could be lengthened again and again by adding more clauses (the verbs are in bold):

> John **was** cross with his dog because it **had eaten** the pie which Sarah **had made**.

> Even though he **is** an easy-going man, John **was** cross with his dog because it **had eaten** the pie which Sarah **had made**.

> Even though he **is** an easy-going man who **loves** animals, John **was** cross with his dog because it **had eaten** the pie which Sarah **had made**.

> Even though he **is** an easy-going man who **loves** animals, John **was** cross with his dog because it **had eaten** the pie which Sarah **had made** while he **had been shopping**.

We now have a sentence with six working verbs in it. That means that there are six clauses – one main and five subordinate. Here, the main clause is still *John was cross with his dog*. All the other clauses merely help to explain the situation. The main clause could stand alone as a fully functioning sentence, just like the one about Rex. It makes sense by itself. Subordinate clauses, however, can't stand alone because they don't make sense by themselves.

INTRODUCTORY WORDS

Subordinate clauses can often be spotted by means of the words that introduce them. Each of the five subordinate clauses in the sentence above about John has an introductory word (or words) that explains how that clause fits the meaning of the sentence: *because, which, even though, who, while. Here are some more possibilities*:

although	where	since
even though	despite	unless
if	until	before

Here's a sentence by George, an Open University student, from his essay on *architecture in the 1920s and 1930s*. By using the words *who* and *which* to relate ideas, George was able to build up a lengthy sentence that functions accurately. The verbs are in bold so that you can more easily spot the separate clauses:

The architect Mies van der Rohe, who **used** the International style vocabulary of flat roofs, white walls, windows flush with walls to suggest volume, and the visible continuous steel supports which **were** part of Le Corbusier's architectural vocabulary of expressed structure, **created** a block of flats which **was** later **copied** all over Berlin.

Here's the analysis:

main clause — The architect Mies van der Rohe **created** a block of flats

subordinate clauses — who **used** the International style vocabulary of flat roofs, white walls, windows flush with walls to suggest volume, and the visible continuous steel supports

which **were** part of Le Corbusier's architectural vocabulary of expressed structure

which **was** later **copied** all over Berlin

Note the very long clause in which the working verb is *used*. This clause contains the word *suggest* which is, of course, also a verb, but it comes as an infinitive – *to suggest* – so it can't have a clause to itself.

Note also that the final clause in the list doesn't contain two verbs but one verb split apart by the word *later*.

▶ Changing the emphasis

Can you spot the main clause in the following sentence?

> I love chips, even though the fat is bad for me and I gain weight every time I eat them.

The most important thing I'm telling you here is that I'm very keen on chips. The main clause is *I love chips* and the main verb is *love*.

There are three more working verbs here: *is, gain* and *eat.* So there are three subordinate clauses:

> even though the fat **is** bad for me
> and I **gain** weight
> every time I **eat** them

Now, just as with John and the pie, you might not agree with me here. You might feel that gaining weight is the most important thing I've mentioned. In my sentence, however, I wanted to *foreground* the information that I'm keen on chips. I wanted the other points to appear less important – that is, subordinate.

If I'd wanted to stress the point on weight gain, I'd need to construct the sentence slightly differently in order to put the focus on weight:

> I **gain** weight every time I **eat** chips, although I **tell** myself that it **does**n't matter and that a little fat **will** not **hurt** me.

Now, the main clause is

> I **gain** weight

and there are four subordinate clauses:

> every time I **eat** chips
> although I **tell** myself
> that it **does**n't matter
> and that a little fat **will** not **hurt** me

The chips are now in a subordinate clause. Notice that the word *not* isn't part of a verb so doesn't show in bold, but it has split apart the two parts of the working verb *will hurt*.

ACTIVITY 8

Try your hand at underlining the **main clause** *in each of the following sentences. It might help to put a ring round all the verbs first. (The main clause will not always be at the beginning of the sentence.)*

1 There are fairies at the bottom of my garden where I haven't cut the grass.
2 Although it is freezing, I refuse to wear woolly undies.
3 Place all gallstones in the bucket provided after you have sewn up the patient.
4 As I came out of the supermarket, I bumped into a small horse.
5 A problem shared is a problem halved, as long as the trouble is either legal or is not divulged to a serving police officer.
6 It's hot.

▶ Co-ordinate clauses

There can sometimes be more than one main clause in a sentence. It's easy to spot these because they will be linked by words like *and, but* or *or*:

My dog Rex **fancies** the cat *and* he **hates** the hamster.
The customer **gave** me an odd look, *but* he **said** nothing.
You **can study** in the library *or* you **can go** home.

In each sentence, the two clauses have the same value – they are each as important as the other. So we call them **co-ordinate clauses**.
Subordinate clauses, as well as main clauses, can be co-ordinate if they are linked by words like *and, but* or *or*:

After you **have added** all the ingredients *and* **put** the mixture in the tin, **bake** the cake for an hour and a half.

Main clause: **bake** the cake for an hour and a half

Subordinate After you **have added** all the ingredients
clauses: and **put** the mixture in the tin

There are co-ordinate subordinate clauses in my sentence about the chips (above):

even though the fat **is** bad for me
and I **gain** weight

There are also co-ordinate subordinate clauses in the *revised* sentence on gaining weight:

that it **does**n't matter
and that a little fat **will** not **hurt** me

▶ Nominal clauses

These are sometimes called noun clauses because the whole clause functions as an item as if it were one noun. In this way, a nominal clause can act as either the subject or object of a verb (see extended subjects and extended objects above). For example:

That nations must co-operate in order to achieve lasting peace is obvious.
nominal clause: that nations must co-operate in order to achieve lasting peace

▶ Adjectival clauses

These are sometimes known as relative clauses. Just like an adjective (see Chapter 13), an adjectival clause describes or explains (qualifies) a noun or pronoun, like this:

The athlete *who won the race* was accused of taking steroids.
That is the girl *whose father taught her Chinese.*
Josh bought the book *which Ray had recommended.*

The nouns that those clauses describes are *athlete, girl* and *book.*
Adjectival clauses usually begin with one of the following words:

which, that, who, whose, whom

Sometimes, a preposition (a linking word) comes first:

This is the boat *in which* the refugees sailed.
Those are the people *with whom* Nelson Mandela had discussions.

The words *where* and *when* can also sometimes be used to begin
adjectival clauses:

I saw the house *where* she used to live.
It was the day *when* the factory burnt down.

▶ Adverbial clauses

Adverbial clauses describe working verbs, infinitives and adjectives.
They can tell us about a long list of different types of information: time,
place, manner, reason, purpose, conditions, results, concessions and
comparison. For example:

I'll make some coffee *when I've finished this report.*	**time**
I planted the apple tree *where we can see it from* *the window.*	**place**
This machine will work *if we give it a kick.*	**condition**
The clock stopped *because I didn't wind it up.*	**reason**

Typical words for introducing adverbial clauses are:

because, as, since, if, unless, whether, although

PHRASES

Phrases are much easier to understand than clauses. In traditional
grammar, a phrase is a group of words that obviously fit together but

don't include a working verb. In the sentences below, the phrases are in bold type:

> Seth moored his boat **at the edge of the lake**.
> **Tomorrow morning**, I'll start painting the dining room.
> The boys were playing football, **despite the rain**.

SUMMARY

A sentence must always:
- make sense by itself
- contain a working verb
- contain a subject for that verb

Subjects and objects
- A **subject**: the person or thing doing the doing, having or being
- An **object**: the person or thing on the receiving end of the doing
- An **indirect object**: the person or thing that is less close to the subject than a direct object and is often prefaced by the word *to*
- *I*   is a subject
- *me* is an object

Some problem areas
- an *ing* verb
  at the beginning of a sentence, it must have at least *two* parts
- word order
  descriptions and explanations must sit beside the person/thing they describe
- referring to the right person/thing
  make sure a pronoun lies close to who or what it refers to
- sentences that fork
  use a matching construction on each prong

Clauses
- main
  the most important statement in a sentence
- subordinate
  a clause that contains less important information

- co-ordinate   a clause (either main or subordinate) that has the same value as its partner clause

- nominal, adjectival and adverbial clauses   these do the job of nouns, adjectives or adverbs

main verb   the working verb in the main clause

phrase   a group of words *without* a working verb

15 Punctuation

This chapter will show
you how to:

► use all punctuation
  marks accurately
► cope with
  apostrophes
► strengthen the
  meaning of what yo
  write

INTRODUCTION

At school, most of us were told that punctuation
is used to show a reader where to take a breath.
Well, there's some truth in that, but it's not the whole story by any
means. Punctuation is used in order to make our writing make sense.
If you were to find a book that had no punctuation in it, you would find
that it was very difficult to understand.

When we talk, we vary the tone of our voices, pause on certain
words for emphasis, frequently change the expressions on our faces,
and may even start waving our arms around or moving about. All this
helps a listener understand what the words mean and even how we
feel about what we're communicating.

But when we're writing, our meaning has to come across via the
words we use and the way we fit them together. All that concerns us is
that there should be *no possible confusion in the meaning* of what we
write. For this, accurate punctuation is absolutely essential.

FULL STOPS

Full stops (American English: periods) are used to separate one statement – plus any related information – from the next. For example:

> Sooner or later, people want to learn to use the Internet. They
> then have access to a vast range of information – ranging from
> courses offered by colleges in distant countries to diagrams of the
> combustion engine.

In the above sentence, I've used a full stop to separate a statement
about the desire to use the Internet from one that explains the results

of using it. The desire and the effect are separate items. Each needed its own sentence.

Here's another example:

> Jo has finally applied to major in modern European history. This was a tough decision for her because her main hobby is going on archaeological digs and she's also fascinated by the medieval period. She eventually decided to study modern history because she wants to teach in secondary education, and she thinks she'd be more likely to get a job with a background in twentieth-century events.

Those three sentences focus separately on:

1 Jo's application to study modern history
2 the reasons why her decision was difficult
3 the reasons why she chose the modern period

Each sentence is concerned with one small but specific area of information on Jo's application for a university place.

Whenever I'm having to read something I find difficult to understand, I find that full stops can be incredibly helpful for understanding meaning. From the beginning of a sentence, I run my eyes down the page until I come to the next full stop so that I know where the next chunk of meaning finishes. Then I can go back to the beginning of the sentence and start finding out how its parts fit together and what it means.

This technique not only allows me to see how much information I need to take in one chunk, but it also makes me feel more comfortable by showing me exactly where the next logical stopping-point is. I can be confident that, when I have understood this sentence, I will have put in place the building block for understanding the next one and, in this way, I can slowly progress through a complex text.

COMMAS

Commas are an essential part of good writing. But, contrary to popular belief, they're not straightforward to deal with. Commas can be some of the trickiest things to get right. Used properly, however, they can be crucial in terms of helping to put across detailed or complex ideas.

▶ Lists

The simplest use of commas is for separating parts of a list:

> I went shopping and bought oranges, apples, pears and bananas.

You've probably been taught never to put a comma before the word *and* in this type of construction, so the punctuation in my example will look correct to you. Actually, the use of a comma before *and* is optional in a list (and essential in other places – see below). In a simple list like the one above, a comma is usually unnecessary, but it can be very useful in some cases in order to make it clear that the last two items in the list are quite separate.

Look at this:

> Knowledge of the identity of objects and features in the environment is obviously valuable to us. Not only does the apparent stability and permanence of most of them create a feeling of security; it also enables us to react to them rapidly and appropriately. We learn by experience what are the uses of houses, shops, and other buildings. (Vernon, 1971 p 13)

In the final sentence, the writer has put in a comma after the word *shops* – which comes before the word *and*. This makes it quite clear that she is talking about three categories of buildings:

> houses
> shops
> other buildings

If she'd omitted the comma after *shops,* it would be possible to read this sentence as talking about two categories:

> houses
> shops and other buildings

This might not seem a crucial distinction when we're talking of things like pears and bananas, but it can be really important when we're trying to distinguish between several complex ideas. On the other hand, it might just be crucial with the fruit. Let's suppose that you are responsible for seeing that fruit and vegetables are packaged for distribution to retailers and you've left the following note for one of your team:

> *Please pack the oranges, apples, pears and bananas in boxes from the store.*

Your team member might have ended up with three boxes of fruit when you'd wanted four. A comma after *pears* would have made your meaning clearer.

▶ Descriptions

Commas are also used to separate two or more descriptive words. For example:

Josh stared at the long, dark snake.
A single, shrill, piercing whistle was heard in the wood.

Notice that a comma is not used between the last descriptive word and the item described. Nowadays, however, commas in lists of descriptive items are frequently omitted altogether.

▶ Marking off extra information at the beginning of a sentence

It's very common for a sentence to begin with some introductory words that set the scene but are not part of that sentence's main statement. These can be marked off with a comma. In the following example, the words *During the summer* fulfil this introductory function:

During the summer, Malcolm laid out his new garden.

The crucial statement here is *Malcolm laid out his new garden*. It's a statement showing what Malcolm did. The fact that he did it during the summer is interesting and important, but it's not as important as the fact that he completed the job.
We all know the next example:

Once upon a time, there lived an old king who had a lovely daughter.

Those last two examples both relate to time. Here are two that relate to place:

Underneath the cushion, I found the scissors I'd lost.
Beyond the town, the mud road stretched into the distance.

Commas are very useful for marking off all kinds of extra information from the main statement in a sentence:

Stretching up on his hind legs, the dog peered over the low fence.
Wrapped in blankets, the walking wounded shuffled to the helicopter.

▶ Marking off extra information at the end of a sentence

Here, the main statement comes first and the extra information follows it:

Six boys were following the old man, jeering and catcalling.
Meera used to make all the family's clothes, helped by her ancient sewing machine.

▶ Marking off extra information in the middle of a sentence

It's often necessary to fit an extra piece of information into the middle of a sentence. In this case, two commas are necessary – one before and one after. The problem here is that people often forget the second one. Here's how it needs to be done:

Maria, the girl who defied a brutal regime, walked to the river.

Here, the main statement is:

Maria walked to the river

The extra information is particularly interesting, but for the sentence to be easily read and make complete sense, the two commas are essential.

I wonder if you agreed with me when I said that the statement 'Maria walked to the river' was more important than the fact that she 'defied a brutal regime'. In terms of Maria's whole life, a trip to the river seems a minor occurrence when compared with her bravery. But in this particular sentence, I'm *focusing* on the walk and I've made that the main statement in my sentence. So Maria's bravery is of secondary importance in that particular sentence.

Now look at the following examples:

Paul, the man Josie had always loved, eventually married Kate.
I ran, stumbling and moaning, back to the hut.
My dog Bruno, who barks ferociously, wouldn't hurt a fly.

Notice that, in each case, you could leave out the extra information and the sentence would still make perfect sense:

Paul eventually married Kate.
I ran back to the hut.
My dog Bruno wouldn't hurt a fly.

By putting commas around the extra information each time, I've demonstrated that I want my readers to concentrate on the other material in the sentences. For example, I want people to concentrate on Bruno's gentleness rather than his bark.

▶ Changing meaning by using a comma

The effect of what we write can be subtly changed by the way we use commas. Look at the following two sentences and see if you can work out why I've used a comma in the first but not in the second:

Maria went for a long walk, taking her lunch in a small bag.
Maria went for a long walk across the fields to the river.

This is where the fun starts. Lots of people would want to put a comma in the second sentence as well as the first, but there's a subtle difference. We're taught that a sentence always makes a statement. It would actually be more correct to say that a sentence always contains a statement. It may also contain other information as well, as we've seen in those examples above.

In the first sentence here, the statement is

Maria went for a long walk

and the words

taking her lunch in a small bag

give us some extra information. But in the second sentence, the statement is the whole sentence. The information on where Maria went is crucial to and part of that statement. That sentence, as it is written at present, must be taken in one go.

But we could write this story slightly differently and so change the *emphasis.* We might want to say:

Maria went for a long walk, slowly crossing the fields to the river.

Now the 'fields' and the 'river' become slightly less important. They are now extra information. The main feature of the sentence is the 'long walk' and the itinerary takes second place. The change in emphasis has been achieved in part by changing (in this case adding) punctuation.

▶ A common problem with commas

There's a problem with the following sentence that many people wouldn't spot. I wonder if you can see it: *I went into town to do some shopping last week, it took me ages.* We've said above that a sentence always contains a statement. Well, sometimes it contains more than one. The statements here are:

I went into town to do some shopping last week
it took me ages.

The problem here arises partly because we've all been told that the reason for using punctuation is to allow the reader to take a breath. So if I read that sentence aloud, pausing at the comma, anyone listening to me would understand perfectly. This is because they'd hear two separate statements *as if they'd been separated by a full stop.*

If there are two equally important statements within one sentence, we must show how the second relates to the first. I can sort out this problem by adding the word *and*:

> I went into town to do some shopping last week, and it took me ages.

Now it's ten to one that you're thinking, 'That's wrong. When I was at school, we were told never to put a comma before *and*.' Well, if you think back to the simple use of commas to separate items in a list – for example, oranges, apples, pears and bananas – I think you'll see that it was in relation to *lists* that the rule was drummed into you. That rule about not putting a comma before *and* only applied to *lists* (and, as I said above, the practice is optional there anyway).

So let's look at some more instances of sentences containing more than one important statement:

> Sue's grandma still rides a bike, she's 93.
> I'm going to get rid of my car, it's so old it's falling apart.
> There was a queue at the traffic lights, I took a left turn to miss them.

All these sentences need sorting out because the meaning isn't quite clear. There are two possible solutions. I could either replace the comma in each sentence with a full stop, or I could add a connecting word (or words) in each case to explain how the second statement relates to the first, like this:

> Sue's grandma still rides a bike. She's 93.
> Sue's grandma still rides a bike, *even though* she's 93.

> I'm going to get rid of my car. It's so old it's falling apart.
> I'm going to get rid of my car *because* it's so old it's falling apart.

> There was a queue at the traffic lights. I took a left turn to miss them.
> There was a queue at the traffic lights, so I took a left turn to miss them.

Can you spot the problems with commas in the following piece of student writing? Claire has written a poignant description of a time when she had to travel without her children:

> *It felt most strange watching my children wave me off, they looked so small standing on the vast now empty platform. As the train pulled away, they had tried to keep up by running alongside, they were aware that this was not possible but had tried anyway.*

In the first line, Claire needed to separate the two statements with a full stop. Short sentences can have impact and would work particularly well here because both statements about the children would then be emphasised, and we would be forced to take the information more slowly and so to empathise even more with the writer. There's also a problem with the comma after 'alongside' because there's an important statement on each side of it. I think that Claire could improve her piece with a full stop here too.

> It felt most strange watching my children wave me off. They looked so small standing on the vast now empty platform. As the train pulled away, they had tried to keep up by running alongside. They were aware that this was not possible but had tried anyway.

Commas need very careful handling. A good rule of thumb is: *never use one unless you know exactly why you are doing so.* They're better omitted than used incorrectly.

ACTIVITY 1

Add commas, if and when necessary, to the following sentences:

1. Marian has travelled in France Spain Australia India and the USA.
2. We were watched by a lean ageing kangaroo.
3. After two weeks on buses and trains it was a relief to smell sea air.
4. Jason our guide walked fast and spoke little.
5. Air disasters it is well known are fewer than accidents on the roads
6. Taking a foreign holiday despite problems with accommodation currency and language can be a liberating experience.
7. Day after day the grey rocks dotted here and there with small plants formed a backdrop for our trek.
8. Taking a foreign holiday can be a liberating experience.

SEMICOLONS

A semicolon is usually thought of as indicating a longer pause than that given by a comma. Well, that's partly true, but a rather better definition would be to say that it indicates a slightly shorter pause than that given by a full stop. The reason for turning the definition around is because it now carries an implicit reminder that, when you use a semicolon, whatever you write on *each* side of it *must* function *as if it were a separate sentence.* That means that there must be a clear statement, including a subject and working verb (see Chapters 13 and 14) on *each* side of the semicolon – like this:

> Many Westerners like Eastern food; Indian restaurants and takeaways, for example, have opened in most British towns.

The working verb in the first statement is 'like' and its subject is 'many Westerners'. In the second statement, the working verb is 'have opened' and its subject is 'Indian restaurants and takeaways'.

The use of semicolons is generally a matter of choice. They could almost always be replaced by full stops without harming the sense of what you write. Their usefulness lies in allowing you to keep within one sentence statements that are very closely related to each other. Like all other punctuation marks, they are used to assist meaning.

Semicolons could be used as another way to sort out the problem with commas shown in the previous section. Here's another way to improve those problem sentences:

> Sue's grandma still rides a bike; she's 93.
> I'm going to get rid of my car; it's so old it's falling apart.
> There was a queue at the traffic lights; I took a left turn to miss them.

Semicolons can also be used in certain lists:

> I went shopping for apples, pears and bananas; flour, sugar and spaghetti; milk, cheese and yoghurt.

In this case, the semicolons separate one *group* of items from another type.

Semicolons can also be very useful for separating sections in a long and complex sentence where:

(a) the sentence follows a pattern
and
(b) you need to use commas within the separate sections.

For example:

> It was decided that a steering group should be formed, consisting of six members; that publicity, particularly via the local media, would be essential; and that a celebrity, preferably from TV, should be approached to be patron of the new society.

The pattern shows up clearly if I make the sentence into a table:

It was decided	that a steering group should be formed ...
	that publicity ... would be essential
	that a celebrity ... should be approached ...

I've used semicolons (above) to separate those three areas. You need semicolons, however, *only when the individual sections themselves contain commas*. The following sentence needs none:

> It was decided to form a steering group consisting of six members, to seek publicity via the media, and to approach a TV celebrity for the position of chairperson.

ACTIVITY 2

*In the following paragraph, it would be possible to replace **two** of the full stops with semicolons. Which two? Why?*

> Many people have strong opinions on the use of the private car. Some feel that it has liberated the individual and brought with it a new level of personal freedom. Others feel that the threat to the environment posed by fuel emissions must be curtailed. Governments can find themselves caught between these mutually exclusive standpoints. They don't want to be seen as autocratic and reactionary. At the same time, they are aware of global warming and of the fact that they are likely to be held responsible for environmental decline.

COLONS

Colons are handy for introducing lists:

> I bought various items at the hardware shop: nails, paint, brushes, a screwdriver, a hammer and some string.

They are also useful for introducing quotations, like this:

> When Hamlet sees his mother die and realises the poisoned drink was meant for him, his response is swift:
>
> > O villainy! Ho! Let the door be lock'd.
> > Treachery! Seek it out. [V.ii.317]

If you look through this book, you'll see that I've used colons a great deal for introducing instructions and explanations. Here is another example:

> Make the sauce as follows: first melt an ounce of butter in a saucepan, then add a tablespoon of flour, and finally slowly add about half a pint of liquid.

There's a further use for colons in which they indicate a kind of balance between the two halves of a sentence and in which the second half explains the first. For example:

> I'm an optimist: my glass is generally half full rather than half empty.
> Television can be seen as having both positive and negative aspects: it is an unrivalled means of communication, but it can ultimately dull the responses of viewers.

BRACKETS

Brackets can be used in order to add extra information in a rather similar way to the use of a pair of commas:

> Dale (who was always a difficult child) refused to go to school until he had been bribed with the promise of hard currency.

Brackets can also contain information that qualifies what is being said in a sentence:

> Britain's Queen Victoria was (in most respects) a strong woman.

Or they can add extra information which, while being important, doesn't strictly fit into the grammatical construction of the sentence as it stands:

> Queen Victoria (1819–1901) ruled during a period of industrial expansion.
> In my garden (I have a small plot at the side of the house) I grow vegetables and roses.

You'll notice that the examples on Dale and Queen Victoria's strength can be read straight through, including what's in the brackets, without harming the sense. The next example doesn't read quite so smoothly, and the section in brackets in the final sentence is grammatically quite separate from the main sentence. All of these are acceptable, but the first two are rather neater than the others.

DASHES

These can be used in a similar way to brackets to add a separate piece of information to a sentence. When information is in brackets, it can seem to be cut off from the rest of the sentence. Using dashes can keep the information in the foreground. When you use a pair of dashes in the middle of a sentence, you'll need to make sure that whatever lies between them fits into your sentence smoothly and grammatically, like this:

> Britain's Queen Victoria was – in most respects – a strong woman.

A dash can sometimes be particularly handy, however, for adding a piece of information at the *end* of a sentence *without* having to fit it carefully to the grammar of the sentence. This use of a dash can be dramatic, but if you do it too often in essays, your work may look slipshod. Keep it up your sleeve for occasional use only. It's done like this:

There were a number of pieces missing from the puzzle – sixteen, in fact.

Accurate punctuation ensures that meaning is clear – inaccuracies can cause confusion.

Always leave a space before and after a dash so that it won't be confused with a hyphen.

HYPHENS

Hyphens are used in various ways to join two words. They look similar to dashes, but they are actually slightly shorter and there is no space between a hyphen and the letters on either side of it. Hyphens can be a bit tricky because of the number of different rules on how and where to use them. Their use is subject to change over time, and, in general, they are being used less and less frequently nowadays. The British tend to use more of them than the Americans.

Sometimes, two words that began life separately are, for a time, written with a hyphen and finally come to be known as just one word. For example, the word *today* was once written *to-day*. Language changes all the time – new words come into use and certain words fall out of use, sometimes becoming so old-fashioned that they don't seem relevant to our lives any more.

Hyphens have three uses:

1 at the end of a line where there's no space for an entire word

For example:

The British comedian Eddie Izzard has suggested that when your cat is behind your couch purring, the situation may not be as innocent as it seems. Although you may think your moggy is peacefully resting, he may actually be drilling. 'Some of them go down as much as forty feet,' he said.

When splitting a word in this manner, aim to break it smoothly in relation to both the sound and the appearance of the word. It would have looked a bit strange if I had broken *peacefully* like this: *peacefully*.

2 in words that are regularly written with a hyphen

For example:

book-keeping
re-export

In both of these words, the hyphen is used to avoid awkwardness with a double letter. This is often a clue as to whether or not you need to use a hyphen. But it's not a hard and fast rule; many people now write *cooperate* rather than *co-operate.*

3 for joining two or more words to make a new one

For example:

a sky-blue dress
a half-eaten sandwich

Some people, however – especially companies who advertise their products – have begun to omit hyphens in these cases and to write the words separately. This can cause confusion. If the hyphen is omitted, it must be possible for both words to be *separately* applicable to the word being described. If I had written, *A sky blue dress*, I would have implied that the dress was both *sky* and *blue.* The first of these is clearly nonsense. If I omit the hyphen from my description of the sandwich, I would imply that it was both *half* a sandwich *and* an *eaten* one – which also sounds pretty silly, because if it was *eaten,* it wasn't there at all.

If you say aloud to yourself the examples of the dress and the sandwich, you'll probably notice that, when we combine two words to describe something, we run them together and speak them more quickly than when we are using them separately. Thinking about the sound can be a rather useful way to help to decide whether you need to join with a hyphen words that are usually separate.

EXCLAMATION MARKS

The only place to use exclamation marks is in dialogue – in stories or drama. As far as academic writing is concerned, we need to demonstrate important points through our writing itself and not rely on exclamation marks to do the work. In fact, these marks are actually frowned upon when they appear in essays because they indicate strong emotion, and the best essays are generally logical and unemotional.

Exclamation marks are, however, very handy in stories for showing when someone is shouting or screaming, like this:

> 'Let go!' yelled Mick.

or

> 'Fire!' shouted the Principal.

or

> 'Help!' screamed Pat.

QUESTION MARKS

These are sometimes called *interrogation marks* – particularly in American English. The main thing here is to remember to use them. It's amazing how easy it is to forget to use a question mark after a question. The lack of one is, however, horribly apparent to a reader. As with an exclamation mark, never use a full stop as well as a question mark, and don't forget that a question mark always terminates a sentence, so you need to follow it with a capital letter.

Questions can be a real problem in essays. There's a section on how to deal with reporting questions that others have asked in Chapter 16 and another on raising questions in essays in Chapter 2.

APOSTROPHES

Apostrophes have two jobs to do – and these are quite distinct. One is to show when there's a letter (or letters) missing from a word. This will usually be in conversational speech or informal writing. This is called **contraction**. The other is to show when something *belongs* to someone or something. This is called **possession**.

▶ **Contraction**

This is really simple. In the following sentence, I've used an apostrophe to show that the letter *o* is missing:

I didn't get where I am today by ignoring apostrophes.

If I had written this in full, I would have put *I did not get ...* You might have noticed that there are a good many contractions in this book because I'm writing conversationally – as if I were talking to you.

The following table gives a selection of the kind of examples that are found in everyday speech:

You'll find this easy.	You will
We *won't* be long.	will not
I *wouldn't* do that if I were you.	would not
He'll be here next week.	He will
They'll do their best.	They will
The children *aren't* ready.	are not
I *wasn't* at work today.	was not

▶ **Possession**

This is where you may be having difficulties. You probably have some vague memories from school about putting an apostrophe before or after an *s* but it's ten to one that you can't remember why or when; and a lot of people have become so muddled as to think that every plural word needs an apostrophe. That is certainly not the case. Apostrophes used for possession show when something belongs to somebody.

Because there's been such confusion over possession, I'd like to suggest that you ignore that old 's' rule and use a rule that is newer and simpler. All you need to remember is to put an apostrophe *immediately after the owner*. And don't start thinking about where to put it until you've actually written the words down. Take the following sentence:

The dog's tail got caught in the door.

Whenever you write down something where possession seems to be involved, you just ask yourself one simple question: who is the owner? In this case, we need to ask: who owns the tail? The answer is the dog.

So you put the apostrophe immediately after 'dog'. Listen carefully to your answer each time and then follow it exactly. It's really simple:

1 Jacks scooter was lying on the grass.
   Q Who owns the scooter?
   A Jack
   Jack's scooter was lying on the grass.

2 From the hill, we could see hundreds of cars lights on the motor-way.
   Q Who (or what) owns the lights?
   A the cars
   From the hill, we could see hundreds of cars' lights on the motor-way.

3 We could see the elephants trunks waving over the wall.
   Q Who owns the trunks?
   A the elephants
   We could see the elephants' trunks waving over the wall.

4 Peoples tastes differ.
   Q Who owns the tastes?
   A people
   People's tastes differ.

If you try to *combine* this rule with the old 's' rule, you'll confuse yourself. Make a clean break, apply the new rule, and, I promise you, you can't go wrong. By the way, if you've ever worried about using an apostrophe for the *Smiths* or the *Joneses,* the following might help:

> I borrowed old Mr Smith's lawnmower last week. Then I lent it to Mrs Jones' aunt. The Smiths' son was furious, but the Joneses' daughter thought it was all very funny.

Smith is a fairly easy name to cope with as it doesn't end in 's'. Where a name does end in *s*, it sounds a bit odd to add another one to indicate possession. So all we need is an apostrophe – *Mrs Jones' aunt.* It would not be wrong, however, to add another 's' if you prefer – *Mrs Jones's aunt.* The name *Jones* is changed to *Joneses* (showing that the word is plural) when we want to talk about the family. An apostrophe is added to this if, and only if, we want to indicate possession. If we write *the Joneses' daughter,* we mean the daughter of Mr and Mrs Jones.

▶ It's and its

The meanings of these two, similar-looking words are very different. The first is a **contraction** and the second shows **possession**. There's just one problem here: how do we remember which is which? Well, again, there's a very simple solution. Each time you write *its,* you just ask yourself, 'Do I mean *it is*?' (Occasionally, you might mean *it has*). If the answer is 'Yes', you put in an apostrophe and move on. If it is 'No', you just move on anyway. The important thing here is not to hesitate and start wondering if you really have got it right. Just ask yourself the question and act decisively on the answer.

CONTRACTION

The contraction *it's*, meaning *it is*, is used in conversation, in stories, and in informal writing such as letters to friends. I've used it a good deal in this book because I didn't want to sound formal. In your essays, however, stick to writing *it is* because that is the correct form for academic writing.

POSSESSION

The word *its* (without an apostrophe) is one of a group of words that deal with possession. Some of them also end in 's', but none of them uses an apostrophe. The others are: *my, his, her/hers, our, ours, your, yours, their, theirs.* They are called **possessive adjectives**, but it's not necessary to remember that term. Here's the word *its* used to show possession:

> The cat ate *its* dinner.
> The ceremony moved towards *its* ending.
> The storm was at *its* height.

As a general rule, use an apostrophe only when you are certain you know where it goes. An apostrophe in the wrong place looks much worse than one omitted.

Note: Until quite recently, items like *VIPs* and *the 1990s* were always given an apostrophe (*VIP's, 1990's*). Now, however, it has become usual to omit the apostrophe. I think this is neater.

ACTIVITY 3

Add apostrophes where necessary to the following sentences:

1 Its only when I laugh that it hurts.
2 Its a lovely day today.
3 Johns fathers got his brothers coat.
4 When its raining, that dog always stays in its kennel.
5 Its easy to see how the cat shut its paw in the Browns gate.
6 The hyenas eyes were visible in the bushes everywhere we looked.

SUMMARY

a full stop is used to	separate one statement and its closely-related information from another
a comma is used to	separate items in a list
	separate two or more words used descriptively
	separate any two statements that are linked by *and, so, but, because,* etc.
	mark off extra information from the main statement at the beginning or end of a sentence
	mark off extra information in the middle of a sentence (two commas)
a semicolon is used to	keep two statements closer than a full stop (*Note:* whatever is on *each* side must have a subject and working verb)
a colon is used to	introduce a list, an explanation, a quotation, some instructions, or to demonstrate balance between two statements
brackets are used to	incorporate extra information
dashes are used to	incorporate extra information at the end of a sentence (one dash) or in the middle (two dashes)
a hyphen is used to	split a word at the end of a line
	show the separate parts of certain word
	join two words to make a new word

an exclamation mark is used to	demonstrate passion in speech in either fiction or drama
a question mark is used to	indicate a question (usually used when giving actual speech or in drama)
an apostrophe is used to	show contraction (a letter or letters missing) or possession
its is used to	show possession
it's is used to	stand instead of *it is* or *it has*

16 Getting Conversation on Paper

This chapter will show you how to:

► Use the rules for writing down what someone says
► Change what someone has said into reported speech

INTRODUCTION

We all know that we need to use speech marks (sometimes called inverted commas) when we write down what someone says – **direct speech**. But getting it right is not always straightforward. This chapter will give you clear examples so that from now on you'll find it simple. The ability to write direct speech accurately can be important in essays. You might want to quote something said on TV or radio by a politician or academic. Writing direct speech creatively and convincingly is also essential for writing articles and short stories.

Reported speech is the term given to relating what someone has said accurately but without using speech marks. The method can be very useful for essays and essential in reports, formal letters and committee minutes.

SETTING OUT DIRECT SPEECH

The term **direct speech** refers to the *actual words* that somebody says. Everything they say is shown *inside* speech marks:

"The garden is going to look wonderful."

Using the double speech marks allows you to distinguish actual speech from quotations – for which you use single marks (see Chapter 3). You can also see that the speech begins with a capital letter and ends with a full stop, just like any ordinary sentence. And notice, too, that the full stop is *inside* the speech marks – this is most important.

There are also hard and fast rules on how we show who is speaking:

Tom said, "The garden is going to look wonderful."

Here, I've begun with the speaker's name followed by the word *said*. I've added a comma and then I've carried on just as before. We can also do this the other way around. But here there's an extra rule to remember. Look at this:

"The garden is going to look wonderful," said Tom.

This time, I had to put a comma at the end of the speech instead of a full stop, because I was going on to explain at this point (rather than at the beginning) who spoke. Just like the full stop, the comma goes *inside* the speech marks. And because I've used a comma, there's a small 's' on *said*.

Here are two more examples of those two ways for showing who speaks:

Tom said, "There's a lot of earth to shift."
"There's a lot of earth to shift," said Tom.

Whichever way you write this, the *punctuation mark* that follows the words spoken is *always inside* the speech marks.

Imagine that Tom and his neighbours in some flats are reclaiming a piece of waste ground where they live. It's hard work, and Tom, who's in charge, won't always be speaking calmly. We can show this in two ways: by the use of an exclamation mark to show that he's raising his voice, and by changing the word *said* to indicate something more expressive:

Tom shouted, "Don't leave that saw there!"
"Don't leave that saw there!" shouted Tom.

Perhaps you've spotted a further problem here. I wasn't able to use a comma following the word 'there' in the second sentence because I needed an exclamation mark to show that Tom shouted. An exclamation mark functions just like a full stop in that it marks the end of a sentence. So you might reasonably have expected the word *shouted* to begin with a capital letter. This, however, is the one exception to the rule on capitals following question marks and exclamation marks. The word *said,* or any substitute for it, always starts with a small letter when it follows somebody's actual words.

Here are some more examples:

> "Mind your backs!" yelled Jeff.
> Jeff yelled, "Mind your backs!"
> "Where do you want these planks?" asked Angie.
> Angie asked, "Where do you want these planks?"

There's just one more basic rule for setting out speech. Sometimes, when writing, we want to put *he said* or *she said* in the middle of what a person says, rather than at the beginning or the end. We do it like this:

> "I want to help," said Tom's six-year-old son, "when you build the pond."

This construction can add a little tension because we have to wait until the end of the sentence to find out the full implication of what is being said. You can see that we don't use a capital letter to start the second half of the sentence. That's because it's *not* the beginning of a sentence. If we could actually hear the boy speaking, we would hear:

> "I want to help when you build the pond."

The following example is constructed in the same way:

> "This garden," said the TV reporter, "is being constructed entirely by the residents of the Brook Lane flats."

Notice that, in each of these split items of speech, there are two commas – one after the first part of the speaker's sentence and one after the small section that shows the speaker's name with the word *said* – or whatever word is used to replace this.

At this point, you might like to have a go at the following activity to practise these rules for speech. Refer to my examples while you do part A. Then see if you can do part B without looking anything up.

ACTIVITY 1

Add speech marks, all necessary punctuation and capital letters to the following sentences.

Part A
1 jack said my partner is expecting a baby
2 i was born in tunis said pierre
3 where is the post office asked the tourist
4 the toddler yelled i want an ice cream
5 that dog said john always disappears when i want to bath it
6 why asked tom have you put the beer under my bed

Part B
1 mary said the eggs are in the fridge
2 high tide will be at three this afternoon said the sailor
3 come back here yelled the policeman
4 sam asked politely how much extra will I have to pay
5 I havent laughed so much said ben since the chicken coop collapsed
6 the main difficulty explained the leader will be getting the tents across the river

Here's an example of how a local newspaper might report on a community project using direct speech:

The residents of the Brook Lane flats are working flat out. Since the beginning of the year, they've been transforming an unsightly piece of waste ground into a gorgeous garden. Angie Stevens, who works on the plot every weekend, told me, "I never thought I'd be doing this."

Angie's partner, Tom, was voted Chief Gardener. "We've had a lot of support from the Council," he explained. "They donated spare paving stones for the path and they're going to organise an opening ceremony."

Even the children have been getting involved: "My twins rush home from school every day to help," said Jeff Rogers with a smile. When I asked what the residents would be doing next, Jeff grinned. "We've got our eyes on the Town Hall gardens," he laughed.

Remember that the words inside speech marks are those that were actually spoken. Of course, in newspapers, journalists sometimes give approximations of the words someone said, but doing that could get you into hot water in academic work.

ACTIVITY 2

The following is part of a reporter's magazine article on Bob Crooks, a glassmaker. Punctuation marks, capital letters and speech marks have been omitted. Copy out the extract, putting them all back in.

i sense theres an excitement for bob crooks in work where hes in dialogue with his material mixing colours and never being one hundred per cent sure of the final outcome because of the speed of the materials reactions
i dont want to battle against the material he says so in the final heating i let the glass do what it wants to do its by this means that bob is able to create the fluid forms hes known for hes influenced by geometry architecture and the natural world I cant make anything as beautiful as what's in nature he goes on but I like taking elements of different things and turning them into something whole

---

INDIRECT or REPORTED SPEECH

Reported speech makes a statement *about* what someone said. For this, we do away with speech marks, but we must keep as close as possible to the original words:

Actual speech   Ron said, "The library is closed."
Reported speech   Ron said that the library was closed.

Here, there have, been some specific changes:

a word has been added   *that*
tense change   the verb *is* has changed to *was*

When we write reported speech, we need to add the word *that* before the body of what was said. If you want a more informal effect, you can omit *that,* but it's best to use it in all academic work.

We also have to go back in time because we are now referring to something that happened earlier. In the example above, the present simple tense has changed to the past simple. The future tenses (see below) can be a little tricky, but you doubtless get it right when you speak. There, *will* changes to *would*.

Here are the key issues for reported speech, followed by an example of each:

1 time change
2 pronoun change
3 place change
4 the format for questions
5 the format for greetings

EXAMPLES OF EACH ISSUE

1a Time (tense) change

Actual	The MPs said, "We <u>are</u> winning the battle for votes."	**Present continuous**
Reported	The MPs said that they <u>were</u> winning the battle for votes.	**Past continuous**
Actual	The MPs said, "We <u>won</u> the battle for votes."	**Past simple**
Reported	The MPs said that they <u>had won</u> the battle for votes."	**Past perfect**
Actual	The MPs said, "We <u>were winning</u> battle for votes."	**Past continuous**
Reported	The MPs said that they <u>had been winning</u> the battle for votes.	**Past perfect continuous**

1b Time change: future tenses

Actual	"We <u>will</u> put forward improved policies on housing and taxation," promised the members of the new party.	**Future simple**
Reported	The members of the new party promised that they <u>would</u> put forward improved policies on housing and taxation.	

Actual	"We <u>will</u> be reducing VAT immediately," said the new Prime Minister.	**Future continuous**
Reported	The new Prime Minister said that the party <u>would</u> be reducing VAT immediately.	

1c Changes to specific times

Actual	"I bought a new car <u>yesterday</u>," said Ruth.
Reported	Ruth said that she had bought a new car <u>the previous day.</u>

Actual	"I bought a new car <u>today</u>," said Ruth.
Reported	Ruth said that she had bought a new car <u>that day</u>.

Actual	The tennis coach said, "It's raining <u>now</u>."
Reported	The tennis coach said that it was raining <u>then</u>.

or

The tennis coach said that it was raining <u>at the time</u>.

2 Pronoun change

Actual	"<u>I</u>'m finishing <u>my</u> essay," said Nick.
Reported	Nick said that <u>he</u> was finishing <u>his</u> essay.

Actual	"<u>We</u> went to the cinema," said the children.
Reported	The children said that <u>they</u> had been to the cinema.

Actual	Beverley said, "<u>I</u>'m exhausted."
Reported	Beverley said that <u>she</u> was exhausted.

3 Place change

Actual	"I'm sure I put the money in <u>this</u> box," said Anne.
Reported	Anne said that she was sure she had put the money in <u>that</u> box.

or

Anne said that she was sure she had put the money in <u>the relevant</u> box.

Actual	Rob said, "The letters are all <u>here</u>."
Reported	Rob said that the letters were all <u>there</u>.

4 Questions

Actual   "Where's the science block?" <u>said</u> John.
Reported   John <u>asked</u> where the science block was.

or

John <u>asked</u> for directions to the science block.

Actual   "Why is Sam going?" <u>said</u> Ben.
Reported   Ben <u>asked</u> why Sam was going.

Actual   "What's the time?" <u>said</u> Ben.
Reported   Ben <u>asked</u> what the time was.

or

Ben <u>asked</u> for the time.

In each of the examples on questions, the questioning word (*where, why, what*) is often repeated in reported speech, but the order of words is different. Note also that we *never* use a question mark in any kind of reported speech. A reported question isn't actually asking anything; it merely points out that a question has been asked by someone at some point.

5 Greetings

Actual   "Good morning, ladies and gentlemen," said Mr Fox.
Reported   Mr Fox <u>greeted</u> everyone.

▶ Some exceptions

- If your friend Alice says to you, "I like cats," and you tell your brother, Ned, you'll probably say, "Alice likes cats." So you've copied the present tense because the situation (Alice liking cats) is permanent rather than relevant to a particular occasion.
- If Alice says to you, "I'll come and see you on Thursday," and you report *this* to Ned before Thursday, you'll probably say, "Alice says she'll come round on Thursday." If Alice doesn't appear, however, it changes to "Alice said she'd come round today." (i.e. *she would*)

ACTIVITY 3

See if you can now turn the following eight brief statements made by Kwame into reported speech using the rules above. The first one has been done for you.

1 I drive to work every day," said Kwame.
   Kwame said that he drove to work every day.
2 "I'm driving a Ford, now," said Kwame.
3 "I drove to Italy last month," said Kwame.
4 "I've driven 500 miles this week," said Kwame.
5 "I've been driving for ten years now," said Kwame.
6 "I was driving at night when the brakes failed," said Kwame.
7 "I'll drive to Spain next year," said Kwame.
8 "I'll be driving a Porsche next year," said Kwame.

SUMMARY

Checklist for writing direct speech
- put speech marks around the *exact words spoken*
- begin with a *capital letter*
- keep punctuation *inside* speech marks
- use a lower-case 's' for *said*
- when following the speech with *he said/she said,* add a *comma* before closing the speech marks
- when using *he said/she said* before the words spoken, add a *comma* after *said*

Checklist for reported speech
- add the word *that*
- go back one tense
- change *will* to *would*
- check pronouns
- check time and place
- check any questions and omit question marks
- check greetings

Part Four
Moving On

17 Your CV

This chapter will show you how to:

▶ gather relevant materials
▶ organise layout
▶ write a basic CV
▶ vary your text for specific jobs

INTRODUCTION

Sooner or later, everyone needs a CV, and the good news is that, once you've got the basics in place, writing later CVs should be a reasonably painless process. You just build on your earlier work.

Once you have a CV in place, you can use it to apply for valuable part-time experience while you're still at college or university. Students who've gained some experience in their chosen field early on are likely to be looked at especially favourably by employers.

Your first task will probably be the most time-consuming. You'll need to gather together every scrap of information you have about your education and your work experience – whether that's been paid or voluntary. If your first thought is that you possess nothing, or that you've never done anything worth mentioning, don't worry – that's a common response. This chapter will explain how to gather information and create a document that shows you in the best possible light. And that goes for everybody. There are no exceptions.

WHAT IS A CV?

The initials CV stand for *curriculum vitae*. This is a Latin phrase that just means *the course of your life*. A CV will show an employer what jobs you've done, what schools and colleges you've attended and what qualifications you've got or are studying for.

A CV is a document that:

- contains essential information about you
- presents you in the best possible light
- is essential for job applications
- is 50 per cent of the means by which you get an interview
- can be referred to by both parties during an interview

If you're planning on working in education, central or local government or other public bodies, you're likely to have to fill in an application form rather than sending a CV. All the information for this, however, will be contained in your CV (except your statement – see Chapter 18), and it's just a matter of copying from your CV what you need in the order shown on the form. So do prepare a CV.

SELLING YOURSELF

The job of a CV is to secure you an interview. You may find the idea of selling yourself a bit strange or unpalatable, but whether you like it or not, a CV is the first stage in your sales pitch. The whole object is to persuade an employer to want to see you. For you to reach the interview stage, your application must demonstrate how that employer would benefit from having you on the payroll.

Imagine the scenario: you send off your application for a job on which you're really keen. Then you watch the post for a response. Meanwhile, your prospective employer is receiving anything up to 200 or more applications and must choose five or six applicants to call for interview. He or she will bin any CVs that are untidy, misspelt or ungrammatical without even bothering to read them through. From the remainder, s/he'll be looking for:

- relevant experience
- qualifications
- professionalism

Your letter (the statement on a form) will be looked at too, of course, and you can check this out in Chapter 18. It makes up the remaining 50 per cent of the means by which you secure that interview.

ITEMS YOU'LL NEED

There's a lot involved here, so the list may look a bit daunting. But this is a one-off process. Once you've completed this initial stage, you'll never have to cover this ground again. In the following list, the first six items are essential, but beyond that, just aim to find as much as you can.

Getting your materials together may take a few weeks if you have to search the attic or make contacts for information. But since you'll be dealing with documents that may be vital for your future, do give each item the importance it deserves. The good news is that much of the work you do here will be useful for your covering letter as well as for your CV.

Here are the kind of things to look for:

- a list of past employment (names and addresses of employers, roles, dates)
- job titles
- key tasks you performed
- the names of schools and colleges you've attended since the age of 11 (with dates)
- educational certificates
- a note of your level of competence in IT
- a note of any school/college achievements
- sports certificates
- music, drama, art or handicraft certificates
- any other certificates (e.g. for attending courses, day schools, workshops, etc.)
- a note of any prizes you've received (for absolutely anything)
- a list of modules you've taken in undergraduate courses
- positive letters from employers
- a list of evening classes you've attended
- a note of goals you've achieved
- any letters of thanks addressed to you
- a note of any position you've held such as secretary or treasurer of a committee
- a note of any voluntary work you've done
- details of any charities, etc., you've worked for
- details of home care you've undertaken – looking after children or other dependants
- experience of teamwork
- a note of any languages you can speak and at what level
- experience of working to deadlines
- a list of your hobbies (past and current)
- a list of your interests (e.g. historic buildings, alternative therapies, wildlife conservation, etc.)
- a note of membership of clubs and societies (past and current)
- a list of your skills and abilities (e.g. driving, playing an instrument, instructing others, making clothes, gardening, etc.)
- anything else which you feel might be relevant

Just as with writing an essay, you're going to need plenty of material so that you can (a) pick the best bits, (b) give a full picture of your abilities, and (c) choose relevant items for particular jobs. Once you've amassed everything you can get hold of, find somewhere to keep it safe. There's no knowing what you'll need in the future.

▶ Lost certificates

If you've mislaid certificates, you'll need to get copies. In order to do this, you'll need to know the name of the awarding body – for example, City & Guilds, OCA, RSA or AQA. You can get the address either from the Internet or your local reference library. If you don't know the name of the awarding body, phone the school or college where you sat the examination and tell them the year that you sat the exam. If you find that your school has been razed to the ground, phone the local education offices.

▶ Lost addresses of employers

It's best to show full addresses for posts you've held in the last five years. For employment further back, just the name of the town is probably enough. It depends partly on how many jobs you've had and partly on the level of the work. The fewer the number, the more important it is to give full addresses. If, for example, you lived in Nottingham for three years and worked as a bar person in six pubs during that time, you could get away with listing just the town, the job and the outside dates:

2008–2011	various employers	bar work
	Nottingham	

If, however, each of the jobs you'd held in Nottingham between 2008 and 2011 gave you valuable experience and was a step up from the previous one, it would be important to show employers' names and addresses clearly. If you're stuck for an address, try the Internet or your local reference library.

YOUR DUTIES AND KEY TASKS: ACTION WORDS

When you've got together lists of your past jobs, you'll need to note down the main duties you performed in each. A prospective employer will want to know what you've actually done. So list the duties you've undertaken, starting each with a verb (an action word – see Chapter 13) like this:

- prepared spreadsheets
- supplied clients with product information
- liaised with outside companies

If you're coming back to work after a break or you've been bringing up children, it's easy to feel that you have little to show here. But don't underestimate your experience. When faced with writing a CV, Anne, a student on an environmental science course, began by saying, "I've done nothing in my life. All I've done is watch TV." When pressed, however, she revealed the following information:

- she was bringing up four children
- she was secretary to her local residents' group
- she sometimes helped out at her children's playgroup
- she did the paperwork for her husband's small farm
- she helped out on the farm

And once she'd worked on her CV, these activities came out like this:

2002–2009	cared for under-fives	home responsibilities
	undertook secretarial duties	family business
	assisted with early-years education	local playgroup
	kept business accounts	family business
	cared for farm animals	family farm

Whatever you've done, it can be made to look interesting and useful, especially when put into formal language. If, for example, you've stood on the street week in, week out selling *The Big Issue*, that shows a lot of determination and initiative.

GAPS IN YOUR WORK HISTORY

A prospective employer will be hoping to see that you've been in continuous employment with no gaps. He or she will understand, however, that you might have had home responsibilities, been travelling or been involved in other reasonable activities. Notice how Anne dealt with this problem (above). She's demonstrated that her years at home looking after children have been packed with useful activities that will have developed her skills and made her a more useful employee.

YOUR SKILLS AND ABILITIES

People sometimes land jobs for the strangest reasons. You might have applied to teach French in secondary education and been appointed because you once attended dance classes and so could also help with the school's drama productions. Your prospective boss in an insurance firm might finally choose you because your previous experience as a fisherman means that you'll be useful in dealing with fishing claims. This is why it's important to make a full list of your skills: you might need one of them for a CV, for your covering letter, or even in an interview. It can sometimes be useful to list things under the following headings:

- coping with data
- working with people
- developing ideas
- working with things
- the arts

Anne might compile the following list:

childcare	negotiation
animal care	organisation
bookkeeping	communication
planning	money management
word processing	record keeping

YOUR PERSONAL PROFILE

Your *Personal profile* (at the head of your CV) showcases your key abilities and achievements in the light of the job being applied for. In three or four lines, you will explain the kind of person you are together with an outline of your skills, abilities and achievements. The *profile* reads rather like an advert and generally contains no working verbs.

Let's suppose that you've worked as a legal secretary and managed a small office and that you're now in the second year of a degree course in personnel management and applying for part-time work in personnel. Your *Personal profile* might read like this:

> A confident and conscientious administrator with proven office experience and a keen interest in all aspects of personnel work, who can work under pressure either alone or as part of a team.

If you've helped run a playgroup since your children were born and are about to take your degree in event management, you might write:

> An efficient organiser who has built on skills gained managing and advertising a play-group and about to graduate in event management. Adaptable and resourceful, with a portfolio of events promoted while studying.

Maybe your work experience was mainly cleaning, bar work and bringing up your children, which involves people skills, organising and budgeting. You might decide to construct a *Personal profile* that focuses on your college or university experience. Let's suppose you're studying interior design. You might write the following:

> An innovative and effective designer who has collaborated on designs for a college common room. Able to plan, budget and take full account of client needs.

▶ Career profile

Sometimes, this personal piece is headed *Career profile*. This heading can be used if you already have considerable experience in the field of work you're applying for. Maybe you've served in the armed forces and are now moving into civilian life but in a similar field to your original training. Perhaps you've worked as a skilled mechanic and are about to gain a BSc. in engineering. You'll want to show that you're building on a strong background:

> A highly motivated engineer with successful experience of leading teams in the Armed Services. Shortly to graduate with a BSc. in engineering and looking to take on a management role. Confident, ambitious, diligent and resourceful.

Here's another *Career profile* that shows clear goals and lots of determination:

> A language specialist, fluent in both French and German, who has lived and worked in Europe and will shortly have a BA (Hons) in Russian. An experienced linguist who is seeking work as a translator or interpreter.

TARGETING YOUR INFORMATION

It's very important not to invent things on a CV. It's difficult enough to remember exactly what you've said on paper when you're in an interview, and the truth has a way of surfacing when you least expect it. Don't worry if you haven't had much paid employment. Unpaid work experience or voluntary work can be important. So be sure that anything relevant to the job you're applying for shows up somewhere on your CV.

It's perfectly acceptable, however, to leave things out or to put stress on something that you want to showcase. You can reword things for different applications or change the layout of your information in order to either emphasise or diminish an item's importance.

Once you've put together a basic CV, you can vary it for different job applications. For example, the fact that you've kept an allotment for growing vegetables could be useful if you apply for a marketing job in the fresh food industry, but you'd probably leave it out if you applied to market computers.

ICT

What some of us know as IT (information technology i.e. competence with computers) is now called ICT – information and communications technology. As you probably realise, this is becoming more and more important. So be sure to mention your level of competence somewhere on your CV. If you aren't very skilled but you can say that you are currently on a computer course, this could be just enough to make you interesting to an employer if he or she is sparked by other areas of your CV.

YOUR INTERESTS

Near the end of your CV, you'll need a short section showing your hobbies and interests. Obviously, you'll list anything relating to the job you're applying for, but it's also important to include anything of a social nature that demonstrates that you enjoy interacting with others. If you have several hobbies that you pursue alone, consider omitting one or more of these. Then think hard about including something you do that involves people. Include the names of any groups or societies that you belong to, like this:

Walking
weekly walk
member of the Ramblers' Association from 1998

Charity work
active member of Cancer Research from 2004

REFERENCES

You'll need to ask two or three people if they would be prepared to act as your referees. One of these should be someone in a position of authority on your course – probably the head of department or a senior lecturer. If you've been in work recently, another referee should be your latest employer. Two referees are essential and you may need an extra one, as some employers ask for three.

Your referees need to be able to comment on your abilities and on the way you interact with others. If you're really stuck, think about people in authority from somewhere you've done voluntary work or about tutors from evening classes you've attended. If the worst comes to the worst, use your bank manager or doctor – but that really is the worst-case scenario because employers really want to have an idea of what you'll be like in a work situation.

Never include actual references with your CV. Just give names, job titles, business addresses, emails and phone numbers. And do check that you give up-to-date information for these vital contacts.

For a speculative CV, where no job has been advertised, it's fine to say you'll send names of referees on request. When applying for a specific job, however, it's essential to give full information.

LAYOUT

You've got to grab an employers' attention with the top half of your first page. They want something that's interesting but that's easy to read and that conforms in general to what they expect to see. They need to be able to scan a CV quickly, which means that it mustn't look cramped and that it has to fit on *no more than* two sides of A4. There are two exceptions:

(a) CVs for academic or research posts which might be twice as long as others in order to include details of publications, conferences attended, etc.
(b) CVs sent out on spec (to whet an employer's appetite) which should be one page only, giving your key selling points.

The sections of your CV will be roughly as follows:

- personal profile
- key qualifications
- current post (if you are in any work)
- past employment
- education and training
- personal details – e.g. hobbies, etc.
- referees

You can vary the order if necessary. Aim to put your strongest selling points first.

Past employment and *Education and training* sections are listed with the most recent first and then working backwards. Your *Qualifications* section needs to include the name of each award, the awarding body, your grade and the date of the award.

If you did well in certain GCSEs (which you'll put under *Education and Training*) you might decide to note them something like this:

2002 10 GCSEs – including Maths and Physics at A* – AQA

A levels, however, would need to be listed separately with your relevant grade for each. Access to Higher Education courses need to show your main subjects.

If you're not computer literate or don't have access to a computer, you'll need to persuade a friend to type your CV for you or pay to have it done. Whatever happens, make sure you have extra copies plus a copy on disk because you're likely to need this CV again and again (with changes as you go along). It's the first edition of a document that you'll use all your life.

THE LANGUAGE OF A CV

The main thing to know about language for CVs is that you won't be writing full sentences. The whole point is to give an employer an easy read. S/he will want to glance through your CV quickly to get an immediate feel for whether or not to put it on the possibles pile. If you write full sentences and paragraphs you lessen your chances of getting an interview. An employer is likely to assume that anyone who is unable to sum up his or her own life experiences simply and clearly will probably be unable to deal with detailed tasks at work.

You must also write formally and use the correct terms for jobs and their relevant duties. Proof-read your work several times because it's horribly easy to include errors. Get a friend or family member to proof-read it too.

HINTS AND TIPS

- use white A4 paper
- use clear type – 12 point in Arial, Times New Roman or Verdana in black throughout
- follow instructions from the job advert/further details exactly
- use **no** Tipp-Ex, glue, Blu-Tack, etc.

- send a top copy prepared on computer
- use bold for headings
- adjust your layout so that no section is split over two pages
- be as concise as possible while giving full information
- stick to the truth
- use appropriate language
- show you're already pursuing your main interest via part-time or voluntary work or hobbies
- show you know about the field of work – via experience, study, reading, etc.

Don't include:

- italics or fancy fonts
- underlining
- the word *Address*
- references (only the names and contact details of referees are wanted)
- photographs/pamphlets/anything else

Sending any separate papers that aren't asked for in the advert is a pretty sure route to the waste bin. If the instructions say 'no CVs', sending one will almost certainly ensure that you are *not* invited to interview, however exciting your CV. Employers want staff who can follow instructions.

There's no specific requirement to include your age on your CV, but if an application form asks for your date of birth, you'll need to give it. You might want to leave it out, but ask yourself: would doing this be worth the risk of not getting an interview?

EXAMPLES OF CVS

There are obviously different ways of setting out CVs and what you do will depend partly on personal preference and partly on the job you're applying for. As already suggested however, it's wise not to depart too far from what an employer will expect.

Note: In the examples below, names and some of the data have been changed.

Tracey Hitchens

6 Hillside Terrace
Newton Abbot
Devon
TQ5 3TH

01434 000000

t.hitchens@telephone.com

PERSONAL PROFILE
A responsible and competent administrator with experience of a variety of organisations, who has particular knowledge of the financial sector and is skilled in dealing with staffing issues.

EMPLOYMENT HISTORY

TCD Ltd Unit 6 Larch Road Plymouth PL3 4AD	March 2008– June 2010 (while studying for my degree)	Cleaning Operative	Responsible for local building society offices

Fiveways Nursing
Home
Back Road
Tavistock
Devon
	April 2006–
	August 2007
		Administrator/
		receptionist
			Admitted residents
			dealt with post
			inputted wages on
			  computer
			booked agency staff
			kept records
			liaised with doctors
			carried out
			  secretarial duties
			  for management
			  and staff

National Bank
Chertsey
Surrey
	November 2005–
	November 2006
		Customer
		Service
		Officer
			oversaw sub-branch
			handled cash
			balanced tills
			served customers
			dealt with problems
			organised security
			liaised with head
			  office
			implemented new
			  IT system

Sewing Guild High Street Dartmouth Devon	April 2004 – November 2005	Machinist/shop assistant	manufactured curtains & soft furnishings served customers
The Care Group Exeter	August 2003 – April 2004	Care Worker	provided home care for elderly and sick, covering: personal care, cleaning, shopping, etc.
Home responsibilities	1988–2004	Parent	brought up my children
Oxfam	" "	Volunteer shop assistant	served customers
Air Training Corps	" "	Volunteer treasurer	handled & banked cash/kept accounts
Savings Bank Guildford Surrey	1984–1988	Cashier	dealt with customers

QUALIFICATIONS

2010	BA (Hons) Humanities	IIi
2000	Arts Foundation Course, Open University	Pass (73%)
1985	RSA Stage 1 Elementary Typewriting	Pass
1984	8 GCE O levels, including English and Maths	Pass

EDUCATION

2007–2010	College of St Mark and St John, Plymouth – BA course in History with English Language and Linguistics
1999–2000	The Open University
1979–1984	Burdock Comprehensive School, Guildford

HOBBIES
Netball
member of local team 1994–2004 – played in county matches

Painting
member of watercolour group – exhibiting annually – 2000–present

REFEREES
[Here, Tracey listed names & work addresses, phone numbers, email addresses & mobile numbers for 2 referees.]

Here's a rather different CV from someone who has a range of work experience. She wanted to showcase her skills and abilities so that a prospective employer would see her expertise at a glance.

Hilary Crawford

18 Bullers Park
Kingsbridge
Devon
PL8 5PT

01436 000000

h.crawford@telephone.com

PERSONAL PROFILE
Self-motivated, versatile and methodical all-rounder, with expertise in providing advice and guidance to diverse client groups. Experienced in establishing and implementing effective administrative systems in a range of occupational areas including the financial, commercial and educational sectors. Highly motivated to succeed within a demanding environment while complying with operational procedures and maintaining excellent standards of service.

SKILLS PROFILE

Administration
- Established the work-placement programme for a government-funded training organisation: recruiting clients, generating placement opportunities with local employers; matching clients according to employers' specifications, conducting health and safety inspections.
- Developed an industrial placement provision, University of Plymouth.
- Provided administrative support to a team of 4 financial advisers, ensuring compliance with financial services regulations.

Communication and teamwork
- Undertook client assessments to ensure that both employer and employee gained maximum benefit from the placement opportunity.
- Liaised between students and academic staff to ensure effective transmission of information.
- Conducted individual and group presentations for peer and academic review.
- Generated sales leads by cold-call telephoning.
- Provided enhanced directory-enquiry assistance in high-volume call-centre environment.
- Established and retained a base of 400+ home-shopping customers through the provision of exceptional customer service.

ICT
- Devised placement handbook and database to ensure adherence to university guidelines.
- Produced a range of management reports and statistical information using complex spreadsheets to illustrate cash flow, man-hour projections and project spend.
- Extensive use of Internet and e-mail, for both research and communication purposes.
- Rapidly assimilated and implemented new software.

Organisation
- Combined reading for a full-time honours degree with raising a pre-school child and running a successful home shopping franchise.
- Arranged customer appointments and managed diaries for a team of financial advisers.

EMPOYMENT SUMMARY

The Number (UK) Ltd	Customer Service Representative	2010–2011
Kleeneze Europe Ltd	Independent Distributor	2007–2010
University of Plymouth	Industrial Placement Co-ordinator	2004–2007
Wesleyan Financial Services	Customer Service Co-ordinator	2003–2004
CC Training	Placement Co-ordinator	2001–2003
Career break	Independent traveller	1999–2000
British Aerospace	Price Control Analyst	1995–1999
Ministry of Defence	Administrative Officer	1993–1995
Legal and General	Insurance Administrator	1991–1993

QUALIFICATIONS
BA (Hons) English Language and Linguistics (1st Class)   2010
University College of St Mark and St John
University of Exeter

Advanced level English Language and English Literature (B)   2000
Stoke Damerel Community College, Plymouth, Devon

9 GCE O levels including English (A) and Maths (B)   1989
Cleverham Community College, Battle, East Sussex

HOBBIES AND INTERESTS

At the gym
regular squash and exercise

Writing
contributions to a variety of national magazines

Travel
extensive travel in Africa, Asia and Australia – great interest in different cultures

ADDITIONAL INFORMATION
Date of Birth: 22 April 1973
Driving licence: Full and clean
Health: Excellent
References: Available on request

The next CV gives a variation on how to set out employment history.

Mark Godfrey

18 Preston Villas
Morland Park
Bristol
BS6 8HK

01735 000000

m.godfrey@telephone.com

Personal Profile
An experienced project manager, responsible for the design, planning and construction of a wide variety of products to produce solutions best suited to customer specifications. Able to work under pressure and adhere to strict deadlines and budgets to ensure maximisation of profit. Industrious, reliable and conscientious, with an outgoing personality and keen sense of humour. Highly motivated to work in an environment that will enable existing skills to be fully utilised, whilst allowing new ones to develop.

CAREER SUMMARY
2011–present   Flint Engineering, Bristol: Project Manager/draughtsman
Design, development and construction of a diverse range of engineering projects involving structural steelwork. Responsible for working with clients to ensure the effective implementation and delivery of the project within budgetary constraints.

2006–2008 – Various contracts, Bristol and Avon: Fabricator/welder
Involved in the design and production of structural steelwork, sheet-metal work and a wide variety of other components. Operated a range of machinery including guillotine, brake press, drills, saws, oxygen-propane cutting equipment, plasma and all forms of welding equipment. Also worked on the running of lathes and milling machines. All fabrication taken from drawings to strict tolerance.

2003–2006 – Motor Accessories, Bristol: Senior Fabricator/ welder
Involved in the production of high-quality vehicle accessories. Responsible for the fabrication and welding of bright mild steel and stainless steel accessories.

1996–2003 – Morgan's Precision Engineering, Bristol: Apprentice Fabricator/welder (structural engineering)
Four years' training and gaining proficiency as an apprentice fabricator/welder. Following completion of apprenticeship, worked on structural fabrications always from drawings and to very precise specifications. Highly accomplished in the processes of MIG, TIG and MMA.

QUALIFICATIONS

2011	BEng – Engineering Design IIi	
	University of Bristol	
2006	City & Guilds level 3D AutoCad	
1996–2000	Structural Engineering	BS 4871 & BS 4872
	Fabrication and welding	Various positions

EDUCATION

2008–2011	University of Bristol
1989–1996	Rivermouth Comprehensive School, Bristol
	9 GCSEs grades A–C, including Maths and English

HOBBIES AND INTERESTS

- socialising with friends
- vehicle maintenance
- playing snooker in a local pub league
- playing squash – regular visits to the gym

FURTHER INFORMATION

Date of birth: 05.04.78
Driving licence: Full and clean
Health: Excellent

REFERENCES

Available on request

SUMMARY

This chapter has covered:

- definitions of a CV
- selling yourself
- materials needed for writing a CV
- lost certificates and addresses
- your duties and key tasks
- your skills and abilities
- your *Personal profile*
- angling the information
- references
- layout
- the language of a CV
- hints and tips
- examples of student CVs

18 Letters and Statements for Job Applications

INTRODUCTION

It's hardly possible to over-stress the importance of everything you write in a job application. Chapter 17 explained that your CV forms 50 per cent of the means whereby you gain an interview. Your covering letter (or statement if you are submitting an application form) supplies the other 50 per cent. It's here that you can demonstrate your best qualities in their best light.

As you probably realise, you'd be extremely lucky to get an offer from the first employer you approach. Look on your job hunt as a project. The more persuasive your letters, the greater your chances of finding employment quickly.

THE STATEMENT ON AN APPLICATION FORM

Some employers (for example, local and national government offices) always send out application forms, and in most cases, these ask for a *Personal statement* that stands instead of a covering letter. The crucial thing is to do whatever is wanted. If you send material the employer doesn't ask for, you run the risk of having your application put straight on the 'No' pile.

A statement is actually very similar to a letter. You'll just leave out the date, addresses, and so on. So read the sections below. Usually, the application form will explain that you can add an extra sheet. If your typed statement would fit in the space provided, photocopy it on to the form, having first made a copy of the form and practised on that because it's fatally easy to miscalculate the space and ruin your work. Otherwise, write *Please see attached sheet* in the space provided and attach the sheet to your form with a paperclip. Head it *Statement* so there's no confusion and put your name on it.

CHARACTERISTICS OF A GOOD LETTER OR STATEMENT

I'll use the word *letter* throughout this section, but everything you find here relates equally to statements. You can see how to set out a letter in Chapter 6, and many of the points in writing essays from Chapter 2 will also be relevant here – such as structure, paragraphing, linking and so on. Your letter needs to be:

- well organised
- clearly expressed
- easy to read
- interesting
- lively
- error-free
- free from negatives

It must show that you are:

- keen
- intelligent
- knowledgeable
- dependable
- sociable
- committed

It needs to highlight:

- your interest in both the job and the organisation
- your knowledge of the work
- your relevant experience/abilities
- other relevant achievements
- your career aspirations
- reasons why the employer would benefit from employing you

Pay special attention to any information you've been sent about the organisation. Look it up on the Intertnet as well, or try your local reference library. A letter that demonstrates a good knowledge of the organisation will start to nudge ahead of those that don't. And always write a letter to a named person. If a name hasn't been given, phone and ask for it. On statements, however, omit names.

WHAT ARE MY BEST QUALITIES?

You're going to have to sell yourself, so you need to be clear in your own mind on the qualities you have to offer. Start by going back to the lists of skills and abilities you made when preparing your CV. Things you've done in the past will help show the kind of person you are. Then think about the obvious things:

Are you: cool in a crisis?
              reliable?
              meticulous?
              confident?
              a good team player?
              resourceful?
Do you: work easily without supervision?
Have you: a pleasant sense of humour?

Here are some more qualities that might be true for you. You'll need to be able to give examples of how your qualities have shown up in various things you've done. Think about how you've coped with difficulties and challenges. Are you:

responsible	diplomatic
flexible	self-disciplined
adaptable	able to see the big picture
reliable	a good communicator
sensitive	a quick thinker
highly skilled	very experienced

You might feel a little uncomfortable about blowing your own trumpet, but if you don't tell employers what you're like, they won't know. It's do or die at this stage.

You won't need to mention all your qualities in one go. Aim to throw one in every now and then as it relates to different aspects of your experience and to the job you're applying for. In your final paragraph (see 'Your conclusion' below) you might mention a few of these qualities when summing up the benefits you would bring to the post.

TRANSFERABLE SKILLS

Don't worry too much if you have little experience of some of the things on the job specification. You're going to show how things you've done in the past can be related to the requirements of the job you're applying for now. It's always possible to use skills in a different context.

For example, if you've run a household, brought up children or organised a fête to raise money for charity, you can show that you have organisational skills. If you've managed an office in a building firm, you can apply the experience gained there to managing one in a totally different field and at a higher level. You might also give examples of how you've adapted to new systems and learnt new skills in the past. This would demonstrate your flexibility.

WRITING YOUR LETTER OR STATEMENT

▶ Getting started

If you've not been sent a job specification, you'll need to phone and ask for one. You can then go through this and highlight key items so that you can be sure to address the most important ones in your letter. If you've also been sent a person specification, you can address each point as you go along. Anyone reading your application is likely to have a person specification beside them and will be looking to see how you match up. Covering issues in order can make the reader's task easier and so make it more likely that you'll be looked on favourably.

You'll also need to have your CV or completed application form to hand as you write so that you can refer to your key points. Your letter or statement needs to point out essential information that you want the employer to notice. You then need to fill this out with more details and perhaps an example or two.

▶ Your first draft

Just as with an essay, you'll need an introduction, a conclusion, and a middle section that contains the meat of your letter. After a brief introduction, start with your most important points and put the least important ones near (but not at) the end. Remember that whoever reads your letter will be totally focused on the vacant post. Make sure that whatever you write focuses on it too.

Your most important points will be any experience you have in the particular industry or area of work and your relevant skills and qualifications, including any you're studying for. When you refer to points from your CV or form, explain how these can be related to the job itself. This is your evidence. Just as with an essay, you need to make it really easy for your reader to understand what you're getting at. So don't leave him or her to make the leap between what you've done in the past and how it has prepared you for this post. Spell it out.

Your language will be fairly formal and your tone needs to demonstrate your enthusiasm for the post together with a quiet confidence in your ability to carry out the work. Use active verbs as you did in the 'duties' section of your CV. And here, unlike in essays, you will frequently need to use the word *I*.

▶ Your introduction

Keep your introduction brief. If you are writing a letter, you can begin by saying something like:

> I would like to apply for the above post and I enclose my CV. I am now completing my final year of a BA in Communication Studies and am aiming to work in ...

If you're writing a statement, however, omit the first sentence above because all details will be on your application form.

▶ Ways of beginning a paragraph

Aim to use good links as you would in an essay, and try to avoid beginning every paragraph with the word 'I'. If you're stuck for the opening of a particular paragraph, you might consider trying something like one of these:

- Having always had a great interest in animal husbandry, I am now ...
- As a member of the County's athletic team, I was ...
- Having recently discovered my ability to design large-scale projects, I ...
- It has been my ambition to become a social worker for some years now and ...
- Teaching is a profession in which my key strengths come into play ...

▶ Your conclusion

Just as in an essay, the conclusion is where you sum up your points. Here, you want to leave the reader with a sense that you have all it takes to do the job. It's often a good place to note that you have a pleasant sense of humour, and, if applicable, that you work well as a member of a team. Be sure to end on a positive note.

▶ Avoiding negatives

It's fatally easy to write yourself out of a job by suggesting that you lack experience in the relevant field, that you don't expect a high class of degree or that you are not quite sure that you have the qualities to undertake the work. As with a CV, omit, wherever possible, mention of things that don't help your case; then make the most of your positives. For example, a lack of experience when applying for a job might be treated something like this:

> While working as a clerical assistant in a large legal firm, I became especially interested in the effect of legal processes on clients. It was this that gave me an interest in the relationship between people and organisations and decided me to pursue a career in personnel. While at university, I have been lucky enough to gain an insight into practical personnel work by shadowing personnel officers in two very different industries.

Even a problem like redundancy can be made to work in your favour:

> If I had not been made redundant from a firm of insurance brokers where I had worked for ten years, I would not have had

the opportunity to undertake part-time work in a residential home. While there, I soon discovered my ability to empathise with residents and their families plus a strong desire to take on a more formal role in assisting at crisis points in people's lives and to become a social worker.

If you have experience of one aspect of a job but not another and the employer wants both, say how keen you are to become proficient in the new area and how quickly you learnt the other one.

▶ Redrafting

However long your earlier drafts, aim to keep your final draft to one side of A4 if possible. You'll need to check spelling and grammar especially carefully, as any mistakes will give a bad impression. The employer doesn't know you at this stage and so will assume that what you send is the best you're capable of. So aim for a professional and polished submission.

It's essential to use black ink or typescript for your final draft as an employer might want to photocopy your letter for the members of an interviewing panel, and black is the only colour that comes out well. It's also the case that a lot of people have a violent dislike of coloured ink – including blue.

You'll see in the examples at the end of the chapter that the letter has the job title in bold as a heading, but that on the statement there's no heading. I suggested above, however, that if your statement is on a loose sheet, you put *Statement* at the top. You'll also need to put your name on the sheet in case it gets separated from your form by mistake.

▶ Before posting

Even if, like most of us, you're up against the clock when getting an application in the post, don't omit to make copies of whatever you send. Photocopy the whole of an application form (not just your statement) because you'll need to be sure exactly what you put on it before you attend an interview, and make sure you have a hard copy of material in case your computer goes down at a vital moment.

Don't discard your letter – even if you get the job. Further letters for other jobs can be quickly constructed by making a few changes when you need to, whereas going back to the first draft stage means you'll have hours' more work to do.

SPECULATIVE LETTERS

In some cases, you may want to send out what's known as a *spec(ulative) letter* to various companies to search for jobs that haven't been advertised. You might be lucky and land a job that hadn't reached the advertising stage. On the other hand, this can be a way of interesting a company in what you have to offer. The kind of job you want might not be available at once, but you might get an offer of something else or be contacted at a later date when what you want *is* available.

You'll need to learn something about each company you approach (use the Internet and/or your local reference library) and then phone to get the name of someone responsible for the area of work you're interested in. Always write to a named individual and always send a top copy – never send photocopies of letters. After a week or two, it's a good idea to follow up with a polite phone call asking the person you wrote to if s/he has had a chance to look at what you sent.

Your letter should be less than one page in length and should very briefly state your career aims, your experience and personal qualities, your knowledge of the industry, your interest in the particular company and your keenness to work in the field. Obviously, you'll enclose your CV.

EXAMPLE OF AN APPLICATION LETTER

Your covering letter will be sent with a copy of your CV, so the employer will have all your data to hand. You can therefore refer to your CV at relevant points in your letter. Below is Doug's application letter to a housing trust for a job in IT. The employer's job specification for this letter was as follows:

- Making sure that the company is optimising its network and systems
- Training staff
- Installing equipment
- Overhauling finance and housing systems
- Advising on design of website
- Making sure the company's IT is secure, efficient, user-friendly

And here's the person specification:

- A relevant degree
- Experience of managing Windows 2007 and a Microsoft Exchange Server 2010
- Experience of supporting systems running on the above
- Experience of developing IT provision to meet the needs of a business
- Ability to communicate complex technical information in layman's terms

---

44 Riverside
Winchester
WA2 7BB
3 October 2011

Melanie Prior
Personnel Officer
Woodleigh Housing Trust
Andover
AN6 5UV

Dear Ms Prior

IT Infrastructure Analyst

I would like to be considered for the above post and enclose my CV. My early career was as a senior mechanic and MOT inspector in the motor trade. Following an industrial accident, however, I retrained as an IT technician. Having now attained a BSc (Hons) in Information Technology at the University of Derby, I feel that my new career can move forward.

I have recent successful experience of managing Windows 2007 and working with a Microsoft Exchange Server 2010 as I worked part-time for the university while studying for my degree. Together with the IT Manager, I set up systems for an expanding communications department and also transferred all data from an outdated system covering food and hospitality on to Windows 2007. Since then, I have been supporting these systems. I feel that this has given me an excellent background for overhauling the Trust's finance and housing systems.

Prior to this, I was an IT technician in a large comprehensive school, responsible for setting up systems for a complex timetable as well as revised timetables for examination periods. I also managed the databases of pupils and staff. During my time at Foxley Comprehensive School, I assisted in installing new computers for the school's IT room, and while working at the university, I played a major part in the installation of a new library cataloguing system, so I feel very competent to install whatever the Trust decides to go ahead with.

The need to be aware of costs and to make full use of a network and its systems in relation to management are issues I have had to bear in mind in my work for educational organisations. If appointed, I would look forward to developing the Trust's use of IT and to finding ways the systems could be optimised whenever possible.

Advising on the design of a website for the Trust would be particularly exciting. I have designed sites for friends and have taken on small commissions which have all been successful. The opportunity to be involved with a more complex site would give me great satisfaction.

As an IT enthusiast, I enjoy helping others to make use of the vast possibilities of ICT. While at Foxley Comprehensive, I assisted staff in IT evening classes, and while at university, I answered queries from staff and students. In my previous career as a senior mechanic, I trained new recruits and developed training materials. So I have the necessary skills to deliver face-to-face training and printed materials in layman's terms for staff.

I find myself very much in sympathy with the ethos of Woodleigh Housing Trust and would enjoy being a part of the enterprise. I am dependable, adaptable, quick-thinking and diligent, and I have a good sense of humour. I would be pleased to discuss my application further at interview.

Yours sincerely

Douglas Barford

Douglas Barford

Doug has demonstrated in his letter that he has the experience and personal qualities listed.

EXAMPLE OF THE STATEMENT FOR AN APPLICATION FORM

The only real differences between a letter and a statement are the omission of addresses, the date, the salutation and the valediction. Below is Sheila's statement. She was applying for a post as a Key Stage 2 teacher. The job advert listed the following required experience and qualities:

- good classroom management skills
- an ability to use ICT

- an understanding of child-centred learning
- an ability to use the whole classroom for learning
- adherence to Equal Opportunities legislation

I will qualify as a teacher this summer with a BEd. I believe I am an all-rounder who is ideally suited to Key Stage 2 teaching. I am a good classroom manager and have a special interest in local history.

I have just completed my final teaching practice with a year 4 class. This was very successful. The head teacher was especially pleased with the children's work on memories as a result of visits to two residential homes. The children then took home their simple questionnaires to parents and carers.

I also received excellent comments on my classroom practice. I feel that good classroom management is essential for learning to take place, and I have dealt successfully with cases of challenging behaviour without having to enlist help from other members of staff or compromise the planned teaching session. I also value structured play for enhancing clear thinking and promoting social skills.

I like to make my classroom inviting so that merely being there can be an exciting learning experience for the children. I believe every child should be interacting in some small way with classroom displays on a daily basis, so I use a response system where each child can write a comment on items they like. I encourage the children to bring items from home to enhance displays. Putting the child at the centre of learning is an approach that I find really pays off. Having an experienced classroom assistant has been a bonus for me as it has given me more time to focus on the children as individuals.

I am highly adaptable and can offer to help out with drama and PE across the Key Stages from Foundation Stage to the top end of Key Stage 2. In my teens, I joined my county athletics team and I now play netball. I have been a member of my college drama group and last year I took part in a local pantomime. I have taken extra ICT training over the last two years, and am now competent to support children up to Key Stage 3. It goes without saying that I adhere to Equal Opportunities guidelines. I am also flexible, energetic, enthusiastic and self-motivated.

I have worked as a secretary in the planning department of a local authority. So I have good administration skills. During my teaching practice, I kept comprehensive records of the children's work and I have had good relationships with parents which I was able to develop further in discussions of the children's progress at a parents' evening.

At college, I have enjoyed the companionship of other students and I am keen to become a member of a thriving staffroom as well as to give of my best to the children. I would be happy to supply any further information you need and hope to have the opportunity to discuss my application to teach at Marley Head School at an interview.

SUMMARY

This chapter has covered:

- the statement on an application form
- characteristics of a good letter
- assessing your best qualities
- demonstrating your transferable skills
- getting started
- your first draft
- your introduction
- ways of beginning a paragraph
- your conclusion
- avoiding negatives
- redrafting
- writing speculative letters

Appendix 1
Spelling Strategies

If you have *severe* problems with spelling, see the people at your college's study support section, who should be able to recommend a book that will give you specific help or tell you where to find a drop-in class for English skills. You might also look at the section on dyslexia at the start of this book. If, however, you're like many people and know that your spelling just isn't very good, you'll find some tips here to help you. People learn in different ways, so use the methods that suit you best.

There are lots of useful tricks you can use to help you remember how to spell particular words. Memory aids are called mnemonics (for pronunciation, ignore the first '*m*').

THE COMPUTER SPELL-CHECK

If you're able to use a computer, you'll certainly find its spell-check facility useful. This will pick up a lot of misspellings – particularly things you've mis-typed – and will improve the look of your assignments. But there are certain things to beware of. A computer won't recognise many technical words and will change some things you may have spelt correctly to the closest word it knows. It might also be set up for American spelling which is fine if you live in America, but not much help if you need the British system. It's usually possible, however, to change the language setting to the one you need.

The main problem with relying solely on a spell-check facility is that you won't be improving your own spelling. This won't matter while you're submitting course work, but can leave you at a serious disadvantage when you come to exams. You'll probably get the best value from a spell-checker by using it *in conjunction with* your own programme of spelling improvement.

MNEMONICS

Mnemonics is the word for any system of using rhythm, colour, patterns of letters or numbers, or visual pictures as memory aids. You may already know the mnemonic for remembering whether to put *i* before *e* in the middle of a word: '*i* before *e* except after *c*'.

This mnemonic has a strong rhythm to it, and it's this that makes it easy to remember. So we can work out (without having to learn them) how to spell words like *retrieve, achieve, conceit* and *deceive*. (There are a few exceptions to this rule, however, such as *eight* and *seize*.)

The key to a good mnemonic is to make it simple, enjoyable and amusing. If you can add a mental picture that is highly coloured, funny, silly – or even sexy – that's even better. If you want to remember how to spell the word *mnemonic*, for example, try this:

mind   **N**ed's   **e**lephant +   monic

You might visualise a tiny man with a huge, ungainly elephant.

It doesn't matter what you choose as long as it will stick in your mind. The more bizarre your mnemonics, the easier they will be to remember.

YOUR PERSONAL SPELLING AID

Another very valuable tool for learning to spell well is a notebook. Divide each page into two down the middle. On the left-hand side, keep a running list of words you've misspelt (spelt correctly now) and underline the letter or section of each word that's been causing you problems. Then work out and write down in the right-hand column a mnemonic for each one. Finally, have your notebook handy whenever you're writing an assignment. You'll need to take especial care over names and technical words related to your own subject. You might use the back of your notebook for these.

VISUALISING A WORD

Some people find that if they spend a few moments looking at a word and then close their eyes, they can see it clearly in their mind's eye. If this works for you, do use this method for learning. It's quick and simple.

SPOTTING THE PARTS OF A WORD

Sometimes, you can clearly see that a word has several sections to it. So you can remember its spelling more easily by splitting it up. For example:

promises	prom	is	es
fluctuate	fluc	tu	ate
cartilage	car	til	age

SAYING WORDS ALOUD

When you're alone, try saying difficult words aloud, using a sing-song voice and really exaggerating each section of the word. You can devise chants, too. For example, the word *necessary* is often misspelt. Try chanting 'One *c* and two *s*'s in *ne – ces – sary*' to help you remember.

SOME TYPICAL PROBLEM AREAS

You'll need to know the following terms for this section:

vowel   a, e, i, o, u, y
consonant   any letter *except* those above (the letter y can also function as a consonant, e.g. yacht)
prefix   an addition to the beginning of a word, e.g. _return_/_undo_
suffix   an addition to the end of a word – e.g. *loud_ly_/sense_less_*
syllable   one section of a word, containing a vowel, that could function as one 'beat', e.g. in the word *particularly* there are five beats: *par tic u lar ly*.

You might like to reinforce the beats of syllables by banging your hand on the desk or table as you say them. Or you can count them out on your fingers. Doing something physical like this usually helps.
There are many rules for English spelling, but it's certainly not

necessary to remember them all in order to spell well. Sometimes, however, people find them handy, so I'll give two here to start you off. The first one is really easy. You may already know it.

▶ The plural of words ending in y

A word that ends with the letter *y* is made plural by changing the *y* to *ie* before adding *s*. For example:

Singular	Plural
city	cities
lady	ladies
body	bodies

Unfortunately, of course, there are one or two exceptions. But, in this case, they aren't difficult to remember. Words that have a vowel *before* the *y* don't change. For example:

Singular	Plural
donkey	donkeys
monkey	monkeys
tray	trays
boy	boys

▶ Double letters

Remembering whether or not to use a double letter can be a real bugbear. For a difficult word where the double letter is somewhere in the middle, the best thing is to copy it out, split it into syllables, and devise a suitable mnemonic.

Other problem areas for knowing whether or not to double a letter are prefixes and suffixes.

▶ Prefixes

These are easy. A prefix is an item made up of a few letters that we put on the front of various words. When adding a prefix, just slot it straight on. Sometimes, this will mean that you end up with a double letter; sometimes it won't. For example:

moderate	+im	immoderate
noticed	+un	unnoticed
marine	+sub	submarine
terrestrial	+ex	extraterrestrial

▶ Suffixes

A suffix is an addition at the end of a word. The rules are as follows:

Do double the letter when adding a suffix beginning with a vowel to a two-syllable word where the stress is on the *second* syllable, e.g.:

admit	admitted
deter	deterred

or in a one-syllable word that ends in a vowel followed by a consonant, e.g.:

trim	trimmed
spot	spotted

and

Don't double the letter when adding a suffix beginning with a vowel to a two-syllable word where the stress is on the *first* syllable, e.g.:

market	marketed
budget	budgeted

Note: for words of two syllables ending in l, the spelling can depend on where you live, e.g.:

British spelling:	travel	travelled
American spelling:	travel	traveled

▶ Some commonly misspelt words

Here's a list of some words that are very frequently misspelt. It isn't exhaustive, but should get you thinking. You might like to put them in your spelling notebook – with suitable mnemonics.

accommodate
achieve
acknowledge
persuade
committee
privilege
existence
separate
fulfil(led)

gauge
occur(red)
address
business
prejudice
embarrassed
receipt
February
usually

independent
necessary
argument
possession
definite
recommend
extremely
until

Appendix 2
Common confusions

accept   receive or agree to
except   apart from, with the exception of

Tom said, "I *accept* all the blame for all the marks on the wall *except* the one the dog made."

affect (verb)   change in some way
effect (noun)   the result of something

If I spend less, this will *affect* my bank balance. Hopefully, the final *effect* will be that I clear my debts.

practice (noun)   the usual way of doing something or the repetition of an activity
practise (verb)   to do (something) repeatedly in order to gain skill

John *practises* the guitar every evening. It's his *practice* to do this after he's had something to eat.

principal   head of a college, director, or most important person in a company
principle   standard by which people behave

The college *principal* prides himself on his *principles*.

their   (possession)   e.g. *their* essays
there   (place)   e.g. over *there*
they're   (contraction)   *they are*

Ant and Dec are appearing in Birmingham. *They're* hosting *their* new show *there*.

to (preposition)	indicating place
to + a verb (infinitive)	to do (something)
two	number
too	more than enough/in addition

Mel is packing and organising the children. In half an hour, she will be off *to* London *to* see her *two* cousins so she's *too* busy *to* clean the car *too*.

simple	something that is easy to understand or do
simplistic	something that is oversimplified

The MP gave a rather *simplistic* explanation of an issue that is in no way *simple*.

where (adverb)	indicates place
were	(past tense of verb *to be,* often used as an auxiliary – helping – verb)

We *were* having lunch in the pub *where* I first met Sam.

past	no longer in existence/beyond (place)
passed	past tense of the verb *to pass*

It was ten *past* three when we *passed* the clock tower, just after we'd gone *past* the church.

dependant (noun)	someone (e.g. a child) who needs the financial support of another person
dependent (adjective)	word used to describe a thing or person relying on someone or something else for some reason.

Geraldine Smythe's *dependants* (her five children) will be *dependent* on her legacies to them which will be administered by her solicitors.

should've (contraction)	should have
could've (contraction)	could have
would've (contraction)	would have

These last three are very frequently written (and spoken) incorrectly as *should of, could* of and *would of.* The reason this happens is because of what we hear. It can sound as though the word *of* is at the end of *should've, could've* and *would've.* It isn't.

I *should've* finished my essay yesterday, and I *would've* if I *could've* done.

Answers

CHAPTER 13: VERBS AND OTHER PARTS OF SPEECH

▶ Activity 1

1 wash
2 foretell
3 long
4 migrate
5 sends
6 desire

▶ Activity 2

1 b is
2 h has
3 d cross
4 d goes
5 b are
6 b is
7 h has
8 h owns
9 d buzz
10 b is

▶ Activity 3

1 past
2 present
3 past
4 future
5 present
6 future
7 present
8 future

Note: No. 5 is present tense because the sentence concerns a habitual action.

▶ Activity 4

1 past perfect
2 present perfect
3 past perfect
4 future perfect

5 present perfect
6 past perfect
7 future perfect

8 present perfect
9 future perfect
10 present perfect

▶ Activity 5

1 present simple
2 past simple
3 future simple
4 future continuous
5 past perfect continuous
6 past perfect

7 future perfect continuous
8 past continuous
9 present continuous
10 future perfect
11 present perfect
12 present perfect continuous

▶ Activity 6

1 A
2 P
3 P
4 A
5 A

6 P
7 P
8 P
9 A
10 P

▶ Activity 7

1 Mrs Steele, letter, Queen
2 Bees, honey
3 Carlos, France, years
4 Mary, bike
5 Julius Caesar, Rome

▶ Activity 8

Concrete
1 water
2 fruit
3 atmosphere
  bar
  smoke

Abstract
life
health

4 monk	understanding
5 members	strategy
6 Paul	philosophy

► Activity 9

1 beautifully	5 harder, harder
2 slowly, silently	6 high
3 quickly	7 dearly
4 fast	8 rather, rashly

CHAPTER 14: WRITING CLEAR SENTENCES

► Activity 1

2, 3, 7

► Activity 2

subject	*verb*
1 Jimi Hendrix	died
2 Beatlemania	swept
3 Fraser	plays
4 Duke Ellington	is
5 Mick Jagger	performs
6 Salsa	is

► Activity 3

1 Carl	5 a belt of rain, high winds
2 Ron	6 Maxine
3 the cowboy	7 The children, the buns
4 Pam	8 To work at a satisfying job

▶ Activity 4

1 the casino	4 a fight
2 the suspects	5 the events
3 their winnings	6 sentence

▶ Activity 5

1 you	4 us
2 class IV	5 me
3 her client	

▶ Activity 6

1 Lucy ran home, crying all the way.
  Lucy ran home. She was crying all the way.
2 Ken's dog had been annoying the neighbours, barking all morning.
  Ken's dog had been annoying the neighbours. It had been barking all morning.
3 Brad ran down the road with the cheque, laughing all the way to the bank.
  Brad ran down the road with the cheque. He was laughing all the way to the bank.
4 The children came home covered in mud looking absolutely filthy.
  The children came home covered in mud. They looked absolutely filthy.
5 English grammar can be difficult, causing all sorts of problems.
  English grammar can be difficult. It can cause all sorts of problems.
6 I couldn't think how to get the cork out of the bottle. I had tried everything I knew.
  I couldn't think how to get the cork out of the bottle. I had been trying everything I knew.
7 The wolf set off through the forest, looking for the cottage belonging to Little Red Riding Hood's grandmother.
  The wolf set off through the forest. He was looking for the cottage belonging to Little Red Riding Hood's grandmother.

▶ Activity 7

1 Nursery schools are places where children learn some of the basic skills they will need for primary school. These include recognising their names, making simple models, and getting along with others.
2 My local school has started a monthly newsletter. Teachers believe that this will help make local people more aware of all the activities available for children and parents.
3 This essay will look at both sides of the argument in order to show the complexity of the issues involved. These crucial issues affect every aspect of our lives.

▶ Activity 8

1 <u>There are fairies at the bottom of my garden</u> where I haven't cut the grass.
2 Although it's freezing, <u>I refuse to wear woolly undies.</u>
3 <u>Place all gallstones in the bucket provided</u> after you have sewn up the patient.
4 As I came out of the supermarket, <u>I bumped into a small horse.</u>
5 <u>A problem shared is a problem halved,</u> as long as the trouble is either legal or is not divulged to a serving police officer.
6 <u>It's hot.</u>

CHAPTER 15: PUNCTUATION

▶ Activity 1

1 Marian has travelled in France, Spain, Australia, India and the USA.
   [It's OK to put a comma after 'India' if you wish.]
2 We were watched by a lean, ageing kangaroo.
3 After two weeks on buses and trains, it was a relief to smell sea air.
4 Jason, our guide, walked fast and spoke little.
5 Air disasters, it is well known, are fewer than accidents on the roads.
6 Taking a foreign holiday, despite problems with accommodation, currency and language, can be a liberating experience.
   [It would not be wrong to put a comma after 'currency'. Since there is little chance of a misunderstanding, however, it's probably best to omit

it. Note that the comma after 'language' is the partner to the one after 'holiday'. Those two mark off extra information.]

7 Day after day, the grey rocks, dotted here and there with small plants, formed a backdrop for our trek. [The first comma marks off extra information at the start. The next two mark off extra information in the middle of the sentence.]

8 Taking a foreign holiday can be a liberating experience.

[It would be wrong to put any commas in No. 8 because there is no extra information in the sentence. This is similar to the sentence 'Maria went for a long walk across the fields to the river.' Everything here is part of the main statement. It's also the case that the phrase 'Taking a foreign holiday' is the subject of the sentence, so it mustn't be separated from its verb.]

▶ Activity 2

The full stops after 'freedom' and 'reactionary' could be replaced by semicolons. In the first case, you might decide to keep within one sentence the statements concerning the two views on the motor car. In the second case, you could keep together the explanations of the difficulties in which governments can find themselves.

▶ Activity 3

1 It's only when I laugh that it hurts. (contraction)
2 It's a lovely day today. (contraction)
3 John's father's got his brother's coat. (possession/contraction: father has/possession)
4 When it's raining, that dog always stays in its kennel. (contraction)
5 It's easy to see how the cat shut its paw in the Browns' gate. (contraction/possession)
6 The hyenas' eyes were visible in the bushes everywhere we looked. (possession)

CHAPTER 16: GETTING CONVERSATION ON PAPER

► Activity 1

A

1 Jack said, "My partner is expecting a baby."
2 "I was born in Tunis," said Pierre.
3 "Where is the post office?" asked the tourist.
4 The toddler yelled, "I want an ice cream!"
5 "That dog," said John, "always disappears when I want to bath it."
6 "Why," asked Tom, "have you put the beer under my bed?" *[Notice that the question mark doesn't come after the word 'Why' because that's not the end of the question.]*

B

1 Mary said, "The eggs are in the fridge."
2 "High tide will be at three this afternoon," said the sailor.
3 "Come back here!" yelled the policeman.
4 Sam asked politely, "How much extra will I have to pay?"
5 "I haven't laughed so much," said Ben, "since the chicken coop collapsed."
6 "The main difficulty," explained the leader, "will be getting the tents across the river."

► Activity 2

I sense there's an excitement for Bob Crooks in work where he's in dialogue with his material, mixing colours and never being one hundred per cent sure of the final outcome because of the speed of the material's reactions.

"I don't want to battle against the material," he says, "so in the final heating, I let the glass do what it wants to do." It's by this means that Bob is able to create the fluid forms he's known for. He's influenced by geometry, architecture and the natural world. "I can't make anything as beautiful as what's in nature," he goes on, "but I like taking elements of different things and turning them into something whole."

▶ Activity 3

2 Kwame said that he was driving a Ford then.
3 Kwame said that he had driven to Italy the previous month.
4 Kwame said that he had driven 500 miles that week.
5 Kwame said that he had been driving for 10 years then.
6 Kwame said that he had been driving at night when the brakes had failed.
7 Kwame said that he would drive to Spain the following year.
8 Kwame said that he would be driving a Porsche the following year.

Bibliography

Blake, W. (1970) 'The Chimney Sweeper', in *Songs of Innocence and of Experience*, Oxford: Oxford University Press.

Buzan, T. and Buzan, B. (2005) *The Mind Map Book*, revised edition, London: BBC Active.

Cottrell, S. (2008) *The Study Skills Handbook*, 3rd edition, Basingstoke: Palgrave Macmillan.

Duffy, C.A. (2005) *Rapture*, London: Picador.

Grayling, A.C. 'Why a high society is a free society', *Observer*, 19 May 2002, http://observer.guardian.co.uk/comment/story/0,,718108,00.html. (Accessed online: 3 June 2005).

Greetham, B. (2009) *How to Write Your Undergraduate Dissertation*, Basingstoke: Palgrave Macmillan.

Ibsen, H. (1981) *A Doll's House*, in *Four Major Plays*, Oxford: Oxford University Press.

McArthur, T. (ed.) (1996) *The Oxford Companion to the English Language*, abridged edition, Oxford: Oxford University Press.

MHRA Style Guide: A Handbook for Authors, Editors and Writers of Theses, 2nd edition (2008), London: Modern Humanities Research Association.

MLA Handbook for Writers of Research Papers (2009) New York: Modern Language Association of America.

Pears, R. and Shields, G. (2010) *Cite Them Right*, 8th edition, Basingstoke: Palgrave Macmillan.

Shakespeare, W. (1982) *Hamlet*, Arden edition, Jenkins, H. (ed.) London & New York: Methuen.

Swan, M. (1980) *Practical English Usage*, Oxford: Oxford University Press.

Vernon, M. D. (1971) *The Psychology of Perception*, 2nd edition, Harmondsworth: Penguin Books.

Williams, K. and Carroll, J. (2010) *Referencing & Understanding Plagiarism*, Basingstoke: Palgrave Macmillan.

Williams, L. (1996) *Readymade CVs*, London: Kogan Page.

The Writing Centre, London Metropolitan University; www.londonmet.ac.uk/writingcentre (Accessed: 12 August 2011).

Note: This bibliography has been prepared in accordance with the Harvard referencing system.

Index